MICHENER

Barnaby Conrad
1974

MICHENER

A Writer's Journey

By
Stephen J. May

Foreword by Valerie Hemingway

UNIVERSITY OF OKLAHOMA PRESS : NORMAN

Also by Stephen J. May

Pilgrimage: A Journey through Colorado's History and Culture (Athens, Ohio, 1987)

Footloose on the Santa Fe Trail (Niwot, Colo., 1992)

Zane Grey: Romancing the West (Athens, Ohio, 1997)

Maverick Heart: The Further Adventures of Zane Grey (Athens, Ohio, 2000)

Library of Congress Cataloging-in-Publication Data

May, Stephen J. (Stephen James), 1950–
    Michener : a writer's journey / by Stephen J. May ; foreword by Valerie Hemingway.
        p.   cm.
    Includes bibliographical references (p.) and index.
    ISBN 0-8061-3699-5 (alk. paper)
    1. Michener, James A. (James Albert), 1907– 2. Novelists, American—century—Biography.   I. Title.

PS3525.I19Z76 2005
813'.54—dc22

2005043061

Frontispiece: James A. Michener, 1974. Charcoal drawing from life by Barnaby Conrad.

The paper in this book meets the guidelines for permanence and durability of the Committee on Production Guidelines for Book Longevity of the Council on Library Resources, Inc. ∞

1   2   3   4   5   6   7   8   9   10

Contents

Illustrations

All photographs are courtesy of University of Northern Colorado Special Collections.

Foreword

The first time I heard James Michener's name, it was spoken by Ernest Hemingway. We were in Spain, and Hemingway was discussing contemporary American writers who had made their mark on literature, who were innovative and courageous, whose works explored new territory; Michener's name was among them. It was many years before I would read one of Michener's books and many years again before I was privileged to spend some time with Michener, experiences that turned out to be positive and illuminating.

Though decidedly different in demeanor and in the style and content of their work, in many areas Michener and Hemingway had a natural affinity; for instance, in their appreciation and knowledge of the art of tauromachy and in all things Hispanic. Hemingway wrote *The Sun Also Rises, Death in the Afternoon, For Whom the Bell Tolls;* Michener countered with *Iberia* and *Mexico.* All five books show how an American writer could absorb the Hispanic culture and, in a unique way, bring it to life for the reader. Both writers were acutely aware of the impact they had on their readers worldwide. They were intensely interested in the art of writing, and Michener, younger by almost eight years, had unbounded admiration for Hemingway.

The two writers barely knew each other, having met only once, at Toots Shor's restaurant in New York City. The occasion, which started ignominiously, was recalled by Michener in his introduction to Hemingway's posthumous *The Dangerous Summer*. Only when Michener engaged in tales of the bullring and his torero friends did Hemingway's interest grow and did he warm to the younger writer.

Hemingway's and Michener's styles are dramatically different; the one spare, the other loquacious. In contrast to Hemingway's succinctness, Michener's works are outsized, of massive proportions. He was a long-lived, long-winded, prolific writer. His books typically run to over a thousand pages. Michener unabashedly proclaimed in his autobiography, "Even in the writing of a novel I persistently write more than is required, then cut back toward the bone. When a recent publication asked me for six sharp pages on a pressing topic, I warned them: In six pages I can't even say hello."

Michener's novels contain almost as many facts as an encyclopedia. While brevity was not his virtue, he was thorough. Whatever his subject, he researched it with diligence. He lived in the states and countries he wrote about—Alaska, Afghanistan, Hawaii, Poland, Spain, South Africa, Texas, to name a few. He truly could assert "the world is my home" when he aptly titled his autobiography. He might well have added a subtitle: "Writing Is My Life." In a coherent and exciting way no other writer has equaled, Michener brings the world to the untraveled reader. Not just the present-day world but world history and geography, combining the myth and imagination of the past with the pertinent questions of contemporary life. His writings have entertained, informed, engaged, and delighted at least two generations of Americans. And his books continue to sell at an unprecedented rate. I have yet to enter a bookstore and find his work missing. I recently counted twenty-three separate Michener titles in two different editions at our local shop. The storyteller lives on.

The first time I read Michener I was camping in Montana in the late 1970s. *Centennial* was a Book of the Month Club selection I purchased inadvertently because I had neglected to return the "Please don't send" card. I threw the book into my suitcase as we left New York. Day after day that August, the rain came pouring down relentlessly on our tents set up safari style beside the river at White Sulphur

Springs. I took out the book and began reading. There could not have been a more propitious moment of introduction to Michener's work. I felt the damp earth and sensed the presence of forgotten ancestors. Although *Centennial* took place to the south and east of where I was, nothing before or since has ever made the land with its secrets and mysteries become so real for me. The magic that Michener wove into his epic tale added a thrilling dimension to a potentially disastrous vacation. I went on to read *Iberia, The Source,* and one after another of Michener's books with equal pleasure and fascination.

Michener had a love and understanding of the subjects he wrote about. He built on his own experience as a young man in the South Seas and Asia during World War II. Throughout his life he sated his wanderlust in search of material for his books. He supplemented his firsthand knowledge with meticulous research. Hemingway advised aspirant writers, "Write what you know about best. Start with one true sentence!" Truth endures, in history and in literature. Recently rereading Michener's novel *Caravans* (1963), based in Afghanistan in 1946, I found it as fresh and true today as when it was written. There is a chilling description of a vengeance beheading. Anyone who is puzzled by the mentality behind the beheadings we witnessed in Iraq in 2004 should read this book to get a glimmer of understanding as to why such cruelty and barbarity exists in the twenty-first century. *Caravans* is even more relevant today than when it was first published.

Friendship, encouragement, and generosity were the hallmarks of Michener's personal relationships with aspirant writers. In later life when he was well established, it gave him great pleasure to help others, but always with a stern father's expectation that his help would propel his protégé to make his or her own way, as he, Michener, had done in the great American tradition. He explained his position to a friend of mine whom he helped on many occasions: "All young artists like you need as much support as you can get in this, one of the world's toughest professions, so any time I can help I will."

I met Michener in his Austin, Texas, home late in his life. Despite his age, illness, and exhaustion from a recent dialysis session, he was gracious and interested. We had a chance to converse over a couple of days. At first he was diffident about Ernest Hemingway, defensive, even critical. As he became more at ease, his mood lightened, and he recounted the things they had shared: love of literature and history, war, old-fashioned ideals, bullfighting, Spain, wanderlust. Michener reminded me of what he wrote in his autobiography, *The World Is My Home:* "I try not always successfully to follow the pattern of Ernest Hemingway, who achieved a striking style with short familiar words." He also repeated his own maxim: "Good writing, for most of us, consists of trying to use ordinary words to achieve extraordinary results." I could not help liking him and admiring his spunk and erudition as he approached his ninetieth year.

For the two years before he died, I had worked as Ernest Hemingway's secretary, and the following four years I sorted out Hemingway's papers, initially to assist his official biographer, Carlos Baker, with his research. At that time, I learned the essentials of the biographical art. Delving into the past, particularly into a writer's personal and private papers, is intrusive and can make the perpetrator look like an eavesdropper, a snoop, a nosey parker. The art is in evaluating the whole and extracting the pertinent information. Life is a complicated process and the life of a writer most complex of all. To understand the subject, to empathize, to admire with a critical eye, to be able to isolate the chaff from the wheat, to put in enough and not too much, to capture the life as well as the work, to leave the reader with a sense of the mind behind the books combining the public and private life, these are challenges every biographer faces.

Now, eight years after Michener's death, it is only fitting that a biography should be written encompassing the life and work of this maverick. Stephen May has taken on the daunting task of writing the first full-length biography of a life that spanned ninety years, touched upon many continents, and produced thousands of published pages. Michener created a new concept for the novel as all-encompassing, factual, historical megasaga. His subject matter traverses the universe and reaches back to the beginning of time. Each book is epic in proportion and scope. Yet the man was private. He did not invite publicity. For the most part, he was a loner who lived in the sway of his imagination, displaying courage, tenacity, and unflagging energy.

May subtitles his biography *A Writer's Journey*. He tackles the important questions even though there is not always an apparent answer. For instance, what propelled Michener to become a writer? Why did he persist in writing to the very end in spite of his success, wealth, extreme old age, and ill health? Why did he appear to have no curiosity about his origins? Did he invent a present for himself so vast, and work so compulsively, to make up for his unknown ancestry? How could one man produce so much in a single lifetime? What was the true nature of the man who seemed so self-effacing, so humble, yet who was hurt when he was overlooked by the Nobel Prize selection committee; who was angry when the University of Texas passed over his name in favor of a larger donor when dedicating a building? Michener's autobiography tells very little of himself. It is one of the least revealing memoirs ever written. Stephen May has come to fill in some of the void, to lay forth the story and answer some of the burning questions that arise when we think of James Michener.

May has proved that he was up to the task, which he has judiciously contained in a highly readable, informative volume capturing and holding the reader's attention from the first gripping sentence. May clearly likes his subject, a valuable trait in a biographer. He cuts to the heart of the story, not bogging us down with unnecessary details. Michener's early life was a sad and heart-wrenching one. He was a foundling brought up in poverty by a woman who may or may not have been his mother. Fatherless, he achieved in spite of his disadvantaged youth. He wrote because he had to, and it must have helped to exorcise the orphan's loneliness. As an adult, he filled the void of his early life with the places and people of his novels. He amassed great wealth but lived humbly, almost frugally, giving millions away to charity. The poverty, loneliness, and obscurity of his youth were replaced by the industry, philanthropy, and fame of his maturity.

Stephen May has packed into a book half as long as a typical Michener novel the basic and crucial facts of the writer's life and work, and he has done it with a critical eye and an understanding heart, together with an ease that makes the reading as delightful as it is informative. I have read this biography with pleasure. May has accomplished what every good biographer should do: he has made the writer come alive and the reader curious to know and to read more about and by James A. Michener.

Valerie Hemingway

Preface

No one was more ill suited for literary fame: raised by a single mother, he flitted between poorhouse and shabby rental, battling with his brothers over a sliver of soap. He was, however, athletic, and as a strapping teenager, he developed a passion for sports and for the written word. By the time he was in high school, he had begun to use words with as much precision as he shot a basketball or hurled a baseball. By this time, his intelligence and character were formed, and he possessed a single-minded purpose.

During his formative years, young Michener experienced the freedom and the perils of a fatherless existence: rafting down the Delaware River; hitchhiking and riding the rails from Canada to Mexico; grappling with bullies in the lanes outside Doylestown, Pennsylvania; and working in a local amusement park, where he mastered the con game. He saw drifters murdered and prostitutes beaten up in the darkness behind the tents and trailer homes bordering the circus.

Within twenty years of graduating from Swarthmore College in 1929, James Albert Michener traveled extensively in Europe and the American West, served in the South Pacific during World War II, and wrote an unassuming collection of stories that garnered him the Pulitzer Prize. During the next ten years, he rose to literary prominence, and he remained a fixture in American culture until his death in 1997. Michener's life was nothing short of extraordinary, since his career bridged the gap between being a serious artist and a publishing phenomenon.

It is difficult to pinpoint the exact reasons why Michener decided to become a writer rather than choose some other occupation. Perhaps it was the way his mother read him the stories of Dickens and Twain, stories so close to his own lonely childhood journey that they seemed to have been penned for him. Perhaps it was the power he felt in shaping a sports story for the high school paper, or the sympathy he felt for young unwed mothers who sneaked into the abortion clinic on the edge of town, or for the toothless drunk shambling down to the railroad tracks to hitch a ride out of town. Maybe he reached his decision much later: as a student rambling through the Scottish highlands in the 1930s, or as a teacher in Colorado witnessing the plight of Mexican American laborers toiling in the sugar beet fields, or as a sailor in the South Pacific hunkering down in his Quonset hut as a swarm of Japanese zeros screamed overhead. Perhaps all of these scenes, taken together, helped him decide that the writing life was the only meaningful career for him.

Deciding to become a writer and mustering the determination to endure the writer's life are two very different things, however. I believe the merger of those events occurred to James Michener on the Tontouta airstrip in the South Pacific in 1944, during the dark days of the Pacific war, when victory for the Allies was still precarious and elusive. The plane carrying Michener came in for a belly landing in driving rain. Sparks showered the runway as the plane skidded along and pinwheeled to a halt on the edge of the airstrip. Unhurt but shaken, Michener gathered his wits and reported to the transient quarters to spend the night. Later, unable to sleep and vexed about his near-death experience, Michener left his quarters and wandered aimlessly along the airstrip. The rain had stopped. A mournful tropic wind rustled the palm and breadfruit trees. At the end of the strip, gray and mauve thunderheads, lit by the moon, towered on the mountain summits guarding the runway. Mixed with faint traces of kerosene, the fallen rain glistened on the airstrip. For hours, Jim paced along, asking himself the questions that increasingly had begun to dog him. What did this experience have to teach him? What did he want to accomplish in the time given to him? What did he stand for? He thought he might be good as a clergyman or as a politician. Then again, he was happy in his civilian life as an editor at Macmillan in New York City. Without reaching any decision, except that he wanted to pursue greatness, he returned to his quarters and started to peck out words on his typewriter, words that gathered strength and conviction as he went along, ultimately forming the first few chapters of a book he titled *Tales of the South Pacific*. I think it was in those moments, sitting in his Quonset hut, experiences pouring from him, that he chose his career path.

After *Tales of the South Pacific* won the 1948 Pulitzer Prize for fiction, Michener led an active writing and publishing life. I have attempted to give the reader, in addition to a survey of his entire career as a writer, a full account of Michener's other lives, particularly his involvement with the Advisory Commission on Information during the Nixon administration. Although Jim was never a professional spy, he did pass crucial information to the American government at various times. To my knowledge, this is the first time this has been made public and certainly the first time it has been written about extensively. It was an aspect of Jim's life he rarely, if ever, discussed but one that adds an important dimension to his personality.

As his career progressed, many readers had questions about Michener's working methods. How could a middle-age writer rise from obscurity to win the Pulitzer Prize and establish a career that made him an international literary figure? Did someone else write parts of his novels? How extensive was his team of researchers? How much did he rely on that team? What is his place in twentieth-century literature? Often these and other questions arise about Michener's work, and I have tried to answer them in this book. Of these questions, the last one is probably the most difficult to determine, largely because Michener defies easy categorization. In his first four novels—*Tales of the South Pacific, The Fires of Spring, The Bridges at Toko-Ri*, and *Sayonara*—he was perceived as an important literary figure, in some people's minds as the next Hemingway. In his early nonfiction work from the 1950s—*Return to Paradise, The Voice of Asia*, and *The Bridge at Andau*—he was seen as a journalist. Writing books on Japanese art brought him acclaim from critics in the art world. With publication of *Hawaii* in

1959, *Caravans* in 1963, and *The Source* in 1965, a new Michener emerged, the writer now famous for writing the meganovel, loaded with facts and executed with scrupulous attention to detail and accuracy. By 1980 Michener stood alone in this brand of fiction. Many people tried to explain the secrets of his success, few with any effective results. In this book, I will delve into the Michener success story: a clever blend of scholarship and fiction, written by a man who refused to be just a novelist, or just a nonfiction writer, or just an art critic. He was the most independent-minded of writers, and his art followed suit.

Because Michener was such a prolific writer, I have not attempted to give the reader a synopsis of his novels or report on each one of his books in balanced detail, which might take up as much space as his life itself. Instead, I have concentrated on leading the reader through the creative process of several of his most important works. Each novel has its own peculiar challenges and problems, and I have tried to examine those challenges in some detail. All conversations in the book have either primary or secondary support. Additionally, all weather conditions, descriptions, and colors of things have primary or secondary support.

In this, the first full-length biography of James Michener, I have attempted to capture the man, the artist, the teacher, the philanthropist, the journalist, the world traveler—the person who could be revolted by requests for money and yet give away most of his life savings; the person who walked with kings and presidents and never forgot his barefoot childhood; the person who answered every letter sent to him, frequently typing out lengthy replies running ten pages, single-spaced; and the person who could have lived in a princely mansion and instead chose the comfort of a roomy bungalow, still treasuring his Royal typewriter and a library of books.

Rather than attempt an encyclopedic version of Michener's life, where every word of conversation is recorded and every act documented in meticulous detail, I have relied on the age-old tradition of the narrative biography. I have focused on the story of Michener's life rather than on the litany of facts and dates, which are meaningless. I hope that the result of this approach yields a warm human portrait with all of its accompanying shades of gray and inexplicable nuances.

Acknowledgments

I owe a great debt to many people for this project. I reviewed more than eight hundred thousand items—including manuscripts, partial manuscripts, letters, reviews of James Michener's work, postcards, and notes—in the principal collections of Michener's papers at the University of Northern Colorado and the Library of Congress. Guiding me through this wilderness of data and information were the people that knew Michener much more intimately than I did, and to them I owe a debt of thanks for sharing what they knew with me. In New York: Walter Cronkite, Kate Medina, Lisa Kaufman, Joe and Shirley Wershba, and Owen Laster; in Pennsylvania: Herman and Ann Silverman, Ed Piszek, and Don Conover; in Boston, Errol Uys; in Illinois, Ed Cowman; in Florida, Joe Avenick; in Maryland, John Barth and Michael Roe; in Wyoming, Tessa Dalton; in Colorado, John Dietz, Ken McConnelogue, Gil Hause, Laurie Guthmann, and Richard Bond; in California, Osmond Molarsky, Henry Jensen, and Robert Vavra; in Arizona, David and Karen Groseclose. My very special thanks go out to Gary Pitkin, Dean of the Libraries, University of Northern Colorado, and Janet Waters, Head of Archival Services, who encouraged me all the way and provided the facilities of the James A. Michener Special Collection, which contains Michener's original manuscripts, journals, and correspondence, as well as copies of documents of Michener-related material in the Library of Congress. Assisting me with the collection were two indispensable people, archivist Roiann Baird and her assistant, Richard Gibboney, who not only pointed me in the right research direction but were always willing to exchange ideas about Michener. I would like to extend gratitude also to my literary agent, Elizabeth Pomada; my editors at the University of Oklahoma Press, Karen Wieder, Chuck Rankin, and Steven Baker; and copyeditor Robert Burchfield for guiding the process smoothly. Finally, I would like to thank Valerie Hemingway, who wrote the foreword, read the manuscript critically, and offered her unique insights into the life of James A. Michener.

MICHENER

PART ONE

The Foundling
1907–1939

CHAPTER 1

The Boy

"Who am I?" "Who is my father?" "Where do I belong?" Although these are typical questions that children periodically ask, young Jim Michener hammered them out daily in his soul. This lack of a clear identity and lineage troubled Michener all his life, despite his claim when he was nineteen that he put the entire matter out of his mind. "I decided to hell with it," he remarked. "I was never going to know what really happened, and I wasn't going to worry about it again."[1]

James Michener's birth and date of birth remain shrouded in mystery. One version, the one promoted by Michener when he sought a passport, was that he was the son of Edwin and Mabel Michener, born February 3, 1907, in Doylestown, Pennsylvania. In his heart, however, he believed himself to be a foundling raised by Mabel Michener, who was devoted to him and saved him from being sent straight to an orphanage. Many people in Doylestown believed James to be the birth son of Mabel.

As for his father's identity, James Michener pointed out as late as 1977 that Edwin Michener died in 1902, five years before young Michener's birth, thereby eliminating Edwin as his birth father. "I am not a Michener," Jim contested. "I am not related to them. Actually I do not know who my parents were . . . the date, the locale, and parentage of my birth I have never known."[2]

The most likely scenario of James Albert Michener's birth is as follows: Around 1890 a teenage Mabel Haddock arrived in Bucks County, Pennsylvania, with her parents, Robert and Kate Haddock, who bought a farm in the valley near Doylestown. Their eldest daughter, Mabel, matured into a loving, affectionate young woman who was devoted to her family and the care of animals. At the Quaker meetinghouse one Saturday night, she met and fell in love with Edwin Michener, son of Ezra Michener, a well-respected landowner who raised Guernsey cattle.

Ezra Michener was a descendant of John and Mary Michener, who emigrated from England around 1685 and settled in the area. From that point on, subsequent generations of Micheners prospered as farmers in Bucks County. As the romance between Edwin and Mabel developed in 1899, Ezra Michener began to view the Haddocks as upstart farmers in the valley and to regard Mabel as an unsuitable match for his son. Over his family's protests, Edwin married Mabel in 1900. After their marriage, Edwin and Mabel moved in with the Micheners to help out with chores on the farm. In 1901 Mabel gave birth to a son, Robert Ezra. The following year Edwin developed bone cancer and died shortly after the diagnosis. Feeling unwanted after her husband's death, Mabel took her son and left the Michener farm.[3]

Between 1902 and early 1907 Mabel's movements are shadowy. She probably returned to the Haddocks' farm and there was courted by a few men, including one of Edwin's brothers. In the spring of 1906 she became pregnant out of wedlock. The father's identity remains a mystery. However, late in life, near his eightieth birthday, James Michener received a provocative letter from a childhood friend, Helen Gallagher. In the letter, Gallagher stated that Michener's birth father was one of the more prominent citizens of Doylestown and that Jim knew him, too. In his memoir, Jim referred to him as "Mr. Blank"—a John Doe name. According to the autobiography, Blank was a "respected voice in the community and a veritable pillar of the Presbyterian church." Michener went on to say that if Mr. Blank was his actual father, then so be it. "It was fortunate," he wrote, "if he was my father, that I never knew it, because my free and wild upbringing had given me a surprisingly rugged character, and had I known that he was treating Mrs. Michener in the way some said he did, I would surely have killed him."[4]

As Mabel's pregnancy advanced, she devised a plan to avoid any scandal associated with her clandestine relationship. In late January 1907 she traveled with her son, Robert Ezra, and sister, Hannah, a nurse in training, to Mount Vernon, New York, just north of the Bronx, where her brother, Arthur, lived in a comfortable bungalow on the edge of town. She gave birth to James Albert Michener in Arthur's house on or near February 1, 1907. She then left the baby at her brother's house, probably in the care of Hannah, and returned to Bucks County.

Several days later the infant was "delivered" to Mabel's house as a foundling in need of mothering. To preserve the secrecy of James Michener's birth, she promptly adopted him and raised him as her son. In truth, Mabel was James's birth mother, although she continued to deny the fact well into her later years.

Another possibility, although remote, was that Michener's birth mother was an unwed teenager who for some reason avoided taking her baby to an orphanage. Choosing a public place—a bus station, a library, or as Michener suggested in a later sonnet, "a New York trolley station"—she left the baby for someone to find and take care of. Eventually, the baby found his way to Mabel's.[5]

Whether Mabel was James's biological mother or simply his loving parent may never conclusively be known. Her dedication to his welfare, however, is beyond question. Possibly from shame or guilt for his birth being out of wedlock, she maintained that he arrived at her door without a name or birth certificate. She took in a number of homeless children: at one time Michener counted thirteen living under one roof. James was the only one to receive the last name "Michener." "I grew up surrounded by noisy, loving rambunctious children," he remarked, "who played with me, knocked me about, tussled with me in the mud, and kept me from ever thinking [of] myself as grand or favored or especially bright or entitled to privilege, or as anything but one of a mob."[6] Mabel hooked up with a local real-estate agent, who installed her and her family in decrepit houses. The agent would help her fix the places up then relocate Mabel to another house to resume the process. From childhood through high school, James Michener lived in nine different houses around Doylestown.

Mabel was an impish woman with an unassuming oval face, a dimpled chin, and dark eyes that tended to cross when her gaze became fixed. She wore her brunette hair parted in the middle and pulled into a bun. In formal photographs, she donned a hat piled with flowers and feathers. Otherwise, she sat in the rocking chair on the front porch dressed in a plain dress and apron. Although she experienced the usual ups and downs, she maintained a stoic Quaker demeanor, believing that tomorrow would bring better, happier days. She had an older sister, Laura, a teacher who lived in Detroit, and a younger sister, Hannah, who lived nearby.

Raised exclusively by Mabel Michener, Jim grew up without the benefit of any strong male influence. He found his favorite men in books his mother read to him. Charles Dickens, in particular, spoke to his alienation. Dickens's compassionate but often bungling and inept male figures became his surrogate fathers: the devious Fagin in *Oliver Twist*, the shadowy Magwitch in *Great Expectations*, the improvident Mr. Micawber and malevolent Uriah Heep in *David Copperfield*. Moreover, the plight of Dickens's waifs was his plight. Jim knew Oliver's fear as he carried an empty porridge bowl to the front of the workhouse to ask for another portion. He was well acquainted with the stigma of the poorhouse and the workhouse, of Doylestown children being abused, neglected, and sandwiched in their quarters. As he got older, Jim began to realize that men, especially men in authority—property managers, bank presidents, and doctors—were as weak and ineffectual as the host of Dickens's characters. Only in his mother and a few other acquaintances did he find solace, inspiration, and normalcy.

Years later as a teacher, Michener recalled the influence of *Great Expectations*: "Pip was an orphan and so was I. His problems were solved by his being taken into the home of his older sister and her husband. Mine were minimized by my being taken into the home of an almost saintly poor woman who eked out a living by taking care of abandoned children. . . . Therefore I followed young Pip with a magnifying glass, aware at every turn of the brilliant plot the extent to which the happenings might apply to me."[7]

In addition to Dickens, his mother read him William Makepeace Thackeray, Henryk Sienkiewicz, Mark Twain, and Charles Reade, emphasizing the artful narrative voice of the various authors. The evenings were a time of family togetherness and a reminder of the importance of literature. Michener clung to Mabel's side, drinking in the words. Gradually, he began to assimilate the size, scope, and complexity of the nineteenth-century novel, the kind of unwieldy, "trunk-size" book he would attempt in later years.

In the summer of 1914, as the European powers edged ever closer to war, Jim's rotund and lovable uncle Arthur lugged two special gifts to the Michener house. The first, an ice-cream maker, pleased Jim's heart and stomach for several hot Julys. The second, a Victrola, brought him food for the soul for the rest of his life. The ice-cream maker came with a crank, wooden bucket, steel cylinder, and bags of salt. "I would crank till my arms ached," recalled Michener. When Jim tired, Uncle Arthur took the freezer between his pudgy knees and defiantly muttered: "Let a man take over." Sweat rolled down his cheeks and veins bulged in his neck as he cranked away at the machine. "It's these last hard minutes," Arthur puffed, "that keep the ice cream from forming into crystals."[8] Once the process was finished, Arthur received the honor of licking the paddles. "Pretty good" was his oft-repeated assessment of their labors. After dinner, they would open the freezer to find the hardened ice cream, soothing refreshment on a steamy day in Doylestown.

Arthur's other present, the Victrola, made the Michener household spirited and livable. After toting it all the way from Philadelphia, he brought it into Mabel's front room, where he handed it gingerly to young Michener. "Guard it with your life," he snarled. "Drop it and I'll kill you."[9]

Holding the Victrola like a religious relic, Jim placed it in a special spot in the front room. Arthur read the instructions out loud and then put a record on the turntable. Jim listened spellbound as the powerful voice of Enrico Caruso rose from the Victrola. In the ensuing months, with the help of the Victrola and early records, he developed a deep affection for music. He listened intently to all the famous voices of the day: De Luca, Galli-Curci, Ruffo, Journet, and Scott. When he could not afford the records, he simply pored over the Victrola catalog, committing to memory the thumbnail biographies of the singers and entertainers. Much later in life Michener would admit that his passion for opera actually inhibited his art: "I have been damaged, in some ways, by my fixation on opera, for it has helped to delude me into seeing human experience in a more dramatic form than facts would warrant; it has edged me ever closer to romanticism and away from reality . . . and it has encouraged me toward artistic conventions that I might have done well to avoid."[10]

In the same year that he became addicted to opera, Jim Michener also discovered the world of art. In an old magazine, he found a reproduction of nineteenth-century English painter George Morland's *The Forge*, depicting a farrier shoeing a horse in front of a barn. In another magazine he saw a landscape by the American impressionist Willard Metcalf. He was so absorbed by the painting that he dashed off a note to the artist: "I think your picture of the field and the tree is very fine. It is in a magazine I am not allowed to tear, so if you have a copy you can spare, I would like to have it." He signed it "Jim Michener, age 7." To his surprise, Metcalf responded, encouraging him to develop his sharp eye. Jim clipped the letter to his postcard-size reproduction and added it to the growing collection of paintings that he kept in an old shoebox.[11]

Jim soon broadened his collection to include the Dutch, Italian, and French masters. He preferred landscape painting, particularly the innocuous and enchanting work of the seventeenth-century Dutchman Meindert Hobbema, whose *Avenue at Middelharnus* absolutely enchanted him. His favorite painting in his youth, however, was *The Goldfinch* by the seventeenth-century Dutch painter Carel Fabritius, a mentor of Vermeer. With its simplicity, naturalistic detail, and meticulous handling of color and line, *The Goldfinch* haunted the young Michener.

Ever widening his artistic tastes, Michener encountered Chinese and Japanese prints, which he considered brilliant counterpoints to European and American naturalistic art. In the next few years he studied the Japanese wood-block artists: Masanobu, Kiyonaga, Utamaro, Sharaku, and especially the work of Ando Hiroshige. His early devotion to these wood-block artists blossomed during middle age into a full-blown passion.[12]

Soon Mabel moved again, this time to a different neighborhood in Doylestown, where she secured work as a homebound seamstress and laundry worker. The money she scraped together was soon eaten up in food, rent, and clothing. "We were evicted six times because my mother could not pay the landlord," remarked Michener. "I can remember standing out in the road at dusk wondering where we could find a place to sleep. For a child, that was pretty frightening."[13]

Often the family's meals consisted of gravy poured over pork fat, or a mustard sandwich, or simply a crust of bread. Homemade sauerkraut was saved for special occasions. Dandelion greens stewed in vinegar and salt made a tasty side dish. In summer Mabel could pluck vegetables from her side garden. In winter, however, the children ate whatever was available. Malnutrition stalked the family. Jim's bones failed to develop properly. He got a bad case of mumps, which he later claimed made him sterile for life. Mabel suffered through colds, measles, and dysentery and steered her family through the period of the Spanish influenza. Frequently, illness, poor nutrition, or the burdens of life made it impossible for her to get out of bed, whereupon Jim or one of his "brothers" would take over the chores.

During Mabel's more prolonged illnesses, she would dispatch Jim to stay with her sister, Hannah Pollock, whose husband ran the poorhouse three miles south of Doylestown. Here, ten-year-old Jim received an education that became tattooed on his memory. The Pollocks lived in an ancient stone farmhouse. Across the field from the house in two red brick buildings stood the poorhouse, where the men in the first building and the women in the second waited out their final years. Often Jim was a delight to them, but other times he was treated as a hostile intruder. In the men's house, moods swung quickly. He loved the old men, however, with their tired old eyes, wrinkled elephant skin, toothy grins, and wonderfully engaging stories and conversations. Sometimes the stories were pure babble. Other times they rang with common sense.

One of the men, called the Dutchman, inspired some fear and caution in Michener. "He was a madman," Michener wrote, "but not mad enough to be placed in the mad cells. He was harmless, a kind of wonderfully vacant house that had known much fine living." When the Dutchman talked, everyone listened. The rest of the men knew he had never been to school and considered him to be illiterate. When the Dutchman talked of his school grades, everyone grunted as if he graduated with high marks. "That was one of the nicest things about the poorhouse," observed Michener. "A man could lie his heart out, could tell in fantastic fables all the things he had dreamed of and never accomplished. No one contradicted him, for all men in the poorhouse lived their last years with ancient lies. . . . There was gentle tolerance."[14]

Other characters filled Michener with their wisdom. There was Old Daniel and Toothless Tom. Daniel was over seventy "with a full set of false teeth that clicked when he talked." Despite a persistent pain in his stomach, Daniel coddled the young Michener. Toothless Tom brought apples for him and Jim to eat. Tom gummed them to the core before tossing them into the corner. He had perfected the habit of not finishing sentences beginning with the word "if." "If I was you . . . " His famous clauses punctuated his speeches, filling "the long hall like dead leaves clogging an alley in autumn."[15] Jim witnessed how old wounds and a lack of education and life skills rendered these souls incapable of living beyond the red brick walls. "I made up my mind in the poorhouse," he remarked, "that I would do anything, *anything* to keep myself out of there. These were pathetic people whose lives had soured, and I was not going to end up on the same ash heap."[16] Thereafter, being in second place was not an option. Later in life, as he amassed a small fortune, the grim prospect of returning to the poorhouse aggravated his most placid moods and forced him into some regrettable financial decisions.

The most significant event at the poorhouse occurred i
spring of 1917, when Jim had just turned ten. "Spring in the co
poorhouse is a time of pain," he wrote. "The hearts break and c
flow into the somber faces of the defeated. The men, gaunt fr
their long surrender, look at the stirring earth and compare th
present lot with what they had hoped for. In the evenings they sta
along the walls and watch the fresh-plowed hilltops."[17] The residen
went into the barn and found a barefoot man dangling from th
rafters. He had been dead for nearly four hours. It was one of man
reported suicides at the poorhouse, but this one chilled Michener
to the bone. He could see himself stretched out taut and lifeless, a
martyred and crucified soul amid the chinks of feeble light and the
smell of straw, manure, and horse sweat. At that moment, he saw his
life ending with the same result. No matter what his choices, his fate
was sealed. The hardest cases at the poorhouse involved men who
had suddenly lost everything. "Either relatives came to rescue
these men, or the men sat apart in the poorhouse and shook as if
the cold winds of death were upon them. Within a few days they
hung themselves."[18]

Snobbishness in Doylestown was deeply rooted. Catholics, African
Americans, immigrants, and anyone not anointed by the town elders
were viewed as suspect and generally shunned. Of course, Mabel
Michener, who ran a boardinghouse for a brood of castoff children,
received the brunt of this prejudice. Racial tension was also evident.
The Ku Klux Klan was accommodated at the local church to hold
their summer rallies. Because of the July heat, the Klansmen were
allowed to assemble without their customary hoods.

To many people in Doylestown, Mabel was a public nuisance; to
Jim Michener, however, she approached something akin to a Raphael
Madonna, a mother of such selfless virtue and uncompromising
devotion that he forever compared other women to her. During one
particular July and August, Mabel had thirty youngsters living under
her roof. In addition to her legal "family," she often took in children
whose parents had left town for the weekend or cared for children
for whole summers when their mothers and fathers went abroad.[19]

In the summer of 1918, as the war in Europe ground to a close, Jim got a job with the Burpee Seed Company outside Doylestown. He rose at six o'clock in the morning, tramped the two miles to the seed company, and from 7:00 till 5:00 in the afternoon, six days a week, toiled in the summer sun for seven cents an hour raising phlox seedlings. "I have sown phlox," he later recalled, "thinned phlox, hoed phlox, gathered phlox, and heaven knows what else, and if my birthday were tomorrow and if someone were to give me a bouquet of the horrid flowers, I would punch him in the nose."[20] He earned a grand total of $63 for a summer's work—all of which he gave to Mabel. The labor was pure drudgery. To counter it, he called upon his imagination, an imagination that by the age of eleven had now budded, bloomed, and flowered. While cultivating phlox seeds, he recited poetry—Whitman, Longfellow, Shelley, Keats, Wordsworth, Whittier, Milton, Hardy. He reckoned that by the time he was a teenager, he had memorized over three hundred poems. Another time he rewrote the ending to Homer's *Iliad* so that the Trojans could defeat the wily and capricious Greeks. When his memory for poetry was exhausted, he sang a Caruso aria. In the grips of sheer boredom, Michener was a happy boy.

Jim also tried his hand as a plumber and paper carrier. In the former role, he was apprenticed to a Doylestown handyman who set up shop in the basement of Barrett's Hardware. Jim became so adept at using a long-handled wrench that he considered quitting school and becoming a plumber. His uncle Arthur intervened, wagged the wrench at him, and growled, "Jim, you are not intended to be a plumber."[21] Shortly thereafter, young Michener signed up for a Doylestown paper route. Rising at 4:00 in the morning, he headed down to the newspaper stand that distributed the *Philadelphia Ledger*. Before leaving on his route, he scanned the headlines, feature stories, editorials, and musical reviews. He even had a chance to glance at the previous night's *Philadelphia Bulletin*, which included the latest murders, suicides, marriages, elopements, foreclosures, and government scandals. His paper route led him though the alleys, streets, and byways of Doylestown; he got to know where the rich people lived and which unwed women had gotten abortions. He also noticed the

houses where the attractive girls resided, paying particular attention to their cotton dresses and skimpy slips dangling on the clothesline in the early morning light.

By his twelfth birthday in 1919, James Michener quickly got used to his Huck Finn existence. Mabel never asked questions when he disappeared from home for days on end. She figured he was mature enough to handle himself in most situations. Deeply curious, Jim once sneaked into the nearby courthouse and listened intently to a murder trial. Impressed by how the attorneys argued their cases, he watched the proceedings from the shadows of the upstairs gallery. He remained at the trial on and off for several days before the bailiff, discovering he was alone, ushered him out. Not wishing to return home—what neighbors called "a madhouse with children running everywhere"—he headed to the railroad station, where he helped farmers load their produce in the boxcars heading to Philadelphia. When Jim came home, he returned to routines set by Mabel. A devout Quaker, Mabel gathered Jim and a few of her children and attended services at the Presbyterian church. As late as the 1920s, Doylestown had no regular meetinghouse for Quakers.[22] Michener was always home for holidays, especially Thanksgiving and Christmas. At Thanksgiving the family often devoured a donated turkey with potatoes and greens pulled from Mabel's garden. At Christmas Mabel loved decorating the house in a festive, Dickensian manner. Cheap tinsel, stockings stuffed with candy, and colorful boxes filled the house; the Victrola crooned a famous aria in the gaily lit front room. Because Christmas was first and foremost a sacred holiday— especially one for the children she insisted on a fresh-cut evergreen tree for the house.

However, one Christmas Eve money and decorations were scarce. No tinseled tree stood in the front window. Despite the situation, Mabel decided on her course of action. It was a frigid night; snow had crested into drifts in the front yard. She threw on her shawl, telling the children to go to bed and that she was going for a Christmas tree. Leaving by the back door, she plodded downtown through the snow and ice. She found a man selling trees. Moving through the forest of askew evergreens, she picked one out and calmly told the salesman as she was leaving: "You can arrest me tomorrow if you want, but a home with six kids has got to have a tree." By 10:00 that night, the tree was up and decorated in the frosted window. Around 11:00 the tree salesman, bearing a basket of food and toys, knocked on the door. "I knew you'd come," said Mabel. "God couldn't miss Christmas in a house where there are six children."[23]

Alas, caring for a pack of children ranging in ages from two to twenty exhausted Mabel Michener. Often she had to rely on her own resources to care for the children, many of whom needed constant attention. The children's birth parents repeatedly failed to support her cause. Mabel expected her children to attend college, so she tried to secure scholarships for them when she could. The reality, however, was that Mabel's reach always exceeded her grasp. In the early 1920s she made the anguished decision to close her boardinghouse and have Social Services find suitable homes for her children. Physically broken, generally despised by the townsfolk of Doylestown, she drifted into obscurity, forever adored by the children whom she raised and guided through young adulthood. One of her last acts of generosity was, through her will, to leave all her meager savings to her sons, Robert and James Michener.

CHAPTER 2

The Young Drifter

James Michener's love of the open road began with an asparagus farm and a lanky, tow-headed orphan and schoolmate named Ted Johnson. The asparagus farm was at a dead end of the road running east of Doylestown. The farmer paid the young Michener to harvest his crop, but the lad spent as much time gazing down the road to the west, visualizing how it must twist and turn on its way to the Pacific Ocean. After leaving the farm at night, Jim would head home, clean and fill the kerosene lamps, and, by their light, pore over his maps. Iowa. Nebraska. Colorado. Nevada. California. Their names sung to his lively imagination. He liked states with geometrical shapes and shuddered at ones with irregular outlines: Michigan, Virginia, and Maryland were castoffs.

In the summer of 1920 he and Ted Johnson were hanging around Doylestown when Ted mentioned to Jim: "Nothing much happening in Doylestown. Why don't we see what's happening in New York?" Somewhat astonished, Jim agreed. They packed some things, walked to the highway that led northeast, and began thumbing for rides. In his pocket Jim carried two dimes. With enough luck, it was sufficient currency to get them to New York. After that, it was catch as catch can. "The automobile had just fallen into a price range affordable by most ordinary families," observed Michener, "and when they owned one they wanted to use it often. They enjoyed picking up adventurous young hitchhikers and talking with them and perhaps, if the boys proved interesting, even treating them to a meal. A boy with enterprise could, in those simpler years, travel where he wished without fear of criminals moving in on him or deviates molesting him."[1]

It wasn't just the lure of the open road or Mabel's "madhouse" that urged him on. Other factors were pushing him out of the house. He began feeling estranged from his brother, Robert. When Jim's two aunts, sisters of the deceased Edwin Michener, paid visits to Mabel's house, they invariably offered Robert boxes of candy and ignored Jim. Handing the candy to Robert, one of the aunts muttered to Jim: "You're not a Michener. You don't deserve any." They said other hurtful things to Jim when Mabel and Robert left the room. Jim directed his anger at Robert, whom he idolized but blamed for instigating his aunt's scorn. Over time, bitterness and silent hatred developed between them.[2] In later years Michener wrote Robert several letters that were never answered.

"Ted and I were so exhilarated by our first success," Michener remarked, "that after we were back home for a few boring weeks, we set out again, this time with a little more money, and headed for Florida."[3] Hitchhiking through Virginia and the Carolinas, the two discovered that the fabled southern hospitality was much in evidence.

From time to time they stayed in the homes of the people they met on the road. Often traveling on dirt roads, they snaked through the South, Jim being offended by the shacks once used by slaves that they encountered. In Georgia, Ted and Jim walked into a police station and asked if they could spend the night in the jail. "How old are you kids?" said an officer. Ted handled the situation. "Sixteen," he replied. "Do your folks know you're down here?" The officer then asked them how much cash they had on them. "Spread it out, all of it." The boys laid out a few copper pennies. Ted mentioned they were headed for Florida. "Not through this state," remarked the policeman and tossed both of them into a cell. The following morning, the cop loaded the two on a northbound truck, gave the driver fifty cents to pay for their meals, and sent Ted and Jim back to Philadelphia.[4]

Describing himself as "a happy warrior moving unawares through a succession of minefields," Michener decided that he and Ted should next head for Canada.[5] A lack of motorists in rural Maine slowed their progress. After they finally got to the wooded border, Jim and Ted took about six steps into a Canadian meadow, decided they had seen enough, and turned back to Pennsylvania.

Michener turned into an irreclaimable nomad. Later in life, he wondered if he was stricken with "some psychic maladjustment" or "sickness of spirit" that condemned him to the road. "I have never been clever enough to analyze the impetus, but I doubt that it was related to any deep-seated psychic deficiency. The simple fact seems to have been that once I saw that mysterious road outside my home, the eastern part leading to a dead end, the western to worlds unknown, I was determined to explore the latter."[6]

Since Mabel Michener lived such a harried life and subsisted on next to nothing, she rarely if ever took the opportunity to acknowledge— let alone celebrate—the children's birthdays. Therefore, Jim's teen years were spent in an amorphous timeline when the customary milestones of childhood—the first pair of skates, the first bike, the first wristwatch—were conspicuously absent. His collection of postcard-size art prints was growing, as were his knowledge and appreciation of opera. He walked everywhere, hitchhiked, or rode the streetcar. He attended school religiously, returned home occasionally. When he studied anything, he attacked it intensely. On Sundays he accompanied Mabel to the Presbyterian Church to hear the Reverend Steckel lead them through the intricacies of honor, sacrifice, and civic duty.

In May 1921 Mabel asked Jim if he would like to visit his aunt Laura in Detroit. After consulting his atlas and confirming that it was territory he had yet to explore, he packed his knapsack and headed for Michigan. By now he was so accustomed to thumbing his way to his destination that he approached the journey fearlessly. Just two years earlier, Aunt Laura had boxed up her forty-volume set of Balzac's classics and shipped them to Mabel's house. Jim found them and soon began devouring *La Comédie Humaine, Le Père Goriot,* and *La Cousine Bette,* imagining himself as a bon vivant heading off to similar adventures as Balzac's heroes. "I am indebted to [Balzac]," he admitted, "as I am to any living human being who ever touched me because his books were so . . . filled with violence and compassion and sex and religion and the business of earning a living."[7] Balzac's large canvas of characters with different occupations and social levels impressed young Michener. Acknowledging that he had never read stories so beautifully written, Jim even overlooked Balzac's penchant for melodrama and sentimentality. He soon moved Balzac to the top of his extensive reading list of favorite authors. With his admiration for Balzac at its peak and his worn atlas in his knapsack, Michener thumbed his way to Aunt Laura's house in Detroit. After a sojourn there, he traveled a circuitous route through Iowa before heading back to Pennsylvania.

Back in Doylestown that summer, a friend of Mabel's invited Jim to work at the Willow Grove Amusement Park near Philadelphia. The friend, a lawyer who worked for the trolley company that owned the park, noticed Jim's resourcefulness and pluck. With its bevy of circus animals, tooting calliopes, milling crowds, and hawking vendors, Willow Grove was an upscale Coney Island without the ocean and the latter's knavery and seamy underside. It was set in a lovely wooded area close to the trolley stop between Doylestown and downtown Philadelphia. Crowds came from all over southeastern Pennsylvania and western New Jersey to amuse themselves.

To a fourteen-year-old, the park was Balzac, Dickens, poetry, barge hopping, basketball, art collecting, and opera all rolled into one. Jim reported to work as cashier, quickly discovering the art of shortchanging customers, or "honest stealing" as it was known among the workers. If a man wanted to receive coins for a $2 bill, the cashier would give him back change for $1 and then move him on through the line. Cashiers could make an extra $50 a day by this method, as well as some bonus money by lifting it from the till when no one was looking. While Jim was only the "honest stealing" type, the truly unscrupulous ones developed more elaborate pilfering techniques. "They resold tickets supplied them furtively by the men who collected them," wrote Michener. "They finagled the receipts from the turnstiles; they charged double and treble what they were supposed to and pocketed the difference; and in ways that only the most ingenious thieves could invent, they stole from everybody."[8] Through the practice of "honest stealing," Jim figured he could bilk one in four customers out of some money. He became so adept at it that the park's management asked him to serve as a private gumshoe, turning in other cashiers whom he suspected of cheating clients.

Besides the prospect of making extra money at the turnstiles, Jim found excitement and enchantment near the bandstand by the lake. Principally to make additional income in the summer, many musicians played at Willow Grove, including John Philip Sousa, Victor Herbert, and Giuseppe Creatore. Four times a day Jim would sneak over and join the throngs enjoying the music of these famous musicians. He met Sousa and Herbert, with whom he struck up a lasting friendship. He worked on and off at Willow Grove while attending Doylestown High School in the years 1921–1925. He left Willow Grove only when Swarthmore College awarded him a scholarship.

Michener's experiences at the amusement park found their way into his semiautobiographical novel, *The Fires of Spring* (1949), a work that almost did not get off the ground and one that was much maligned by several critics. In tone similar to Somerset Maugham's *Of Human Bondage*, *Fires* relates the ascent in the world of Michener's proxy, David Harper. The most important parts of *The Fires of Spring* are David's adventures in the poorhouse and at Willow Springs Park, which sparkle with Michener's youthful naïveté confronting social evil.

In his senior year in high school, Jim was president of the class, editor of the school paper, a frequent public speaker, and a star forward on the basketball team. Self-mastery dominated his thinking; in the back of his mind was the gnawing fear that one slip, one stumble, one innocent afternoon of laziness would send him straight into the gutter. The additional fear was that he could never recover from such a fall: it would mean death. Avoiding idleness, cigarettes, alcohol, and attachments with most young women, he buried himself in activity. In spring of 1925, two months after his eighteenth birthday, he spoke to the Doylestown Legionnaires and Rotarians about the importance of encouraging interests and hobbies in young adults. "By minimizing his defects," he continued, "by being kind to him and by bringing out his fine characteristics and desires, this can be accomplished."[9] Also that spring Jim learned that he was going to accompany forty-six other students on a three-day trip to Washington, D.C., to meet the president of the United States, Calvin Coolidge. Although the trip was honoring the top students at Doylestown High, Michener imagined that he was being singled out for congratulations at the White House.

Eight days before he graduated from Doylestown High School, Jim received the news that Swarthmore College had awarded him a $2,000 scholarship. He and Mabel were overjoyed. She had planned to send him to college, but Swarthmore's generous gift was an unexpected bonus.[10] Michener was once asked what prepared him for the Swarthmore scholarship; his reply: "Nothing! Absolutely nothing, I never in my education up to now, ever had any guidance—from anybody. . . . I got the scholarship to Swarthmore because a teacher who had gone there said, 'You're the ideal type of kid that ought to go to Swarthmore,' and she arranged it."[11]

On the morning of June 23, 1925, Jim, as class president, prepared to deliver the commencement address to his fellow graduates. He was above average height and powerfully built. His right arm often dangled unnaturally by his side. His nose was slightly irregular, the souvenir of an after-school altercation. A thatch of mahogany-colored hair slouched into a comma on his forehead. He rarely smiled for public view; if he did, he curled his lip slightly. His face looked optimistic, forceful, and determined.

In addition to garnering top honors at Doylestown High, Michener had continued to cultivate his personal interests. He continually thumbed through his shoebox art collection. He consumed opera records like candy. He had memorized numerous opera scores, including *Aida, La Traviata, Otello, Lohengrin, Carmen, Rigoletto,* and *Madama Butterfly.* He knew by heart several hundred arias, duets, and trios. By his own admission, he had become an addict.[12]

Religion gave Jim a code of ethics, a model for behavior, but it did not inspire him to any metaphysical or spiritual contemplation. Of all the saints, the one he could wholly accept was Saint Sebastian.

When trouble swirled around Jim, he could imagine himself as this Christian martyr, "standing calmly against a pillar while [his] enemies' arrows pierce [his] extremities without ever striking a mortal spot or making [him] wince." This kind of stoic belief dominated his thinking and kept a strict sense of moral virtue always in his gaze.[13]

That June morning of graduation, Jim delivered his speech titled "Diversions in the Student's Life." There was nothing particularly noteworthy or insightful in his words, except that he proposed a $500 scholarship for future students at the school, which was later established.

After his speech, the school principal, Dr. Carmon Ross, shook his hand and offered him a teaching position at Doylestown High after his Swarthmore studies were complete. Jim made no commitment. Privately, however, he was bitter about his and Mabel's treatment in Doylestown. He felt rejected and deprived of a normal childhood. Mabel, of course, was all but driven out of town. He would go to Swarthmore College. He would give it everything he had. He would never come back to Doylestown—at least not as an educator.

CHAPTER 3

The Mind's Journey

When James Michener began classes at Swarthmore College in September 1925, he found a seat of learning described perfectly by Cardinal John Henry Newman as a place "where inquiry is pushed forward, and discoveries verified and perfected, and rashness rendered innocuous, and error exposed, by the collision of mind with mind, and knowledge with knowledge."[1] Originally founded under Quaker auspices in 1864, Swarthmore retained much of its religious heritage while it encountered the demands of the modern age. Set on 330 rolling acres eleven miles southwest of Philadelphia, the campus, with its ivy-covered walls and elm-lined walkways, spoke of wealth, privilege, and tradition.

During his freshman and sophomore years Jim courted the image of a campus radical. He particularly objected to having to join a fraternity. Students at Swarthmore pledged to fraternities, even women, and Michener's cheekiness in raising his voice against them immediately branded him as a maverick. Fraternities were the social center of campus life, but Jim rebelled against the constant partying and their overt discrimination. Reluctantly, he joined Phi Delta Theta, a scholarly fraternity, which he soon bolted. "I saw them as doomed," he remarked later. "In a democratic, academic situation it was criminal to turn the social life of the college over to organizations that did not admit Negroes or Jews, and weren't very happy with Catholics either. I didn't have to be too bright to figure that out, but I did have to have a certain amount of guts to act on it."[2]

The fraternity issue was not one that Jim was willing to relinquish without a scrap. He single-handedly led a campaign to try to eliminate them from Swarthmore. Although his efforts were fruitless, it was one of his first tastes of grassroots political action. "Everyone knew Jim," recalled Tom Hallowell, a classmate and varsity football player at Swarthmore, "and we all admired him even though we didn't agree with him. Overall there was nothing wrong with the fraternities. . . . To a certain extent Jim was right about the discrimination, but we were bound by our charters. . . . I think Jim's protest convinced a few people to drop their memberships . . . [but] nothing drastic occurred, and the fraternities survived."[3]

In the autumn of 1927 Americans had every reason to feel optimistic. A few months earlier, Charles Lindbergh had flown solo across the Atlantic, launching him as an international icon and reviving the possibility that the average American man could become a hero. At Yankee Stadium in the Bronx, Babe Ruth was closing in on a record sixty home runs for the season. The stock market was soaring to new heights. With the premier of *The Jazz Singer*, movies now featured a sound track. "The future was bright," wrote journalist Joseph Wood Krutch, "and the present was good fun at least."[4]

The nation's buoyant mood carried over into Jim Michener's life at Swarthmore. Beginning with his junior year, he had been selected for the Honors Program on the basis of his superior performance in the classroom. Instituted in 1921, the Honors Program helped Swarthmore gain national recognition by the end of the decade. The program stipulated that a student, with aid of an adviser, should direct his or her own education through the careful selection of readings and weekly papers. There were no regular classes or scheduled hours. Students selected two areas of study each semester for their junior and senior years. Michener hailed the program as "an experience in intellectual grandeur."[5]

Jim emphasized studies in English, history, and philosophy. "I was a guy who was almost ordained to do well in the Germanic type of higher education," he observed. "I got an 'A' in everything. I took me about two days to figure out the professor—what his bite was and what he wanted me to do and then I did it. I'm not sure it was an education, but it certainly was [for me] at the time."[6]

Always adept at self-analysis, Jim once explained why he thought the Germanic method was perfectly suited to him: "Education was easy for me. I have a Germanic type of mind, a bear trap. I can organize and assimilate material. I distinguish between the Germanic and French way of thinking. The two systems are quite at odds with each other. The Germanic process is heavily deductive; it's one of amassing data and making deductions from it. The French is inductive and intuitive, very poetic and emotional. Each has its merits and its own flowering."[7]

Relying on his "bear trap memory" and his relentless drive to succeed, Jim learned more in those two years than perhaps at any other time in his life. He read great quantities of poetry and fiction and expanded his knowledge of literature by reading the Scandinavian and Russian masters. In the first semester of his junior year, he was primed to receive great instruction—and when he was ready, the teachers appeared. In philosophy Brand Blanchard led Jim through Plato, Aristotle, and Kant. For history he had the noted professor Freddie Manning, a scrupulous scholar who made him dig for details. In literature Robert Spiller, who would go on to a distinguished career at the University of Pennsylvania, introduced Michener to T. S. Eliot and the work of a young revolutionary novelist named Ernest Hemingway. Spiller effectively used the stories in Hemingway's *In Our Time* to demonstrate the power of the short, direct sentence. It was Spiller who got under Jim's skin and shook his sensibilities. "In my writing workshops," remarked Spiller, "I asked my students to focus on penetrating questions that made them experience raw feelings. I told them not to get lost in their own problems, but to write about what they knew. I said that a writer must have the courage to analyze his own life and write a story about it. This fires him so that he can go into the world and write."[8] For Michener, who tended to overintellectualize and second-guess himself to the point of immobility, Spiller's words were timely and profound. During seminars, Spiller encouraged students to probe their experiences to begin writing. Jim showed up with his diverse group of melodramatic love verses, listening intently to the other students' work and Spiller's comments on it. Spiller recoiled at Jim's traditional and maudlin poetry, but he was glad that his student was beginning to create.

It was difficult for anyone to break Jim's cool, superficial surface. At this time, he was trying to resolve the open question of his parentage. Was Mabel his birth mother? Was he adopted? Who was his father? Such questions vexed him to the point of madness. At Swarthmore he decided to put the matter to rest: he would never know the truth, and it did not matter. In the writing classes, he felt threatened by other students' willingness to share their early experiences. His were too painful, too embarrassing. He remained unaffected and aloof, writing the kind of "decent" prose and poetry that did not run too deep. Twenty years later, when Spiller read Michener's *The Fires of Spring*, Spiller took credit for unleashing Michener's creative talents. Although Spiller was not impressed with the quality of Jim's writing in the book, he called it the beginning of "a very worthy writing career."[9]

Dr. Albert Barnes was something of an enigma to Philadelphians. He was a man of considerable means who enjoyed mixing with the cream of Pennsylvania society, while he disdained money and most people with it. Born into a working-class family in 1872, he graduated from the University of Pennsylvania and afterward made a fortune in the pharmaceutical business. He developed a passion for collecting art. In 1912 he journeyed to Paris, where he met the American expatriates Leo and Gertrude Stein. From the Steins he purchased two Matisse paintings, which formed the basis of his growing art collection. By 1922 he founded the Barnes Foundation, and it blossomed into one of the greatest private collections in the country. In addition to a fine representation of impressionist and postimpressionist painters such as

Renoir, Monet, Rousseau, Degas, Gauguin, and Cézanne, the collection featured works by modernists such as Picasso and Modigliani. When Matisse visited New York, he requested to see the Barnes collection as part of his tour of American museums. Barnes counted among his circle of friends the philosopher John Dewey, the painter William Glackens, and the French art dealer Ambroise Vollard. Despite his fortune and his friends in the art world, Barnes never forgot his blue-collar roots, trusting only people with similar backgrounds.

Late in his junior year at Swarthmore, Jim was talking to a friend who mentioned Barnes's important collection, which immediately kindled interest in seeing it for himself. But Jim, wary of Barnes's hatred of college art programs, was cautious at first. He went to his desk at Woolman House and devised a scheme for viewing the collection. Posing as an uneducated steelworker from Pittsburgh, Jim sent Barnes a letter (via a friend in Pittsburgh, who had it postmarked there) asking him to see the "nice pictures," as he put it. Barnes wrote back, inviting Jim to a private showing at the museum. Still maintaining his ruse, Michener wandered around the collection like a young man in a trance. "Barnes was not only gracious," Jim later wrote, "he gave me a delicious meal, and then he took me into his gallery where a special light played on a Manet, beside which stood a Victrola on whose turntable he placed a record, which offered a symphonic music while he explained the virtues of painting."[10]

When word leaked to Barnes of the ruse, he was not only furious but also allowed the incident to escalate further. Later, after Michener became a writer of note, he claimed Barnes was hoarding his collection, while Barnes, in a letter to Michener, fired back that the Swarthmore student had seen it under pretense. Barnes further argued that Michener's work "glamorized ordinary people" and that it catered to "the smug complacency of snobs."[11] In an unusually shrill response, Michener contended: "I judge from the tenor of your letter that it would do me no good to apply for another invitation. . . . But since the vitriol of your pen seems to be diminishing with age . . . do you think there's a chance that my wife—who is a good artist and not at all like me—might get a chance to see what you're sitting on over there behind the wall?"[12] Trading barbs and insults, the two art lovers continued their battle for several years. At one point, Barnes challenged Jim to a debate on art, which Jim declined.

Before leaving college, Michener toured western Pennsylvania in the summer of 1929 with the Swarthmore Chautauqua, the largest group in the eastern United States of the Chautauqua assembly. Organized in 1909 by Paul Pearson, the Swarthmore Chautauqua was a curious blend of religion, culture, and education. The group traveled and entertained crowds through lectures, demonstrations, and dramatic presentations. Jim relished the idea of being part of a group involved in a variety of activities. Chautauqua had its own special meaning for him, reminding him of some of the bustle and noise of Willow Grove Amusement Park. However, as David Harper observes in *The Fires of Spring*, "this was the year 1929, the last year that the good brown tents of Chautauqua went through the East, and although there was money to burn that year, Chautauqua was slowly dying." Radio, movies, and the automobile were all conspiring against it.[13]

There were other changes brewing in Michener's life. The Hill School (always called the Hill), a prestigious college prep school in Pottstown, Pennsylvania, had offered him his first teaching job in the English department. The department head, John Lester, had personally visited Swarthmore and handpicked Jim from a score of candidates. Michener jumped at the chance to teach at the Hill, accepting a beginning salary of $2,100 a year and all living expenses. Before he began teaching in the fall term of 1929, Michener strode into Lester's office in a pressed suit, with his bow tie somewhat askew and his bristly hair teased into something respectable. Lester told him outright: "We place great emphasis here on diagramming the sentence. It teaches the student how to think, how to keep his ideas in line." Jim confessed he knew nothing about sentence diagramming. Lester shot him a confident glance and said smoothly: "Learn."[14]

For the next two years Michener endured the novice teacher's dilemma of having to learn more from his students than he taught them. The Hill School seemed a comfortable place for a teacher's career to unfold. Located northwest of Philadelphia and situated on a hill with a commanding view of the Schuylkill River valley, the Hill modeled itself on English public schools such as Eton and Harrow, primarily sending its graduates to Harvard, Princeton, and Yale. The teachers, called masters, scurried about in robes, their books clutched to their chests, while platoons of students marched to class tugging on their starched white collars.

At first Jim shared a faculty cottage with Jim Rice, a colleague from the English department. Michener's schedule filled with classes, tutoring, faculty dramatic presentations (including *A Christmas Carol* and A. A. Milne's *The Dover Road*), and student-teacher basketball games. As the Depression cut deeply into the economy, the student population dropped below four hundred, forcing temporary freezes in the hiring of masters. Jim was lucky to have such a lucrative teaching job—and he knew it. "I was a pretty gung-ho guy," he remarked, "and I came there under some difficulties. The preceding guy had been run off campus . . . it was touch and go with a new teacher. They were going to take a shot at me. It was very rough and everybody knew it, including the faculty. The faculty was not supportive; they said 'let the son of a bitch sink or swim—let's see if he's got it.'"[15]

For Michener, his sojourn at the Hill was tenuous at best. He soon moved into new rooms. Part of his responsibility included being a dormitory master, which forced him to hibernate in his rooms from nine o'clock at night until dawn. "That kept me in one place—my place—with no interruptions."[16] In Pottstown, he had bought four hundred classical records for fifty cents each and over a few weeks had lugged them back to his room. He went to the school library and checked out an armful of books—Dostoyevsky, Balzac, Tolstoy, and Dickens continued to be his favorites. However, he was adding Zola, Bjornson, Hemingway, and Dreiser as well. Jim must have sensed this was not exclusively pleasure reading, for he was beginning to look at literature in a much more serious way than at any time before. One book caught his attention: *Huntsman in the Sky* by Granville Toogood, "a very powerful book of the social structure of main line Philadelphia."[17]

He read Toogood's novel at the same time he was trying to write about his own experiences in the same way that Spiller at Swarthmore had urged him. However, Toogood's achievement (he wrote his first novel at about the same age as Michener) absolutely stopped Jim in his tracks. Jim hungered to write, but the novel convinced him that he did not have the "imagination or technique" to create anything of significant length.[18]

On the other hand, Toogood's novel inspired him to look beyond his life at the Hill School and consider the opportunities outside Pennsylvania. He was not truly content with the demands of teaching and the regimen of the classroom. Moreover, he had learned that Swarthmore had awarded him the Joshua Lippincott Fellowship, an annual prize that allowed him to travel and study in Europe.

After some careful deliberation, he decided to accept Swarthmore's invitation. One sticking point was a passport. Since he had no birth certificate or adoption record, his citizenship remained in doubt. After he wrote Mabel about his dilemma, she saw an attorney in Doylestown and convinced him that Jim was her son, fathered by Edwin Michener. Although the lawyer was unsure of Mabel's claim, he nevertheless used her testimony to secure a passport for Jim.

On a spring day in 1931, Michener walked into the headmaster's office and resigned. The headmaster, as well as a cadre of his colleagues, was speechless. Later, as Michener was removing his personal effects from his rooms, his teaching friends told him he was a fool to throw away a good job during the worst of economic times. At that moment, he might have agreed with them.

When Michener sailed for Europe in the summer of 1931, the national economy was far worse than he imagined. Bank foreclosures had quadrupled in two years. Thousands lined up at the Salvation Army or the Red Cross to get a simple meal. Others supped on potatoes, crackers, or dandelions, while still more people pillaged neighborhood trash cans. As the year advanced, the jobless were evicted, furniture and all, from their apartments. The homeless used anything—debris, cardboard cartons stitched with chicken wire—to form makeshift communities, which were infamously referred to as Hoovervilles, in honor of the president who presided over the nation during the start of its worst depression ever. Across the country, as farmers encountered drought, dust storms, grasshopper plagues, and foreclosures, a gloom and gnawing uncertainty settled on the nation.

Jim's destination was the University of St. Andrews in eastern Scotland. As one of Great Britain's oldest universities (founded in 1410), St. Andrews maintained a vigorous program for international students, drawing them from Europe, Australia, and America. When Jim arrived, sans his Victrola but with a well-thumbed Baedeker travel guide, he found the university's ancient gables and turrets rising from immaculate lawns by the edge of the North Sea. As a "research student," he used St. Andrews as a study hall and base of operations, often absconding for weeks or months at a time. Although he primarily came to Europe to study, Jim had travel on his mind from the beginning. He had a shoestring budget, so he drew up a plan of how he wished to spend his *Wanderjahre* abroad. He would tour Scotland in the fall and winter and then visit France, Germany, Italy, and Spain the following summer. In between, he would take short trips to the outer islands of Scotland and to London, where he spent numerous hours touring the galleries and museums.

In the autumn of 1931 Michener prepared to hike the hundred-mile stretch across the neck of Scotland, from St. Andrews on the east coast to Oban on the ragged western coastline. Wearing a sturdy pair of shoes and carrying a compass and a knapsack, he set off one morning, following traditional footpaths and making his way over the rolling countryside. For the next two weeks he ate in pubs along the way, chatted with impoverished sheepherders, slept in fields, enjoyed the hills burnished with heather, and spent his time precisely as he wished. When this first trip ended, he planned his second hiking trip: from Inverness to Fort William, a distance of about fifty-five miles. Abroad in the land of Walter Scott, Robbie Burns, and Robert Louis Stevenson, he treasured the new friendships he made in Scotland and appreciated his friendly hosts, who were "so admirably adjusted to their dour yet splendid land."[19]

Later, as winter advanced in St. Andrews, one of Jim's new Scottish friends suggested that he spend some time on Barra, a remote island on the Outer Hebrides off the coast of northwestern Scotland. Periodic isolation always rejuvenated Michener. In fact, it probably ensured his sanity. "The wee island of Barra" (as his friend called it) was to challenge him like no other previous experience. Arriving there through choppy seas, he found a craggy, windswept island that rarely saw the December sun. Waves chewed at the coastline. Gulls pleaded and bickered on the descending breezes. Barra was a Gaelic strong-hold of Catholicism, rich in legend and song. The islanders spoke little English, so Jim was forced to use hand gestures and generally "feel" his way through a conversation. For three months, without radios, books, and newspapers, Jim absorbed this wild relic leftover from the Middle Ages. The local priest introduced him to Morag Macneil, a blowsy, toothless old woman with deformed feet, who Jim discovered was close to the heartbeat of island folklore. She chanted to Jim her ancient Hebridean songs. Fascinated, Jim began accu-mulating them in great numbers. "Morag was an extraordinary woman," Jim remarked. "She had been born in an era before rural doctors knew how to correct clubfeet . . . Her warm heart, her desire to participate in whatever was happening on her island, and her love of both storytelling and singing made her a special person whose memory I cherish." Jim did more than cherish her—Morag's per-sonality was to appear (with some modifications) as some of his char-acters in later novels, including Nellie Forbush in *Tales of the South Pacific* and Ellie Zahn in *Centennial.*[20]

The Outer Hebrides are lonely islands, dark and forbidding in winter, bright and enchanting in summer. Morag convinced him to sail to a tiny isolated island nearby called Eriskay, "an exquisite little island with a fairy tale name." After he covered every inch of the emerald island, he considered himself a nesomaniac—a lover of islands. From that point on, Michener devoured information dealing with archipelagos, atolls, reefs, and inlets.[21]

In early summer 1932, at the suggestion of a Scottish friend, he enlisted in the British merchant marine. It was a simple process. He wrote a letter to the Bruce Line in Glasgow introducing himself. One of the directors wrote back asking him to show up in Glasgow and be ready to ship out when he got there. He arrived in the Scottish port and became an honorary member of the British merchant marine; he received a shilling a month and free passage to the Mediterranean ports. The shipping company transported coal to Italy and Spain and returned to Scotland with cargoes of lemons and oranges. In Rome and Sienna, he witnessed the glories of Italian painting for the first time; in Valencia, he took in his first bullfight and developed a love of Spain that would endure through the decades.

With his Lippincott Fellowship set to terminate that summer, Jim began casting about in January 1933 for a suitable teaching position in America. One of the schools he applied to was the George School, a private coed Quaker institution located near Doylestown in Newtown, Pennsylvania. In his seven-paragraph letter to the head, Michener emphasized that he was a Quaker and that he had graduated with highest honors from Swarthmore. After a time, the head, George Walton, wrote back and informed Jim that a teaching position would become available in May and that he was under consideration. Unknown to Michener, however, was that Walton wanted a Quaker of deep faith. Walton wrote to Michener's former chair, John Lester, at the Hill School, asking him about the depth of Michener's character. Lester responded that Jim's "main interests are intellectual . . . [he] is not a person to make any Quaker contributions to the new curriculum."[22] Despite Lester's advice, in May Walton offered the teaching job to Michener, a position that he quickly accepted.

Arriving back in America on board the *Mauretania* in early August 1933, Michener witnessed how Franklin Roosevelt's New Deal programs—principally the National Recovery Act and the Works Progress Administration—were beginning to stimulate the economy. Although there were still soup lines and massive unemployment, people felt optimistic. Even in solidly Republican Bucks County, the locals were giving Roosevelt grudging praise.

The George School buildings were sprinkled across 227 acres of wooded countryside in southern Bucks County. Michener's salary started at $1,200, plus room and board—not necessarily a princely sum, but in 1933 it seemed like a gold mine. Unlike teaching at the Hill, where he arrived tentative and unsure in 1929, he strode into his class at the George School a confident, sometimes cocky, young teacher, fed by a steady diet of literature and nurtured by two years' experience drifting around Europe. For the next three years he made the George School his home. He would develop lasting friendships with his students; however, the standoffish faculty was another matter. He involved himself in the activities of the school: as a forward on the faculty basketball team, as adviser for the *George School News*, as a director of the school marionette club, and as a representative to the Progressive Education Association.

Europe had reawakened Michener's love of the arts and social sciences. During his first year at the George School, he began to see academics not as individual subjects but as interconnected parts of a greater whole. He felt cramped by the English program and by the amount of essay grading. "I had moderately large classes," he remarked, "which I taught with all the vigor I could command. I took my responsibilities seriously, reading an infinite amount of world literature to prepare myself. . . . I used to correct themes until I thought that I had read every possible way of putting together inadequate sentences. . . . I was, to put [it] simply, caught up in the awful drudgery of teaching grammar."[23] He felt qualified to teach art, music, literature, poetry, history, and sociology and to synthesize them in classroom instruction. Therefore, he requested that he move to the history department, where he could marry the best of liberal arts with the foremost scholarship in the social sciences. Although Walton had Jim teaching in the English department for the 1934–1935 school year, he moved him to the history department at the beginning of the following term.

In summer 1935 Jim planned to study history at the University of Virginia at Charlottesville, in preparation for his tenure in the George School's social sciences department. While there, he met Patti Koon, the twenty-one-year-old daughter of a Lutheran minister from Lone Star, South Carolina. Within a week, their mutual attraction developed into a romance. All of sudden, Jim had a wildfire on his hands, and none of his experience was of much help to deal with it.

Patti Koon was a gregarious tomboy, stockily built with bobbed hair. Jim described her as an all-around athlete; she had an infectious southern drawl, frequently scorning women who incessantly talked of husbands, cleaning, makeup, and domestic matters. Friends called her "Butch." In some ways, Jim and Patti were hopelessly mismatched; in others, she was exactly what Jim needed. She posed no real threat to his intellectual life; she allowed him time to be alone and curl up with Flaubert or Dickens. They both shared a passionate love of collecting art prints and enjoyed a regular set of tennis.

As June advanced, Jim fretted about how to tell George Walton that he may be returning to the George School with a wife in tow. Jim knew he wanted to marry Patti—and quickly. In a letter to Walton, he chose his words carefully, hoping to sound like a person in full control of his reason: "[Patti] was voted best-liked girl in the university, and I believe I was the third fellow to propose to her since summer school began. She graduated with a very good scholastic record and is personally abstemious and very honest." Michener further characterized Patti as "the daughter of a Lutheran minister" and as someone who would make "a wonderful third baseman for the faculty ball club." No doubt these descriptions troubled Walton, a devout Quaker and believer in women's traditional roles.[24] In late June Walton put aside his doubts and wrote Michener that Patti would be a great asset to the George School. Jim was relieved and overjoyed. He dashed off a letter to Walton, stating among other things that "Patti's fully aware that in marrying me she will be marrying into a group where community living is a real problem. She's always been the minister's daughter and accepted that responsibility very well. She's been brought up strictly and has worked hard. . . . I'm just glad you wrote as kindly as you did. It makes a person feel good."[25]

On July 27, 1935, Jim married Patti Koon in a small ceremony in Charlottesville. After a brief honeymoon, they settled into a small farmhouse near the George School. Jim had wanted rooms on campus so he could be close to his activities, but no suitable quarters were available.

In late August Jim began his third year of teaching at the George School. He had a new bride and a new house, and he looked forward to teaching a new curriculum. As autumn came on, Michener could have echoed his persona David Harper in *The Fires of Spring* that "the old year died and the new one began some time in late October and November when irresponsible gusts of wind ripped the last leaves loose and sent them howling into the long nights . . . this autumn he was being born anew."[26]

CHAPTER 4

Sojourn in the Rockies

Aside from writing a few plays for school productions and advising for the school newspaper, Jim was not writing creatively at the George School—not even short stories—a fact that he deeply regretted later in life. Pushing his writing to the side, he threw everything he had into class preparation and instruction. He gave depth to his lectures for sophomore history by adding perspectives in art, music, and literature. Often preparing for an hour, he burst into the classroom, set his books down on the desk, and began nervously pacing the front of the classroom. Dressed in a shirt and tie, his dark glasses resting askew on his nose, Jim turned his riveting gaze on each student, tossing out names like Charlemagne and Maeterlinck, Handel and Mozart, Rubens and Vermeer. The head, George Walton, thought him "an original, resourceful, brilliant, unconventional teacher, a great inspiration to the more brilliant students . . . and a very inspiring and helpful teacher to slow students." Walton also liked Michener's energy, noting that "students who dislike him dislike his over-enthusiasm."[1] Now that Michener was twenty-nine, the tributaries of his accumulated knowledge in art, literature, music, and history—added to his exploits in Europe and thumbing around the country—were beginning to gorge the mainstream, creating a formidable teacher and mentor.

Jim and Patti's first winter in the cottage near the school was especially severe. The wind howled from late November on; snow piled up at their doorstep, forcing Jim to shovel his way out before class. He gathered his books and trudged through the drifts to campus, madly warming himself as he went. By March 1936 the remoteness began to wear on the couple. In a letter to Walton, he reiterated his desire to teach another year at the George School but reminded him that "another year in the country would be a hardship, but bearable. We have never spoken to anyone this year, in spite of badly nipped ears and wet feet."[2]

That summer, as Jim and Patti played singles and doubles tennis on the George School's courts, a half a continent away in the Rockies, William Wrinkle, director of the College High School at Colorado State College (now the University of Northern Colorado), had an unexpected opening in his social sciences department. The position required the candidate to teach in the laboratory school and, along with his or her spouse, be ready to direct a large dormitory. The candidate would be hired as an associate professor and encouraged to pursue a master's degree at the college in Greeley. Hearing of Michener's background, Wrinkle sent out a "feeler" to Walton, asking him about both Jim's and Patti's character and their suitability for the openings. Walton, faced with inevitability of Jim's departure, scrawled some notes to a few of Wrinkle's questions. In part, Walton noted: "I would not want him to undertake the directorship of any of my boys' dorms. Not systematic, unreliable in routine detail. Not indifferent to duty, but absorbed. [Jim] has immature tardiness, forgetfulness, and a hesitation to enter into planning of social events. . . . No moral faults. High estimate of versatile scholarship and original inspiring teaching methods."[3] Walton had nothing complimentary to say about Patti Michener, a fact that did not seem to deter Wrinkle from attempting to hire Jim.

In early August Wrinkle sent Jim a letter offering him the position. Jim accepted, partly because he wanted to advance his career, and the George School did not afford him that opportunity. His colleagues were surprised, offering him some pointed criticisms about academic life in the West. Nevertheless, Jim and Patti packed their things and headed to the Rocky Mountains to start a new life. On the way, they stopped briefly in Columbus to visit some friends on the Ohio State University faculty, who gave Michener more dire warnings about college teaching out West. One faculty member cautioned him: "The sands of the desert are white with the bones of young men who went west and are trying to get back east."[4]

There were times in James Michener's young life when his eyes opened to a new place like a prairie flower drinking fresh spring rain. Scotland was one. Italy another. Spain definitely. The West was next. But this discovery was gradual. The myth of the West, popularized by a host of romantic writers, suggested that the land beyond the Missouri River could transform character, correct physical weakness, and even have enough magic to clear one's thinking. Writers from Theodore Roosevelt to Owen Wister and Zane Grey championed this idea in their classic works. For Michener in particular, his move to the West benefited him in three areas: it freed his writing; it offered him a bold new landscape to discover; and it boosted his sagging career as a teacher of progressive ideas.

The stimulating teaching environment was the first of these to become apparent to Jim. After he and Patti got settled into their dormitory supervising thirty young men and preparing discussions for ninety high school students in his classes, Jim geared up to teach the fall term.

William Wrinkle was a staunch advocate of the modernization of the college curriculum at Colorado State. He criticized other programs that forced students "to undertake work in mathematics, in foreign languages, and in highly differentiated sciences in which they have little interest and in which there is little expectation that they can find utility or satisfaction." Aided by a faculty of twenty-four professors at College High School, Wrinkle sought to revolutionize secondary education by stressing "meaningful experience" over the "accumulation of knowledge."[5] Consequently, Wrinkle built his program around fields of experience—nature studies, the arts, communications, and vocational training—and eliminated traditional requirements in ancient history, Latin, economics, and highly specialized courses.

For Michener, fresh from the treadmill of diagramming sentences for instruction, it was a new professional life. He took quickly to the idealistic nature of the courses; he felt free to express new ideas to his students and to have them respond without judgment or criticism from him. Instead of pounding knowledge into his students' heads, he was training them to be independent, critical thinkers and good citizens. At the same time, he was teaching himself the same values. For the first time in a while, he felt stimulated, challenged, and acknowledged.

He rarely taught a course without incorporating several disciplines. He introduced Bach into a course on Colorado farming. Gathered around Michener's phonograph, students heard Charpentier, Beethoven, and Gounod compared to Colorado sheep and cattle ranchers trying to calm their herds. Using the same technique, he instructed courses in the Renaissance by combining art and musical approaches. "I believe that social studies," Jim maintained, "and music need to cooperate on this problem of training the imaginations of our school children. . . . Music is perhaps the finest single instrument we have by which to achieve the development of fine, sensitive, perceptive imaginations." His belief in the value of interdisciplinary education placed Michener way ahead of his time. One of his students remarked that "he knew how to get his points across in an interesting way, and he was very intelligent. We expected him to become a great philosopher and a legend of our time."[6]

After he met Floyd Merrill, editor of the *Greeley Tribune*, and began accompanying Merrill on day trips outside of Greeley, Jim felt a new inspiration to write. Partly it was the landscape: the plains, the mountains to the west, the Pawnee Buttes to the north, the great sweeping clouds towering over the horizon. Free of the clutter before him, he saw fresh spaces and new, sweet life. At first in Greeley, he focused on writing articles related to education: "Music in the Social Studies," "Bach and Sugar Beets," and "Sex Education: A Success in Our Social Studies Classes," an article whose subject surprised his colleagues. In Greeley, Michener seems to have made a conscious attempt to further his career by writing professional journal articles. These were followed by his first published work of fiction, "Who Is

Virgil T. Fry?" (1941), a story of a rogue teacher criticized by his colleagues and fired by his boss who is nevertheless worshipped by his students.

Written toward the end of his sojourn in Greeley, the short story was clearly a work whose subject Michener had frequently pondered; but he insisted that the work was a composite of teachers he had known, particularly at the Hill School. "I could visualize the subject of my story," explained Michener, "for I had taught with him and had not particularly liked him. I thought he was prone to showboat. But I was also intelligent enough to know that he had teaching capacities far beyond the prosaic ones I had developed." Michener's first work of fiction—barely nine and a half pages in manuscript form—attempted to "cut right at the heart of our nation's educational problems," according to its author.[7] Noteworthy neither in story nor character development, "Who Is Virgil T. Fry?" nonetheless reveals Michener first go-round with narrative. While he wrote and taught, he also worked on his master's degree in secondary education at Colorado State, which he finished in 1937.

During his first year in Greeley, Jim felt a sense of fulfillment and freedom. Besides, he was on his way to proving his friends wrong. "If I had listened to my friends," he remarked, "I would not have moved to Colorado in the first place, and the time I spent there was not insignificant. A much freer society existed out west than in Pennsylvania, where I had become a semi-sophisticated easterner, politically and socially. The West really helped to make me."[8]

The Depression, coupled with the great drought of 1931–1939, cut deeply into the economic soul of Greeley and eastern Colorado. The lack of rain was accompanied by windstorms that blew away the top soil and reduced the wheat fields to stubble. Although Greeley was on the northern fringes of the Dust Bowl, it was still prone to periods of these vicious storms, called "black blizzards," which could rage for days. Many of Michener's students were affected by both the economic conditions and the severe drought.

One student situation remained vivid in his memory. Much later, he would reflect on it as one of the inspirations for the novel *Centennial.* "I had a minor responsibility for allocating National Youth

Administration funds," Jim recalled, "and I think we gave worthy students thirty-five dollars a month, if they gave us library help, or janitorial service, or tutorial service in return." He quickly discovered that this "pitiful amount meant life and death" to some of his students. He found out that two young sisters were starving themselves so that they could give the money they earned from Michener to feed their parents, who lived on the family farm northeast of Greeley. One day Michener drove out to see how the family was faring. What he found appalled him. "Mother, father, two younger children. No food. No seed crop for the coming year. No money to pay the bank. Only strong humans willing to till the soil, but with no soil to till." As Michener started to leave, the man asked him for a favor. Would Jim mind if he siphoned some gas from Jim's tank? They had no money for the past month to buy gas so that the man could travel to nearby Keota and find work. When writing his novel of Colorado in the early 1970s, he remembered the dignity of that family and their struggle against hopeless odds.[9]

After several encounters with communism and fascism in Europe, Jim arrived in Colorado with his Republican stripes still virtually intact. He could thank Joe Grundy and Bucks County politics for that legacy. However, as he began to move into the community of Greeley, this allegiance to conservatism began to erode. "In Pennsylvania," he commented, "I learned to respect politics; in Colorado I learned to love it."[10]

One of the leading reasons for his disenchantment with conservative issues was his participation in the Angell's club, a group of local businessmen and professionals who gathered at a Greeley restaurant managed by a widow named Nellie Angell. According to Michener, there were "two clergymen—one liberal, one conservative—an admirable lawyer who had pleaded major cases before the Supreme Court, two scientists, one of the cantankerous leaders of the Colorado Senate, a wonderful school administrator, a fiery newspaper editor [Floyd Merrill], and a healthy scattering of businessmen, mostly on the conservative side."[11] Twice a month this diverse group would gather to swap news stories, discuss current events, and spar about politics.

Upon arriving in Greeley and witnessing how the Mexican field laborers were being treated, Jim became an outspoken advocate for their fair treatment. Gradually, in and out of the classroom he adopted other liberal issues (among them, some atheistic views), which began to brand him as anticonservative. When a Bible-thumping evangelist came to town and started castigating the Angell group for its toleration of liberals, Jim was instrumental in running him out of town. "Some of my students," Michener remarked, "were surprised to learn that a relatively quiet man like me had been willing to risk a frontal assault from a master mud-slinger."[12]

During the 1936 presidential campaign, the electricity in the group was especially pronounced. The Republican candidate, Alf Landon, had his group of supporters at the table, who squared off with the Democrats and their reigning hero, Franklin Roosevelt.

"Landon will win by landslide," the conservatives claimed. "The nation has seen through Roosevelt and knows what a charlatan he is."[13] When Roosevelt swung through Greeley on a whistle-stop western tour, Jim and the other members turned out at the train depot to see him. Michener and his group were stunned to see the president steered onto the platform in a wheelchair, his body immobile from the waist down and the braces on his legs flashing in the sun. Most of them had no idea that Roosevelt was unable to walk. The president said nothing of substance, noted Jim, but his presence, his calming voice, and his defiant grin won thé crowd over.

Soon after the Roosevelt's departure from Greeley, the group met again. The election was imminent, and according to the preelection polls, Landon was a shoo-in. Jim remained unconvinced. On the day after the election, as news flashed of Franklin Roosevelt's landslide victory, most of the Angell group slouched around in an incredulous stupor. The *Greeley Tribune*'s headline was "WHA HOPPEN?"[14] From that point on, Michener was neither a conservative in politics nor a believer in preelection polls.

Floyd Merrill, the "fiery editor" of the Angell group, remained one of Jim's best friends in Greeley, even though their political views frequently clashed. Merrill began taking Michener around northern Colorado in the autumn of 1936. Merrill emphasized the advantages of taking photographs on their journeys, so Jim always packed a camera loaded with Kodachrome film.[15] Two subjects that were personally close to Merrill were the complex irrigation systems of the Platte River valley and the American Indian residents of the area. The former topic piqued Michener's interest. Jim was becoming fond of arid and semi-arid areas (including Spain), and he listened intently to Merrill's explanation of how water was brought to the dry lowlands around Greeley. It was a subject that would provoke Michener during future travels, especially in Mexico, Afghanistan, and North Africa.

Over the next three years Michener and Merrill journeyed to the important sites of westward settlement and expansion: Cheyenne, Wyoming, and the Union Pacific Railroad; Fort Laramie; the Oregon Trail, shadowing the Platte River in Nebraska and crossing into Wyoming; the Colorado and Wyoming Rockies; and the battlefields of the U.S. Cavalry versus the Cheyenne, the Arapaho, and the Sioux. This vital tapestry of disconnected information, too much to absorb over a short period of time, nevertheless remained at the forefront of Michener's keen memory. It turned out that in addition to being a major agriculture area of the Rockies, Greeley was also a strategic center for exploring the historical West.

Often, when the pressures of teaching became too great, Michener took walks along the nearby Platte River. In summer, huge plumes of cottonwoods loomed over the river among the spindly willows that bent forward like tired old men. It was Cheyenne and Arapaho country, still filled with the echoes of their culture. In winter, he borrowed a pair of snowshoes and trudged along the river, a dark snake in the blanched countryside. Legions of Canada geese descended on the nearby fields to peck at the desiccated cornhusks. Whether in summer or winter, the Colorado sky—blue, deep, ethereal—dominated the land. Silently and gradually, he began to appreciate the barren landscape.

Jim took frequent trips to Denver to attend the theater and to take his classes to the Denver art museum. He and Patti spent the spring holidays of 1937, 1938, and 1939 traveling by car in Mexico. Accompanied by a Greeley couple, the Gilberts, on the 1937 excursion, the Micheners drove to southern Texas and prepared to cross the border. Instead of encountering a long wait, they were fortunate to meet a customs official—a former resident of Greeley—who waved them through quickly. They motored down to Chihuahua, Jim feverishly training his camera on virtually anything of note: cattle ranches, the sunburned hills and valleys, drowsy hamlets with pigs and chickens scrambling through the streets, and the faces of the people. Deep in Mexico, he made friends with two bullfighters, Rolleri and the graceful torero Flaco "Skinny" Valencia. "With them," Jim recalled, "I traveled the bullfight circuit—the rude *pachangas* [pick-up affairs with no rules] in the country, the exhibitions, the *tientas* [testing the cows for bravery] and the formal fights. They introduced me to world few strangers would be allowed to know."[16] Mexico kindled Jim's love of Spain. He was hungry to write a novel, but the setting had eluded him. He had always wanted to write of Scotland, but as he divulged later, he was unable to explain exactly why his many attempts failed. "I knew the land, the people, and the history, but the magic never came," he commented.[17]

He returned to the heart of Mexico in summer 1937 and 1938 for an extended look at the country. All of a sudden Mexico stood before him, ripe for comment and inspection. He knew the people and the land, certainly not intimately but enough to render it convincingly in fiction. As early as 1937 he began drafting his novel of Emiliano Zapata and the Mexican revolution. After finishing it in 1939, Jim submitted it to Macmillan for publication. The rejected manuscript had a kind note attached: "Not quite ready, but it shows promise. Come back later." Jim shelved the project among some of his other truncated works and temporarily removed Mexico from his list of possibilities.[18]

Although his attempt at capturing Mexico came to naught, his interests were moving in two different directions. On the one hand, he loved the artistic products of civilization: painting, literature, music, and dance; he liked living well among comfortable furnishings; on the other, he prized cruel, arid lands and primitive peoples. His art tended to drift to the latter. He began to love the wasteland, finding there a lack of convention and a meaning that he could not comprehend in the cities of his journeys. He glimpsed this prospect in Scotland and

Spain; Colorado and Mexico heightened that notion; and later the South Pacific would bring it to fruition. In his head he was the maestro, but in his heart he was the matador.

By 1939 and his thirty-second birthday, Jim was seeking new challenges in education. His fifteen journal articles had given him widespread notoriety in higher education and led to Harvard University's offer of a visiting lectureship for the 1939–1940 academic year. After receiving a year's leave of absence from Colorado State, he and Patti headed for Cambridge, Massachusetts, and Harvard's School of Education, where he sought to complete a doctoral degree and teach in the graduate program. His professors in the Harvard program included the prominent historians Howard Wilson, Arthur Schlesinger, Sr., and Kurt Lewis. While in Cambridge, Eleanor Roosevelt invited him and a few other scholars to visit the White House and discuss issues in education. After he engaged her in a spirited discussion about social studies, he met the president briefly.

At Harvard the long grind of a Ph.D. program, coupled with an intense teaching schedule, wore on Michener. Moreover, he wanted to pursue writing more and teaching less, a decision that had been tumbling in his mind for more than a year. Swaying his decision to abandon the doctoral program was Harvard's insistence on a reading knowledge of two foreign languages, a background that Michener did not have. He explained his dismay to his lead professor, Howard Wilson: "I think this is a perfectly asinine series of decisions that will do education no good. . . . I have seen too many such men [Ph.D.'s] wasting the time of their students. I do not have the wish to enter this cat and dog fight unless I was forced to do so."[19]

Ultimately, when the fellowship terminated in August 1940, he resolved to relinquish the doctoral program and return to Colorado State, knowing that his days in education were numbered. "I wasn't bitter about it," claimed Jim. "I had used up academia and realized it was not going to have too much to offer me."[20]

Back in Greeley, Jim and Patti viewed the situation in Europe with alarm. World War II had begun the previous September. German U-boats in the battle of the Atlantic had decimated Allied shipping;

in May 1940 Hitler had invaded Norway and Denmark; on June 5 France had fallen. And in Britain, as the newspapers daily reported, all that stood between the full might of a Nazi invasion was a scrappy band of Royal Air Force (RAF) pilots flying Hurricanes and Spitfires. Democracy was at stake; the world as Jim knew it was at stake.

If Britain fell, there was no stopping the Nazi juggernaut. Remarkably, the British stopped the Germans in the skies over England. As the war lapsed into limbo and America waited hesitantly, Jim resumed teaching at Colorado State. He continued his travels with Floyd Merrill and generally kept a novel manuscript he was working on in his desk drawer; however, he finalized nothing during this time. In the spring of 1941 Macmillan Publishing sent its representative, Phil Knowlton, to Greeley, hoping to hire a book editor for its textbook division. Knowlton liked Michener's background in the social sciences and offered Jim the job, which meant a move to New York City. "He didn't need me," claimed Jim, "but he needed someone like me, about 35, who could fill a gap in Macmillan's chain of command. I was available."[21] Despite several friends' objections, including Floyd Merrill's, he took the position with Macmillan at three times his current salary. Later Jim discovered that Macmillan had narrowed their hiring choices to three, and he was their last choice. The two other candidates took other jobs, leaving the position to Michener.

It was late June in Greeley, always a sizzling time. Cottonwoods sagged in the sun. The breeze, barely a whisper, stirred the cattails along the banks of the Platte River. To the drone of flies, cattle huddled in the dank stockyards. Westward, clouds mushroomed over the distant Rockies. Jim and Patti boarded the morning train that headed out of Greeley, bound for Cheyenne and points east. They were soon roaring through the sea of grass of southern Nebraska, retracing their journey of five years earlier. At thirty-four, his hair thinning rapidly, Jim was closing in on the age (thirty-five) that, by his own admission, a man must choose his primary vocation. As the landscape whisked past him, he was uncertain that his present quest would bring him to that realization. He had always believed in bold leaps into the unknown. Perhaps this one might bridle his free spirit, smooth his rough edges, subdue his often stubborn personality, and help him settle down into something respectable.

But he certainly hoped not.

PART TWO

A Tale of the South Pacific
1940–1949

CHAPTER 5

The Amateur Hero

The Micheners rented a one-bedroom apartment a short walk from Macmillan's imperious headquarters at the corner of Tenth Street and Fifth Avenue. Their six-year marriage was clearly in trouble. Jim embraced the big city with its museums, libraries, bustling streets, posh restaurants, concerts, and theaters. Patti, originally from a small town in the South, hated it. In his free time, Jim wrote at the kitchen table in their apartment. Patti became jealous of the time he spent writing and his devotion to it. Never one to show his emotions, Jim withheld from Patti some of his deepest fears and concerns. Patti was growing in her religious life; Jim was not. Although they loved tennis, music, and art, the time they had to dedicate to these interests began to shrink. While Patti stumbled through her days in New York City, Jim plunged into his job as a fledgling editor.

Textbook editing, however, was considered in the second echelon behind the ultraglamorous world of trade publishing. Jim's office, a disheveled affair with piles of paper erupting to the ceiling, was on the second floor. His job was to find, edit, and perform financial feasibility studies on prospective books for the textbook market. Using his math skills and a slide rule, he became something of an expert at projecting costs for a book.

He divided his task into two columns. In the left column—always signed off by the president of the company—were the estimated costs of sending a book through production; in the right column were actual costs of publishing, plus 35 percent overhead, which included the salaries of the editorial and sales staff. "I became a wizard," Jim commented, "at keeping the left-hand and right-hand costs at a minimum, only to have that dreadful thirty-five percent kill me in the end. The art of publishing is to keep the inevitable costs of the left-hand side so low that the profit per copy on the right-hand side will be large enough to amortize the fixed costs if a reasonable number of copies are sold."[1]

Michener took special pride in both the process and product of book publishing. He once claimed: "I acquired an abiding respect for the concept of a book as one of the finest symbols of our civilization. I saw it as a timeless pledge to the future. I wanted any book for which I had responsibility to look right, to be well printed and properly bound, to feel good to the hand and inviting to the eye. . . . With me the making of a book was an act of dedication, and I had this devotion before I ever dreamed that I would myself be writing books."[2]

In addition to Phil Knowlton, who became Jim's boss, his other coworkers included Harold Latham, the senior editor, and Jim Putnam, a junior editor exuding British decorum. Latham was a towering figure at Macmillan, having landed Margaret Mitchell and *Gone with the Wind* for the firm back in the 1930s. He never married and, for the most part, lived in his office. Although he never talked to the lowly Michener during Michener's first years on the job, he figured prominently in Jim's development as a writer. The second person whose presence affected Michener was Jim Putnam. "Serene, charismatic, and never pompous," according to Jim, Putnam was the only trade book editor who walked down to the second floor and conversed with the underlings in the textbook section.[3] Jim envied Putnam's role at Macmillan, which involved dressing immaculately and meeting the luxury liners at the pier. He would then escort some famous English author to Macmillan's offices on Fifth Avenue and, while Michener watched in awe, parade him or her through the various sections, making introductions here, chatting there. Putnam and Michener became good friends, until the day that Putnam was fired over the publication of a controversial book.

Issues of censorship, usually involving certain religious groups, always nettled Michener. A team of lawyers would show up in Michener's office demanding that parts of the text be changed, toned down, or eliminated entirely. Jim bristled at coercion or threats of any kind. He listened to their arguments and negotiated a suitable alternative without compromising the integrity of the original text. In one instance, however, he found himself taking on the entire state of Texas. When a prominent textbook writer authored a history of the United States, Macmillan sales agents in Texas reported to Michener that the book needed a better Texas angle to compete with other publishing houses. The sales agents also reported that Texas commissioners wanted to downplay the importance of Abraham Lincoln (who at the time was a scoundrel in the Lone Star State) and accentuate the deeds of Sam Houston, Stephen Austin, and Davy Crockett. The field agents wanted a picture of each with full biographies and "glowing accounts of their heroism." The agents made other suggestions that emphasized Texas history and culture. The result was a "sanitized" version that "sold a great many volumes in Texas and very few in Vermont."[4]

Toward the end of October 1941, after the U.S. destroyer *Reuben James* was sunk off the coast of Iceland by a German sub, Jim knew that America's entry into the war was only a matter of months or days. In an article he wrote for *Progressive Education*, he elucidated six reasons for American involvement in World War II: "decency," "economics," "social issues," "democratic government," "self-interest," and "the democratic spirit," which he thought was being eroded by "a dedicated group of convinced Germans."[5] With Jim's ability to handle complex issues in a straightforward and simple manner, the article convinced many people that America's way of life was being threatened. Among the letters he received was one from his former boss, George Walton, head of the George School. An admitted pacifist, Walton at first had thought that the Nazi regime might crumble from within but now was willing to declare "a whirlwind is ready to be reaped." Walton added: "I am not opposing the thrust of your article that the

spirit and purpose of democracy must be as ardent and self sacri-
ficing as that of Germany, but wish there was a little more emphasis
upon a foundation of moral soundness, both in principle and practice."[6]

As war drew nearer, Jim anguished over whether he would serve
in battle or declare himself a conscientious objector, as would be
expected of a Quaker. He had been called for the draft, even though at
thirty-five he was considered old for service. He thought that the draft
board was "out to get" him, an idea that most of his friends thought
was absurd. After the Japanese bombed Pearl Harbor, however, an
outraged Michener made his decision. Wilbur Murra, who knew Jim
through the National Council of Social Studies, claimed that "after
the war broke out, Jim became an ardent advocate of the war as a
moral imperative to stop Hitler and the Japanese aggressors; and he
was determined to have a part in it himself." Ultimately, Jim's decision was based on his travels in Europe in the early 1930s, when he
witnessed firsthand the intense fervor of Nazism.[7]

At Macmillan Jim divided his time between editing manuscripts
and monitoring battle reports. In early 1942 it was clear that America
was preparing for total war in Europe and the Pacific. In March President Roosevelt authorized the removal of Japanese Americans living
along the Pacific Coast to internment camps in Colorado, Utah, and
Arkansas—an event that was to figure prominently in Michener's life
several years later. That same month General Douglas MacArthur withdrew from the Philippines to Australia. In May and June, respectively,
in the battles of Coral Sea and Midway, U.S. forces, despite crippling
losses to ships and planes, assumed temporary naval superiority in the
Pacific. Jim became emotionally pulled into the conflict. In summer,
either from pressure from Jim or by her own choice, Patti Michener joined
the Women's Army Corps, reporting to duty at Fort Polk, Louisiana.

In early August 1942 American forces landed in the Solomons and
on Guadalcanal, in what was the beginning of a prolonged, desperate,
and grueling road to Tokyo. Carefully reading the reports in the *New
York Times*, Michener was intrigued and moved. Now like a blood-
hound on the hunt, Jim traveled to Washington, D.C., several times,
hoping to land a commission in the navy. Michener blamed his age
and poor eyesight as factors in his rejection. Finally in October 1942,

exasperated by his attempts, he enlisted in the navy. He wrote Wilbur
Murra that he had "one chance in four or five" of getting the job he
wanted.[8]

In early 1943, however, a commission as a lieutenant came
through. At thirty-six years of age and peering through his porthole
glasses, Michener was something of an oddity. The navy didn't know
what do with him. As a former college professor and prep school
teacher, he possessed few combat skills. Sitting naked for his physical
exam, doctors poking him with needles and rapping his knees with a
soft hammer, he felt that the navy was ready to drum him out and
dispatch him back to Macmillan. He happened to mention that he
spent time in the British merchant marine sailing the Mediterranean
and had experience at reading and correcting charts. Based on these
exploits, the navy selected him for duty in the Mediterranean.

On leave from Macmillan and virtually on his own, Lieutenant
(senior grade) James A. Michener was sent to Dartmouth for special
training. Afterward, instead of being shipped to the Mediterranean,
the navy sent him to the Bureau of Aeronautics in Washington, D.C.,
where he performed work as a publications editor. By night he combed
the National Gallery of Art; by day he was usually in his superior's
office begging for duty overseas—anywhere out of Washington.

In November 1943 Michener was again transferred to the Aviation
and Supply Depot in Philadelphia. Overqualified for the position of
publications officer and chafing to be posted overseas, he petitioned
Washington for another assignment. In the meantime, he was assigned
work as a mediator. In early spring 1944 his orders came through: he
was to report to San Francisco, where he would take a troop ship to
the South Pacific.

He happened to mention to his superiors that he had been trained
for Mediterranean duty. "You will go the Pacific!" one of them bellowed.
For Michener, who had endured nearly two years of aggravation and
delay, the Pacific would do.

One of the most baffling features of James Michener as a serious
novelist was that he arrived on the literary scene with the skimpiest
of writing credentials. He had written nearly a score of academic

journal articles, several sonnets, a few plays for school productions, a book (*Unit in the Social Studies*), and a short story. He had an extensive knowledge of art and literature, but except for what he absorbed through reading, he had virtually no grounding in description, dramatic pacing, and character development.

Then in early April 1944 on the troop ship *Cape Horn* bound for Guadalcanal, something happened. Something big happened. Whatever triggered the events—the sea, the freedom, the camaraderie of his fellow fighters—Michener discovered the stuff of good fiction. Jim had spent most of his life keeping a safe distance from people. He felt comfortable within himself, locked away in intellectual seclusion. The war forced Michener out of his introversion and into the lives of his fellow sailors and airmen. Even though these men were sometimes overbearing and frequently shrill, he began to connect with people on an emotional level—perhaps for the first time in his life.

The Solomon Islands—Bougainville, Vella Lavella, Rendova, New Georgia, Malaita, and Guadalcanal—flung like pebbles on the cerulean, motionless sea, also played a crucial role in Michener's development as a first-rate novelist. Lying six hundred miles southeast of Guadalcanal in the New Hebrides Islands was a large chunk of volcanic earth named Espíritu Santo, which was Michener's destination. Of course, Jim had known and loved islands. Calling himself a "nesomaniac," he was prepared for island life. But the war had interrupted and in some cases devastated the rhythms of the South Pacific islands, as Japanese and then American forces struggled to control them. As only some islands were affected by the war, Jim would still find the paradise of Robert Louis Stevenson, Somerset Maugham, and Herman Melville.

The *Cape Horn* was a veteran transport ship, known for traveling "bare-ass," or without an escort cruiser, and one that regularly plied the waters between the West Coast and the South Pacific bearing men and matériel. Having only one gun forward, it relied on two methods to avoid detection in open water. It zigzagged instead of heading in a straight line, and all of its garbage was thrown overboard at night in one large bag so that the enemy would not find a strung-out trail in the morning. Cigarette lighters or matches on deck at night were forbidden, as were loiterers at the aft rail who might absentmindedly fall overboard. One did, according to Michener, and the ship sped on.

Accompanying Jim in his cubbyhole on board were Bill Collins, a tall, rangy Merrill Lynch bond salesman from Los Angeles, and Jay Hammen, a gregarious Detroit businessman who surprised everyone by volunteering for the most unsavory tasks. Collins had smuggled six bottles of Southern Comfort aboard and spent rest breaks usually nipping at one of them.

The *Cape Horn* was run by a civilian crew whose diet and accommodations were far superior to the sailors and marines on board. Such injustice was not lost on Michener. He soon found a mutinous ally named Richmond, and together they hatched a plot to gain better rations and a larger supply of the water that was mysteriously being used elsewhere. There were two commanders on the ship— one civilian, the other military—who supervised their respective groups. Michener rarely if ever saw them on deck, leading him to conclude they were both roaring drunk in their quarters.

One day Richmond took his .45 caliber revolver, and he and Jim headed down to the galley. With Michener guarding the front of the galley, Richmond brandished his revolver and ordered the civilian cooks to open the storage lockers. Inside, Richmond and Jim found fine cuts of meat, including steaks, chickens, and pork chops, as well as fruits and vegetables. The two were outraged that the tasty provisions were being kept from the troops. Fearing any kind of ruckus could lead to their court martial, they nevertheless drafted a list of their complaints, roused Collins and Hammen to their cause, and stormed up to the captains' cabins to deliver the list personally. When they reached the cabins, however, the two captains refused to come out or even take the time to tell them to clear out. "We stood for awhile," observed Michener, "looking silly, then backed off and never did confront the scoundrels."[9]

"Hell," said Richmond, "if they want us to run the ship our way, we'll do it." Returning to the galley, the two ordered the cooks to open the lockers, break out the supplies, and prepare a solid meal for the troops. "During the rest of our voyage," wrote Jim, "we continued to feed the crew proper food, never making waves or doing anything conspicuously dramatic." As to why the captains behaved the way they did, Jim explained that a court-martial would have exposed the terrible mismanagement on board the *Cape Horn*, "so it was wiser to let things slide."[10]

Jim reflected with fierce pride on his actions with Richmond during the voyage in the Solomons. "When a basic principle was involved," he commented, "I would dig in, and long after others had surrendered I would still be flailing away. . . . I did not surrender easily, but that characteristic, which manifested itself on numerous occasions, was not a sign of any moral courage; it was more an innate desire to see the thing that someone else might have started brought to a sensible conclusion."[11]

It was dark when the *Cape Horn* anchored in Luganville Channel, the harbor of Espíritu Santo, and the troops began filing ashore. Fearing an attack by the Japanese, the navy had eliminated all lights on the island. Only the outline of the island, huddled in sleep like a coal black animal, had any distinction. The events of that evening proved to be an enormous stroke of fortune for Michener.

According to his account, he and two of his shipmates, Collins and Hammen, stopped in at the captain's quarters to bid the officers farewell. Finding the place deserted, the three lounged in the chairs ruminating about their voyage. As Collins listened to Jim's tales of the voyage, he happened to spy on the captain's desk a form used for sending navy personnel to their next duty station. Collins then had the brilliant—and audacious—idea of creating his own assignments in the South Pacific. Wryly, Collins said: "Michener, in our conversations you've often mentioned how much you love to travel. I'm going to see to it that you get your chance." Collins proceeded to type out orders that would send Jim throughout the Solomon and New Hebrides islands on "tours of inspection." Rummaging through the desk, Collins found an official stamp, which he "hammered" onto the documents. He signed the name "Admiral Collins" on the orders that gave Lieutenant James A. Michener the cushy job of traveling around the South Pacific. Later, Jim received more official orders, but they were largely based on Collins's impromptu signing on board the ship the first night in Espíritu Santo.[12]

When Michener arrived, American forces were subduing Japanese resistance on the nearby Solomon Islands, pushing the Japanese farther northward into the sea. For the next eight months, as a kind of "super clerk" for the navy, Jim hopscotched from island to island inspecting installations, delivering dispatches, and transporting fresh supplies. He carved his niche in the greater war. "I usually got to the islands three days after the fighting was over," he remarked. "It was just like going to a Sunday picnic when I landed, and we just walked ashore. . . . I never did anything that a good woman secretary could have done better."[13] The navy provided him his own Quonset hut, a jeep, and access to aircraft to travel between islands. From his Quonset on Espíritu Santo, he could see the dry husks of palm leaves on the beach, the sailors drilling and parading on the way to mess, and the supply and transport ships cluttering the harbor. Far beyond the harbor on the headlands, the dense dripping foliage heaved and swelled in the afternoon breezes.[14]

Before the American forces arrived, Espíritu Santo slept in isolated tropical peace. Dense jungle ran down to the sea, offering few anchorages. Originally, the island and its neighbors supported a million people. In the nineteenth century, cannibalism was common, as was the slave trade, which, though slow to develop at first, soon flourished. At one point it reached proportions comparable to that of Africa. Australian ships prowled the coastline, hoping to enslave colonies of indigenous people to work in the sugar fields of North Australia. Measles, whooping cough, and malaria were common afflictions, often decimating the populations of the outlying islands. When the war came, Espíritu Santo overnight became one of the biggest bases in the South Pacific. A makeshift harbor was hacked out of the jungle; a flourishing city went up quickly; hospitals and a radio station were added. Within a year after Pearl Harbor, Espíritu Santo's rough edges were reasonably subdued: roads were cut through the island;

American troops were comfortably housed in Quonsets on the south part of the island, while a few miles inland, indigenous tribes carried on a separate existence.

During this time Patti Michener was serving in the army with Eisenhower's command in Europe. Jim and Patti exchanged letters of concern, but there was no great affection between them. In fact, in one letter Patti hinted at a separation when they returned to New York. Loneliness, anxiety over impending action, and the waiting— the interminable waiting—gnawed at Jim. "You rotted on Caledonia waiting for Guadalcanal," laments his narrator in *Tales of the South Pacific*. "Then you sweated twenty pounds away in Guadal waiting for Bougainville. There were battles, of course. But they were the flaming things of the bitter moment. A blinding flash at Tulagi. A day of horror at Tarawa. An evening of terror on Kuralei. Then you relaxed and waited. And pretty soon you hated the man next to you, and you dreaded the look of a cocoanut tree."[15]

To counteract his sense of isolation, Michener studied everything within reach: language, folklore, climate, food, regional oddities, and the people. As he had in the Outer Hebrides in early 1930s, he made South Pacific culture a place of intense investigation. Instead of feeling lonely or anxious, he studied and traveled. In addition to becoming intimate with the snakes, scorpions, and mosquitoes, he got to know the people on a personal level: the erudite Frenchman Aubert Ratard, struggling to keep his copra plantation going in the face of insurmountable odds; the Tonkinese workers who toiled on the plantation; and Bloody Mary, the garrulous, big-hearted island woman who sold human heads for $50 each. "She was not more than five feet tall," wrote Michener, "weighed about 110 pounds, had few teeth and those funereally black, was sloppy in dress, and [had] thin ravines running out from the sides of her mouth. These ravines . . . were usually filled with bezel juice, which made her look as if her mouth had been gashed by a rusty razor. Her name, Bloody Mary, was well given."[16]

Jim visited Ratard's plantation more than fifteen times, spending as much time interviewing the Tonkinese workers as he did lounging with the Frenchman and his family. The Tonkinese, who hailed from the Gulf of Tonkin region in present-day Vietnam, were able workers.

They were indentured laborers who signed up for three years' work in the Melanesian copra plantations, saved their wages, and returned to their homelands as reasonably well-off servants. But the war had intervened, and the Tonkinese workers, unable to be repatriated, grew restless and resentful. For the most part they were working under wage agreements that were negotiated before the war. "An ugly situation developed," remarked Michener. "[It] was understandable, but it was not just."[17]

During his stint in the South Pacific, Jim visited nearly fifty islands in Micronesia, Melanesia, and Polynesia, logging over 150,000 miles in the process. Some of these were top-secret missions delivering or picking up dispatches; some were brief inspection tours of naval installations; still others were missions of goodwill directed at appeasing the indigenous people of the Pacific islands. Dropping from the skies like an uninvited Icarus, he toured Somerset Maugham's Pago Pago and Robert Louis Stevenson's American Samoa, which he "found lacked size, both geographically and in the behavior of its islanders, who seemed cramped and almost afraid of themselves. . . . I remember it mostly as a dark, cold, rainy place."[18] Landing on lonely Pacific atolls proved routine for Jim after a time, but approaching Bora Bora remained a magical experience. "To put it quite simply," he remarked, "Bora Bora is the most beautiful island in the world. . . . To come back to [the island] at the close of day after a long trip . . . and to see the setting sun illuminate the volcanic tower, massive and brooding in gold, is to see the South Pacific at its unforgettable best."[19]

Several missions stood out in his mind, such as the one to a Samoan island where he checked into a hotel "that would have delighted Somerset Maugham or Joseph Conrad." The hotel, the Cosmopolitan Club, was run by Aggie Grey, a gregarious woman in her late forties and a daughter of a Scottish adventurer and a Samoan woman. She would later serve as one of the inspirations for Bloody Mary in Michener's *Tales of the South Pacific*. Aggie featured three important assets: "cold beer, great island music, and a bevy of the most delectable young Samoan women."[20] Here, while nursing a beer (he drank only occasionally) and chatting with islanders or traveling Americans, he heard some of the best stories of the Pacific war. On another journey, his reliable DC-3 landed in Pukapulas, near Tahiti, to rescue the ailing writer Robert Dean Frisbie, whom he whisked off to the naval hospital in American Samoa. On Fiji he intervened in the case of a New Zealand woman who had fallen in love with a Polynesian priest. To prevent an uprising in the capital of Suva, Michener assisted the local authorities in flying the couple out of the country. At another time, while accompanying a heavily armed patrol rooting out some recalcitrant Japanese soldiers on the Treasury Islands, he jotted down a name scrawled on a crude signboard: Bali-ha'i. He thought the name melodic—perhaps it would be of use in the future.

One of Michener's most gratifying experiences in the South Pacific occurred on a lonely Melanesian island. He began a search for a village whose residents had rescued American fliers in the early days of the war. Representing the American government, Jim wished to thank them with a goodwill gesture of food and clothing. "A French planter took me to the island in his small boat," Jim remarked. "We coasted along the forbidding island for two days. Early in the third day we went ashore. . . . We walked through dense jungle for about an hour. An astounding sight greeted us."[21]

A host of laughing Melanesian girls flocked around them. Large bamboo huts stood in the background surrounded by gardens containing corn, watermelon, yams, pineapple, and taro. Soon a graceful white-haired woman approached them. "She was as stately as a queen," said Michener. "Nobility spoke in every motion she made. She was barefoot. Her feet were splayed and hard."[22]

The laughing girls introduced her as "Mother Margaret." After he distributed his gifts to the group, Jim spent a few quiet moments learning of the background of the mysterious woman. Mother Margaret had been educated at St. Leonard's School for Girls near St. Andrews, Scotland—where Jim had spent time as a research student in the 1930s. She was living and teaching on Tulagi when the Japanese swept down and destroyed her school. She hid in the jungle for several days. Outfitting a small boat, she sailed south deep into Melanesia. Near death, she washed ashore on this remote island. With the help of the islanders, she built a mission and a huge garden. She soon taught the young women how to grow crops in the jungle soil, weave blankets, and construct durable bamboo housing. After long hours working, Mother Margaret retired to an austere room where she wrote in Matu a textbook for the girls that instructed them how to read and write. Michener strolled around the village in awe. "Here was teaching that I had never known before," he commented. "Here was the very essence of all that education stands for: a dedicated human being tearing the lessons from the world's past experience and sharing it with children." Before he left the village, Jim promised Mother Margaret and additional gift: "As soon as I get back to Guadalcanal," he remarked, "I'm going to cable for a complete library. You'll have so many beautiful books . . . you won't have room for them all!"[23]

As a roving ambassador, troubleshooter, soldier of fortune—all while in the service of the U.S. Navy—Jim saw his own version of the Pacific war and made no bones about his noncombat role: "I was always mindful of the fact that while I was exploring the joyous wonders of Polynesia many of my friends were landing on quite different islands: Tarawa, Saipan, Okinawa. I never forgot the difference."[24]

While returning from one of these many missions, this time from Bora Bora, Michener made his ill-fated landing on the Tontouta airstrip on New Caledonia, where he ultimately decided to become a writer and record his exploits in the South Pacific. After the incident, Jim returned to Espíritu Santo. For some time, he had been meeting with a few of his fellow officers, similar to the Angell group he had joined in Colorado. They would meet periodically and share ideas about their personal lives and the war. One night, one of the officers asked him what he was doing with his life. He had to admit that he was doing nothing at the time, except flitting about the Pacific. It disturbed him that he was not committing his talent or dedicating his passion to something worthwhile. He reflected on his near-death experience on New Caledonia. He returned to his Quonset hut that night, looked over his notes of his experiences flying around the South Pacific, and began the series of stories that would become *Tales of the South Pacific*. "No one knows the Pacific better than I do," he reminded himself. "No one can tell the story more accurately."[25]

Michener's quarters on Espíritu Santo are worthy of some description. His typewriter sat on a metal desk in the middle of the Quonset hut. In and out boxes stood guard on the ends of the desk. A smelly lantern—to ward off the mosquitoes—hung from a hook on the ceiling. If the lantern didn't work on the mosquitoes, he could use an insecticide bomb he kept in his drawer. A stack of photographs that he used for recalling characters and providing descriptions lay near his notes. His cot was against the wall, with a pair of boots stuck under it. Using his two index fingers, he banged out the stories from 9:30 at night until 4:00 in the morning, seven days a week. As he worked through December 1944, he kept his goal in the forefront of his mind: "to report the South Pacific as it actually was. By nature I stayed away from heroics and I was certainly not addicted to bombast . . . . I wrote primarily for myself, to record the reality of World War II, and for the young men and women who had lived it."[26]

He also knew that he wanted to avoid following in the tradition of those writers—Robert Louis Stevenson, Pierre Loti, Herman Melville, and Jack London—who excessively romanticized the South Seas. He perhaps knew the archipelagos of the South Pacific better than any of these writers. Although he had not been directly involved in combat, he felt his experiences might yield something just as compelling as combat to the reader.

His early notes, collected over several months, were written on the back of navy orders, envelopes, and small notebooks. Often his scrawls covered the entire surface, even running up the edges. He had to use his own deciphering system to render them legible and meaningful. As he typed out the stories, he showed his first efforts to both a fellow officer and an enlisted man who lived in the adjoining hut. The officer usually shook his head and bawled, "Christ, Michener, this stinks! Why don't you change it here and there?"[27]

Jim's other critic was a navy draftee named Fred who specialized in making shell necklaces. One morning they met outside Jim's Quonset hut, and Fred offered to read one of Michener's chapters. With some trepidation, Jim handed him an early chapter. The following morning they met again; Fred handed him back the typescript and muttered: "Not bad; not bad at all." Whenever Jim gave him more work to criticize, Fred always returned it with the same comment: "Not bad," or "You know what you're doing." Fred never mentioned anything to do with plot or character development but simply gave Michener his same general assessment. "I cannot express how much I valued his support," wrote Jim, "for writing in an empty shed darkened with mighty shadows and infested with mosquitoes is a task that cries out for moral support, and he provided it."[28]

His roll call of characters—Tony Fry, Bus Adams, Bloody Mary, Nellie Forbush, Luther Billis, Joe Cable, Atabrine Benny, Liat, and Emile de Becque—resembled people Michener knew in the South Pacific. Even the narrator of the tales was based on an acquaintance. "One might say my manuscript is a memorial to the bull sessions at the Hotel de Gink on Guadalcanal," Michener commented. "Therefore, nothing in the manuscript is entirely fictitious." There were eighteen interconnected stories, plus the prelude "The South Pacific," which opens like a discordant bar from Debussy: "I wish I could tell you about the South Pacific. The way it actually was. The infinite specks of coral we called islands . . . lovely beyond description. I wish I could tell you about the sweating jungle, the full moon rising behind the volcanoes, and the waiting. The timeless, repetitive waiting. . . . But whenever I talk about the South Pacific, people intervene."[29]

Michener worked feverishly on the manuscript well into the first months of 1945. By then, American troops had captured Manila, capital of the Philippines. In other action, the marines were grinding it out on Iwo Jima. In April American forces began the laborious task of blasting the Japanese off Okinawa, a prolonged conflict that lasted almost three months and cost the United States eighty thousand casualties. Just as it became apparent that the Allies were closing in on and preparing to launch the decisive blow on the Japanese mainland, President Roosevelt died suddenly of a cerebral hemorrhage.

In February Jim had turned thirty-eight and was fairly convinced that the navy was ready to retire him and ship him home. He anticipated that Macmillan would have him back upon his return. He wrote George Brett, chief executive at Macmillan, that "if you are of the opinion that I can help at Macmillan, I'll put in for my release [from the navy]. In the meantime I know that some of my work you brought me into the company to do is being unavoidably postponed. I am aware of this and it disturbs me, but if I'm worth a damn, there will be something I can do when I get back."[30] Brett, in fact, wanted Michener back in New York to promote him to a senior editor position.

Meanwhile, Jim was finishing the final chapter of *Tales of the South Pacific.* In early spring, he wrapped the pages in waterproof fabric and slipped them into a sturdy manila envelope. Since Macmillan had an unbreakable policy of not publishing anything by its employees, he at first thought of sending the manuscript to Knopf, whose list of authors Michener greatly admired. However, he reasoned that because he was not technically working for the company, it would be acceptable to send the manuscript to Macmillan's editors. "I mailed it there under a nom de plume," remarked Michener, "and with a contrived return address to which a response could be sent."[31]

As the Pacific war wound to a bloody close, Jim fully expected that the navy would retire him soon. He was shocked, therefore, when the navy offered him the position of naval historian, a job whose territory covered all the islands from New Zealand to Tarawa and from Australia to Tahiti. Called into headquarters on New Caledonia, Jim stood before an affable rear admiral who puffed on his pipe and outlined the assignment: "Michener, without question you have enough points to get out of this war zone and pick up a good assignment stateside. But we have an important job for which you seem ideally qualified. Your aviation duty has made you familiar with most of the islands, more than anyone else we can find. We need a historian, someone with brains and a sense of military movement, to start compiling a history of the navy in these waters. . . . It means another tour of duty, but we'd be grateful . . . if you'd consent."[32] Jim worried that Brett at Macmillan might abandon him in frustration. At the same time, the opportunity to be a naval historian was too promising to relinquish. Michener wrote Brett that as soon as his naval assignment was over, he would be in New York, ready for work.[33] With his manuscript in New York and a new position beckoning him, Jim once again felt that fate had intervened on his behalf.

When Jim's manuscript of *Tales of the South Pacific* arrived at Macmillan, it was immediately dispatched to the slush pile—that notorious morass reserved for unsolicited material from a writer without an agent. It took a junior editor several weeks to wade through the pile and begin to read it. When he did, he was impressed enough to walk it up to George Brett's office and let the chief executive review it himself. Brett read the work by some unknown author with a military return address. Realizing that it was promising but would take some careful editing by the author, he wrote to the author. Jim got the letter and realized that he would have to divulge his true identity, which he did shortly thereafter. Brett was at first displeased by the news; so was Harold Latham, the senior trade editor.

After things cooled, Brett agreed to send the manuscript to several outside readers to make comments on its merits and perhaps to recommend it for publication. Making sure that Michener's name did not appear in the text, he circulated the manuscript to three of his toughest readers. In June 1945 he wrote Michener: "There is a lot of work ahead of you, my lad, if the book is to be made as good as it ought to be, as good as you can make it. But I am only the president around here and not an editor. I have turned the whole file over to Harold Latham."[34] In all their correspondence, Brett stressed that Macmillan published only the best material, and books had to meet his exacting standard. "Remember, Michener," Brett told Jim repeatedly, "we are not an eleemosynary institution. We publish books to make money. And the only way I know how to do that is to publish the best books possible."[35]

While Latham worked on Michener's manuscript, Jim began documenting the history of the U.S. Navy in the South Pacific. He resumed his flying schedule throughout the area, dropping into Bora Bora (where he negotiated a peaceful settlement to a near-mutiny by enlisted men on the island), New Caledonia, and Fiji. He made extensive notes on these trips, tracing the culture and history of each island as well as the navy's role in its development. Back at his base, he typed out his histories, which by the end of summer were expanding into voluminous and unwieldy stories. "All in all," admitted Michener, "I judge that in eight months I caused to be written well over a million and a half words and that in the same time I myself wrote 791 pages of history."[36] These reports, along with maps and photographs, eventually ended up at the House Naval Affairs Committee in Washington, D.C., where they were pored over by a cadre of military and civilian officials. "Long after I am dead," scoffed Jim, "somebody will find them gathering dust . . . and they'll be published as affectionate little records of the absurd."[37]

At Macmillan two outside readers had completed their review of Michener's manuscript—both were favorable—and Brett passed along their comments to Jim in a letter. One reader thought the book contained "mighty fine stuff." There was some concern from both, however, that Michener had embroidered some of the tales too much; they recommended that some of the "thin" material be cut out. On balance, the feeling was that the good qualities outweighed the bad: "The writer's own attitude is interesting . . . the book is interesting for its wealth of details and sidelights. . . . One gets the impression that this book lets the reader behind the scenes more than the average war book does."[38]

In late July Harold Latham sent Jim two full pages of criticism on *Tales*. "All of us agree," prefaced Latham, "that there is much interesting and valuable material in your book. However, it is fairly obvious that it is your first book, and that there are certain faults." Latham singled out Michener's weakness in characterization: "You have imagined your characters indistinctly, with the result that in their various appearances they seem to be different people." According to Latham, some of the scenes were excessively melodramatic; moreover, Jim's sardonic humor did not work in the storyline. He also cited Jim's attempts at philosophizing as "regrettable" and said further: "You have not yet acquired the skill to do this sort of thing and write this kind of conversation without becoming stilted and self-conscious." Summing up his observations, Latham added: "Does all this sound too harsh, as though there were little left worth keeping? I don't mean to say so, because I think a great deal of the book is excellent." He asked Michener to do some additional work on the manuscript and return the changes. Stung by Latham's remarks, Jim took the manuscript and filed it in his desk drawer for several weeks while he mulled things over.[39]

In early August 1945 the United States dropped atomic bombs on Hiroshima and Nagasaki, leading to the formal and unconditional

Japanese surrender on September 2 aboard the USS *Missouri*. While
Jim made preparations for his position to shift from a wartime to a
peacetime footing, he made no revisions on *Tales*. He wrote a flurry of
reports and traveled to Guadalcanal and New Caledonia. After giving
his manuscript careful thought, he finally capitulated in November
to Latham's wishes: "My recent experiences in the South Pacific have
somewhat enlarged my perspective from what it was when I wrote the
manuscript. . . . At this date I realize that my original manuscript has
lost much of its forcefulness and that your interest may have waned
considerably. I hope that is not the case." He then agreed to revise
the manuscript to Latham's specifications. He would make these
changes and be ready for his senior editor position at Macmillan
after his discharge in January 1946.[40]

The delay until the next year vexed George Brett, who adamantly
wanted Michener back in New York posthaste. Since the war was over,
Brett could see no reason for Jim postponing his return to Macmillan.
"We need you and we need you now," Brett fumed. "Things are moving
rapidly. We have a world wide educational program in the 'liberated'
countries. I hope that I may persuade you to present your case as vigorously as possible with a view to getting released."[41]

Realizing that he could request consideration because of his accumulated points and his time in foreign service, Jim formally asked
for his discharge from the navy. The navy was quick to respond, com-
missioning him a lieutenant commander and preparing to send him
back to America by ship. In mid-December 1945 he was on board
the USS *Kwajalein* headed to San Francisco, prepared to assume his
new position at Macmillan and perhaps, just perhaps, have his novel
finally published.

CHAPTER 6

Nobody Shouted "Author!"

On a drizzly day in January 1946, Lieutenant Commander James A. Michener, former naval historian, ex-ombudsman extraordinaire, and now budding novelist, donned a gray flannel suit and headed to Macmillan's offices on Fifth Avenue. His hair was cropped short, with the sides left whitewall, military style. His deep tan, now beginning to fade in the New York winter, spoke of his long months under the tropic sun. His stride was brisk and assured. Buying a newspaper on his way, he stepped through the "big" door of the publishing house—the one used by Macmillan's executives and senior editors.

He had been reunited with Patti in New York. They lived together for a few weeks, until they both agreed to a permanent separation. Jim called his marriage a "casualty of war." Before he left for Pacific duty, their relationship was a fire ready to die out; the war only doused the embers. Patti packed her things and returned to South Carolina. Jim never saw her or corresponded with her again. His reluctance to continue relationships became something of his hallmark. "Life is too damned short," he once wrote in a letter to a friend, "to abuse it with self-injected passions. On the other hand, I do have stubborn beliefs and when they are offended or abused, I simply cut the situation out [of] my existence. I don't hate, but I do amputate."[1] He used this efficient field surgery on anyone in his life. With spouses, it was especially evident. Jim was an absolute stranger to emotional intimacy. He lived in and trusted only his intellect. When it came to affairs of the heart and soul, he was a scared novice. In women, he looked for someone who did not threaten his intelligence; in men, he looked for his equal. Then he spent countless hours trying to make himself superior in some fashion, through either his incredible knowledge, his ability to seize upon historical detail, or his commanding memory. With Patti, he found someone with whom he could share a few of his interests. Once he got past the friendship stage, he was on foreign ground. His various sexual experiences in the South Pacific probably hastened his inability to live with her again. Since he could not father children, he enjoyed a sexual lifestyle in Polynesia free of responsibility. While other soldiers and sailors returned with scars of war, Michener returned with a keen sense of himself and a heightened libido.

In the early mornings before going to work, while listening to Beethoven or Brahms in his apartment on Charles Street in the Village, he revised portions of *Tales of the South Pacific*. In mid-February Granville Hicks, the third outside reader, reported that he was satisfied with the manuscript but would like some further revisions. Based on this final endorsement, Macmillan offered Jim a contract for the book, which included a $500 advance and serialization rights. Once Jim completed his revisions, the manuscript was turned over to Macmillan's veteran copyeditor Cecil Scott, who made the final textual corrections. Among the changes Scott demanded were the elimination of much of the sailor slang; in its place, he and Jim found suitable substitutes. After Scott worked it over carefully, Harold Latham then projected late 1946 as the publishing date for *Tales of the South Pacific*.

Through the summer of 1946 Jim shopped around for an eligible mate. He was surprised to find that most women he dated wanted to keep their careers after marriage, a depressing fact for a man who wanted control of the household. "He knew a number of attractive, accomplished young women," recalled a friend, "including an editor at a major publisher, an elegant little blonde with a doctorate from Radcliffe or Barnard, a widely published short story writer, and a girl who ran her own publicity agency. Any one of them would have filled the bill as the second Mrs. Michener."[2] Not willing to enter a relationship on any of these women's terms, Jim shied away and dated sporadically.

He was reading with delight Thomas Heggen's recently published novel, *Mr. Roberts*, an often irreverent account of the cargo ship *Reluctant* in the South Pacific during the war. Michener recognized in Heggen a literary ally; he also understood with some alarm that *Mr. Roberts* was upstaging *Tales of the South Pacific*, whose publication date was some months away. Heggen's star, however, would rise swiftly and plummet just as fast. *Mr. Roberts* would become a best seller and be turned into a successful stage play by Joshua Logan. Unfortunately, Heggen scuttled several relationships with women, squandered his fortune, and ended up dying at twenty-nine of an overdose of barbiturates in a bathtub in New York. His rise and fall became a sobering reminder to Jim to cling to his steadfast Quaker resolve.

In mid-September Michener learned that the *Saturday Evening Post* wanted to publish two of the stories from *Tales* as early as December 1946. Jim was flattered, but such a move meant that Macmillan would not publish the book until February 1947. He discussed it with Harold Latham, who agreed to move back the publication date so that the *Post* could showcase two of Michener's stories. The *Post* paid Michener $4,000 to run the "Remittance Man" in the December issue and the "Best Man in de Navy" in the January 1947 issue.

Post readers were enthralled by Michener's account. Three million subscribers were introduced to James A. Michener, the author of "an extraordinary book" that for the first time captured the reality of the South Pacific war. His photo accompanied the articles, showing him with his retreating hairline and a brooding stare. Michener received a pile of laudatory fan mail. At Macmillan, there was cautious elation, as the fallout from the *Post* articles settled on New York City. Gearing up for *Tales of the South Pacific*'s debut, Macmillan ordered two more printings to meet demand. But on the whole, the editors predicted *Tales* would rise and subside quickly. Their view was largely based on the success of Heggen's *Mister Roberts*, which they believed had already satisfied the public's interest in the naval war.

When *Tales of the South Pacific* was published in February, Michener groaned at the book's rustic appearance. The cover was awful, the print quality looked primitive; the whole effect was of a company trying to get as many letters on a page as possible. "It was an ugly, monstrous book," remarked Michener, "a disgrace to a self-respecting company and a humiliation to its author."[3] The book was not touted by the marketing department, which spent more time lavishing attention on Macmillan's lead titles. Moreover, a number of the major periodicals—*Time, Saturday Review of Literature,* and *Newsweek*—ignored it entirely. Still, the book found its way onto the desk of Orville Prescott, the influential critic of the *New York Times.*

Writing in the February 3 issue, Prescott, a shrewd judge of fledgling talent, declared that "this long book of eighteen loosely linked short stories is, I am convinced, a substantial achievement which will make Mr. Michener famous. If it doesn't there is no such thing as literary justice. It is original in its material and point of view, fresh, simple and expert in its presentation, humorous, engrossing, and surprisingly moving."[4] Later in the spring Prescott was even more enthusiastic in the *Yale Review.* "These *Tales of the South Pacific* are magnificently entertaining. But they are more than that. Mr. Michener is an acute observer of human character. An adroit literary artist, a man with a philosophy of life which makes him tolerant of many human weaknesses but not of all, he is certainly one of the ablest and one of the most original writers to appear on the American literary scene for a long time."[5] David Dempsey in the Sunday edition of the *New York Times* touted the book as "one of the most remarkable to come out of the war in a long time. The book's only weakness—the interminable length of some of the tales. . . . Fortunately, even when he is uneconomical, Mr. Michener is never dull. Nor is his lengthiness always a fault."[6] There were some unfavorable reviews, focusing on Michener's use of stereotypes in the novel. The *Quarterly Book List* claimed:

Although this group of stories, modestly titled, makes little show of subtlety or depth of insight, the stories, as stories, do "come off." The events that befall the characters are just those that one would expect, from the newspaper accounts of Guadalcanal and the other islands . . . all the stock characters are here . . . the lonesome lieutenant . . . the philosophical drinkers . . . the beautiful island maid . . . the dirty natives who learn to bargain in four-letter Anglo Saxon words with the Marines, and, once more, the philosophical doctor.[7]

As sales increased through the summer, a few literary agents began circling around Jim's boat. One of these, Jacques Chambrun, was notorious for signing unsuspecting young authors to long-term contracts and fleecing them down the road. Michener's copyeditor, Cecil Scott, warned Jim not to sign with Chambrun, who counted among his clients Somerset Maugham. Instead, Jim acted on an invitation from Carl Brandt, Sr., the dean of American literary agents. Brandt wanted Michener with his agency only if the writer could "produce." Furthermore, Brandt stated that he could represent Jim only "if you like to work and work well—toward a purpose—and if you care about your reputation and want to enhance it." Walking Michener to the door of his agency, Brandt ended his discussion with the author by saying: "You have a tremendous future, Michener, if you can learn to tell a story."[8]

Jim strolled back to Macmillan's offices deep in thought. Was he the next Hemingway, as some people were touting him? Could he meet Carl Brandt's expectations? And if he did, would he have to quit Macmillan to do it?

Meanwhile, Jim was polishing some of the material that would become his second novel, *The Fires of Spring*. The working title was "The Homeward Journey," and Jim consciously chose an American setting with distinctly American themes. Expatriate writers bothered Michener, so he yearned to write something that would return attention to American values. In his heart, he cherished the memory of his hardscrabble youth and his eventual success as teacher and author. These features, he believed, were testaments to the American dream. After the First World War, he was keenly aware that a number of writers abandoned America, hoping to find meaning in Europe and elsewhere.

Michener wrote: "Our novelists . . . seemed to hate their own land. Many of them, finding no sanctuary here, fled to a more hospitable Europe. Glenway Westcott, Louis Bromfield, and Hemingway found spiritual homes abroad, and it is noteworthy that Hemingway has not yet written an important novel of America."[9] Michener believed that the years following the Second World War should be a time of peace and literary renewal, when writers turned their attention from foreign battlefields to the American social scene. He maintained that some of the great American works were yet to be written: "What should be the subject matter of a great [American] novel?" Jim asked. "It is impossible to say. Remember that America's two finest novels dealt with the most improbable content: a white whale snarling in seas far removed from America, and a juvenile delinquent drifting down the Mississippi on a raft! No one can predict what ill-sorted subject matter will inspire genius, but one can survey modern America to discover that many of the most important aspects of modern life have been ignored by the novelists."[10] Consequently, during the summer of 1947 Michener shaped "The Homeward Journey" into a product that would reflect this anticipated American renaissance. Moreover, it would tell his story thinly disguised as the journey of an American youth in the 1920s and 1930s. While still in the midst of writing the novel, he penned two short stories, "The Empty Room" and "Yancy and the Blue Fish," both of which he sold to *Ladies' Home Journal* for $1,000 each.

As he worked on his second novel, *Tales of the South Pacific* was encountering unforeseen success. Donald Friede of Metro-Goldwyn-Mayer (MGM) mentioned to Jim that he was recommending it for the MGM prize, which meant instant consideration for a movie. In November 1947 Latham handed Jim the first royalties from *Tales*. Latham, in one of his rare magnanimous moments, mentioned to Jim: "It is not often that a publisher has the privilege of writing to one of his own staff to congratulate him on the success of a book. We are all distinctly proud of *Tales of the South Pacific*, and of the fact that you are its author, and at the same time a Macmillan man."[11] Following discussions with George Brett, Latham then offered Jim a $1,000 advance for "The Homeward Journey."

After some deliberation, MGM rejected the movie option for *Tales*, one executive declaring that "no one could make a movie from this. No dramatic possibilities whatever. No story line."[12] Simultaneously, however, MGM stage designer Jo Mielziner and actor Henry Fonda recommended the material to Richard Rodgers and Oscar Hammerstein II, who had shown interest in Michener's story of the Pacific war. In the late 1940s Rodgers and Hammerstein were the toast of Broadway, having had smash successes with *Carousel* and *Oklahoma!* The two men reviewed the book and found parts that attracted them. Director Joshua Logan and producer Leland Hayward offered to buy the dramatic rights for $500. Michener was cautious. He agreed to accept future royalties (1 percent) but refused a lump sum payment for the material—a stroke of genius given the eventual success of the production. Eventually, Hammerstein focused on two of the tales— "Our Heroine" and "Fo' Dolla"—and began the tedious process of expanding them into a full-length musical.

After the war Jim frequently motored from New York to Doylestown to visit Mabel Michener. Mabel, who died in March 1946, was so senile, according to Michener, that she could not comprehend he was a novice writer. After Mabel passed away, he began staying with her sister, Hannah, on his visits. At a meeting of political liberals in Doylestown, he met Herman Silverman, a builder of swimming pools and a man who would become Jim's lifelong friend. He and his wife, Ann, suggested that Jim stay in their spacious attic apartment when he came to Doylestown.

As it turned out, Oscar Hammerstein II, who lived on a wooded hilltop near Jim's boyhood home, had employed Silverman to build a pool on his estate. Silverman became close to Hammerstein, and Hammerstein mentioned to Silverman the difficulty he was having adapting Jim's book for the stage. It was Hammerstein's method to write the lyrics for the production and then take his material to Rodgers in New York, who would write the music. Hammerstein had focused on two principal relationships for the new musical: Nellie Forbush and Emile de Becque, and Lieutenant Cable and Liat; Bloody Mary would play an important auxiliary role. As Hammerstein and

Rodgers worked on the lyrics and music, they projected that their new musical, *South Pacific*, would premier sometime in early 1949.

Between January and mid-May 1948 James Michener encountered one of the most anguished and exhilarating rides any writer would dare take. He was paying regular visits to Carl Brandt's agency in hopes of selling Brandt his second novel, now titled *The Fires of Spring*. However, Brandt's demands intimidated Jim. Without making any agreements with the agent, Jim left the revised manuscript with Brandt, who predicted great things if Hollywood liked the project. At a friend's recommendation, Michener was also interviewing agent Helen Strauss of the William Morris Agency, a diminutive fireball just starting out in the business. Michener liked Strauss's understated charm and inherent savvy.

In early March, nearly a month past Jim's forty-first birthday, George Brett called Jim into his office at the end of the day. Michener knew it was serious when he entered the spacious, oak-paneled office and noticed a small banquet placed on a table near Brett's desk. Portraits of Macmillan's gentry, past and present, glared down at him. Jim put his food on a small plate and then sat down on the edge of a sumptuous leather chair pulled close to the desk. They engaged in small talk during their meal. After they finished eating, Brett reached inside his lower desk drawer and pulled out the bulky manuscript of *The Fires of Spring*. Placing his hands on top, fingers laced together, Brett mouthed the words that sent a cold wind howling through Jim: "Michener, I have bad news. We have decided not to publish this. My wife read it and did not like it at all."[13]

Jim remained speechless, frozen in his chair. Whether Brett rejected *The Fires of Spring* because he wanted Jim as a full-time editor or whether he truly believed it was an inferior product will probably never be known. Shoving the manuscript aside, Brett continued: "Michener, I've been watching you, listening to reports . . . and I'm convinced that you have a brilliant future as a publisher. I want you to start immediately working closely with me with an eye to your becoming the president of our company."[14]

It was a bomb calculated to have an immediate effect. It did. Jim turned pale and swallowed hard. Without making any commitment, he took the manuscript and told his boss that he would like to think things over. Shortly thereafter, Jim cradled his manuscript and took the bus up to Random House on Fiftieth Street. He walked unannounced into the office of Saxe Commins, a lanky, chain-smoking senior editor who had groomed Eugene O'Neill and John O'Hara and once had let William Faulkner hole up in his office for several days while he revised a manuscript. Any day now, Saxe was expecting from Faulkner the final manuscript for *Intruder in the Dust*. After leaving the manuscript with Commins, who promised Jim he would consider it for Random House's list, Jim went home, packed some things, and walked the short distance to Penn Station, where he boarded a train headed to Colorado.

Out of Chicago the train clattered westward, resurrecting the distant joys of travel and prompting the persistent questions and doubts that had begun to dog Michener. Maybe he should quit writing and accept Brett's offer. Maybe he should leave Macmillan and return to teaching. A friend at Colorado State had offered him a part-time teaching position in the English department. The last thing he was ready to do was to chuck everything and become a full-time writer. He had with him the beginnings of a new novel about Colorado, tentatively titled "Jefferson," but things were not going well with it.

Arriving in Greeley, he sauntered around campus with his English professor friend, who showed him some recent additions to the college. He also gave Jim keys to his mountain cabin, located in Poudre Canyon, north of nearby Fort Collins. For nearly two weeks Jim stayed in the mountain setting, loafing and thinking, living the simple life. Snow squalls blasted through the canyon, giving way to frosty blue skies and a feeble spring sun. Towering cedars loomed over the cabin and lined the canyon below.

In Greeley, Jim picked up a cable from Saxe Commins, who wrote him that he was "wildly enthusiastic" about *The Fires of Spring*. In comparing Michener to Dickens, Commins noted: "Your story is always exciting, penetrating and compassionate; it is completely honest and radiant with character." He also remarked that the manuscript—totaling a hefty three hundred thousand words—needed pruning, but they could work on that when Jim returned to New York. For now, emphasized Commins, "the first glow of enthusiasm for the book is all that matters."[15]

Commins's telegram was the affirmation Jim needed. He recalled his experience on the Tontouta airstrip in 1944 and the promise he had made himself. He wanted his life to have meaning, and presently the only meaning that would truly satisfy him was the life of a writer.

He wrote George Brett that he was turning down his offer of Phil Knowlton's job, a move that he thought surely would get him fired. Michener also thought it would be embarrassing at this stage for Macmillan to publish *The Fires of Spring*, so he was returning the advance on royalties. He mentioned in his letter that he had approached Saxe Commins of Random House, who had recently expressed interest in his new book. Although he left any decision about his termination with Brett, Michener related that he wanted to stay at Macmillan in some capacity, "regardless of condition or salary."[16]

Despite the friction over the manuscript, Brett had a deep respect for Michener. After reading Jim's letter, Brett immediately dashed off a response: "[Thank you] for your continued interest in The Macmillan Company. . . . We shall now, of course, have to go out and try to find the fellow to succeed Knowlton. . . . But I do hope to persuade you to carry on with the department along the lines of the divided interest, you to work for us three days a week and for yourself the other four."[17] Brett indicated he was raising his salary to $7,500 a year.

It was a generous offer on Brett's part. Jim, however, sought out Cecil Scott, his ally at Macmillan, to share some of his insecurities. On March 31 Jim wrote him from his cabin:

As I told you in my first letter, on the night before I left for the west, Mr. Brett extended this very fine invitation and then immediately added that he thought that I was wasting my time trying to write. . . . As he probably told you, he accepted my basic decision, agreed that [the] novel should be published elsewhere, and decided to keep me on, for how long neither of us has said. That's how things stand. I feel a

much older man than when I left New York. It's as if the
dream world in which I lived had been roughly banged
about. But *Oliver Allston* has a remarkable passage in which
[the author] speaks of the man trying to keep one foot in
business and one in art. He says that when the pinch comes,
they always cling to business. I did my damnedest to be the one
who knew where his feet, and his heart, were. . . . I'm terri-
bly sorry, Cecil, but you know it would have been impossible
and untenable for me to hope to publish with Macmillan
after the decision I had reached. As I said in my letter to Mr.
Brett, I know I'm going to regret my decision. I could have
been quite happy as an executive, playing bridge with the
gentry, moving into the countryside. But it didn't work out
that way. Ten years from now I may kick the hell out of myself
whenever I think of Colorado. But I shall have given a few
things a fling in the intervening years.[18]

Back in New York in early April, Michener walked up to Random
House, where he met Saxe Commins to discuss the manuscript. He
liked Commins, and he liked him more as time went on. Uncomplicated, a cigarette usually wobbling in the side of his mouth, Commins
was quick to praise work that he liked. He told Jim that Random
House had decided to publish *The Fires of Spring* and would release
it early in 1949. Michener was overjoyed. Jim signed the contract in
late April, which carried with it a $1,000 advance. He and Commins
then began the process of whittling the book down to a trimmer size.
When the manuscript was finished, Jim dedicated the book to "C.S."
(Cecil Scott) and "S.C." (Saxe Commins).

Jim was back at Macmillan, clinging tenuously to his position.
Brett made overtures about reconsidering Jim's novel for publication.
However, forgiveness was not a Michener trait. Once Brett related
his feelings about the book, there was no going back.

On the morning of May 3, 1948, Jim was shaving and listening
to a spirited movement from Bach's Brandenburg Concertos when
a special delivery letter was slipped under his door. Slicing it open
with his thumbnail, he read with shock and dismay that Carl Brandt

had reached the conclusion that he had no future as a commercial writer and was dropping him from any consideration as a client. Brandt said, among other things, that Michener's work did not show any promise and that Jim's revisions to the manuscript were not an improvement. Michener glanced over the letter one more time and then in a fit of rage tore it to shreds. He stormed into the living room, gathering his senses. He realized that one of his great weaknesses was accepting criticism: "I did not accept advice from others graciously, and especially not when it touched on my writing. . . . I would always be an uncut diamond rather than a polished gem and it was futile to think I would ever change."[19]

With a "mixture of depression and good spirits," Michener walked the six blocks to work that morning. As it turned out, Phil Knowlton was in a crotchety mood. He picked on Jim for using some imprecise language in correspondence Michener had sent out. Michener was about to respond to Knowlton's complaints when Cecil Scott, the erudite Londoner, burst through the door and shouted: "Jim, you've won the Pulitzer Prize!"[20]

Soon bedlam broke through Macmillan's ranks. Editors poured into Knowlton's office to congratulate Jim on his achievement. The phone started ringing and kept on ringing well into the afternoon. Radio stations and newspapers wanted statements regarding the prize. After the hoopla had subsided, Knowlton escorted Jim down to WOR radio, where a soundman plopped the newly crowned writer into a chair for his first literary interview.

"Why do you suppose the Pulitzer committee chose your unusual book?" asked the interviewer. "I really don't know," said Jim modestly. "It's sort of miraculous."[21]

Tales of the South Pacific had indeed scored a miraculous victory, winning the top prize in fiction for a series of stories that added up to a semblance of a novel. At that moment, however, having in the morning been jettisoned by the dean of American literary agents and in the afternoon been awarded the major award in letters, he was not prepared to discount his triumph.

CHAPTER 7

The Page and the Stage

Within a few days of the announcement of the Pulitzer awards, a few cries of indignation were heard in the press. Writing in the Sunday *World Herald*, Victor Haas summed up the general sentiment: "I cannot understand how *Tales of the South Pacific* won any prizes. Mr. Michener's 'novel' is in reality a collection of 19 short stories. . . . Mr. Michener has written some good stories, but I do not find them 'distinguished.'"[1] Many critics agreed with Haas, voicing the opinion that Michener's work was not only a collection of stories but also a mixture of fact and fiction—and therefore not worthy of the preeminent prize in literature.

For many years, the guiding definition for the Pulitzer Prize for fiction had been "a distinguished novel, preferably dealing with American life." Most previous winners stayed within the guidelines for this definition; however, there were exceptions such as John Hersey's *A Bell for Adano* (1944), which depicted an event in an American-occupied Italian town. In 1947, coincidently the year Michener's book came up for the award, the Pulitzer Advisory Board changed the designation of "novel" to "fiction," which opened the door for collections of short stories to be considered.

Still, Jim's book was set in the South Pacific, which did not meet the other half of the criteria. A flurry of debate followed, centering on what constituted a novel and how closely the award should follow the prescribed guidelines.

The controversy shook Jim's confidence. He admitted he was not the new Hemingway, the new Faulkner, or the new Dos Passos. He further claimed that *Tales of the South Pacific* was neither a great novel nor a bold new step in literature. It was nonetheless a faithful chronicle of life during the war in the South Pacific. Stunned by the controversy, he temporarily quit writing. He visited various cities around the country giving lectures and interviews while also scouting for textbook proposals for Macmillan.

After he won the Pulitzer Prize, Jim maintained that *Tales of the South Pacific* could not have won in any year but 1947, when the competition was slim. However, in 1947 the Pulitzer field was crowded with several notable titles that came up for consideration alongside *Tales*, among them were John Steinbeck's *The Pearl*, Laura Hobson's *Gentleman's Agreement*, and Malcolm Lowry's *Under the Volcano*. The frontrunners for the prize were considered to be *The Big Sky* by A. B. Guthrie, *Knock on Any Door* by Willard Motley, *The Garretson Chronicle* by Gerald Brace, and *The Stoic* by Theodore Dreiser. The panelists reading fiction for the Pulitzer Advisory Board included critic and writer Maxwell Geismar, John Chamberlain of *Time* magazine, and Orville Prescott of the *New York Times*, the reviewer who had first championed the worth of *Tales of the South Pacific*. Going into the final voting, *Tales* was in fifth place, behind *The Big Sky, Knock on Any Door, The Garretson Chronicle*, and *The Stoic*. Although these were significant titles, there was no clear favorite among the voters. Then in late April Arthur Krock, the committee chair, cast his vote for Michener's book. "I gave my reasons and the board accepted them," he admitted.[2] Krock's final and persuasive plea for *Tales*, largely based on the influence of Alice Roosevelt Longworth, assured the prize would go to Michener. Jim also felt that had his book been published in 1946 as scheduled, it would have run up against Robert Penn Warren's *All the King's Men*, a work that swept the Pulitzer field and went on to become one of the great books in American literature.

As *Tales of the South Pacific* gained wider fame, it was inevitably compared to other war novels published in the late 1940s and early 1950s. *Tales*, however, proved difficult to categorize. It did not have the explosive punch of Norman Mailer's *The Naked and the Dead*, the meticulous development of James Gould Cozzens's *Guard of Honor* (Pulitzer Prize), the sustained narrative sweep of James Jones's *From Here to Eternity*, or the psychological tension of Herman Wouk's *The Caine Mutiny*. Michener's book was a rare war novel with charm, which probably explains why it was popular with men as well as women and why it was immediately attractive to Rodgers and Hammerstein.

Only much later could Michener appreciate the novel's homely appearance and accept the drubbing it received from certain reviewers. By then the stage version of *South Pacific* was setting records on Broadway, and suddenly everyone had heard of Bloody Mary and Nellie Forbush. Such success made the controversy fade away, but Jim remained suspicious of critics and criticism in general.

When Jim returned to New York from the South Pacific in early 1946, he rented a brownstone at 85 Charles Street owned by Nancy Shores, a charming but erratic alcoholic and sometime writer. Employing Helen Strauss as her literary agent, Shores wrote glossy fiction for such periodicals as *Ladies' Home Journal*, *Collier's*, *Saturday Evening Post*, and *McCall's*. She encouraged Jim to secure Strauss's services as well. From as early as mid-1946, Michener periodically met Strauss for lunch, in hopes of gaining some support for his fledgling career. After he won the Pulitzer Prize, Strauss phoned him for a lunch date. At Sardi's on West Forty-fourth Street, Strauss probed Jim's commitment to writing, while he decided on her suitability as his agent. She realized he was a divided man, split between being a writer and an editor at Macmillan. She also knew that Rodgers and Hammerstein were currently developing *South Pacific* for the stage and that there were commissions to be made in the future.

Helen Strauss had been at the William Morris Agency a little more than four years when she sat down for lunch with Jim at Sardi's. Her clients at one time or another included Robert Penn Warren, Paul Bowles, Leon Edel, Garson Kanin, Ralph Ellison, and Maurice Edelman. She could be aggressive or reserved, loquacious or taciturn, depending on the situation. In Michener, she saw a polite loner but one steadfastly committed to excellence in most anything. She later was baffled by his attitude toward money. "He had a great ambivalence about it," Strauss remarked. "He relished his success but spent little money on himself. He lived modestly. His personal material needs were simple."[3] Ultimately, Strauss viewed her prospective client as one she could both respect and find dependable as a writer. In summer 1948, with a Pulitzer in his pocket, a new book (*The Fires of Spring*) in production at Random House, and a musical ready to premiere the following spring, Jim signed a contract with Helen Strauss and the William Morris Agency.

Jim's romantic life seemed like it was blossoming along with his career. On weekends he frequently returned to Doylestown, once bringing with him Janis Paige of the hit musical *Pajama Game*. They stayed in a single bed in the Silvermans' attic. On July 4, 1948, Jim boarded the train at Penn Station and headed down to the peaceful comforts of Bucks County. On his arm was a twenty-five-year-old architectural student named Evangeline Nowdoworski, who went by the name of Vange Nord. Vange was an attractive strawberry blonde whom Jim had met at a party in Greenwich Village. He quickly fell in love with her and proposed marriage, even though he was still legally married to Patti.

At the Trenton, New Jersey, train station, the couple met Doylestown friends Herman Silverman and Les Trauch. Climbing into the backseat of Silverman's Ford, Jim snuggled Vange close to him during the drive to Bucks County. Vange lit a cigarette, holding it between long, tapering fingers and spewing a trail of smoke out the window. Jim was unusually upbeat, though he didn't talk much about New York. Les turned to Vange and asked: "Are you in the chorus of *Pajama Game*?" Jim snapped back: "If she were in *Pajama Game* she wouldn't be in the chorus."[4]

Bucks County was painted a deep summer green. A slight breeze made the leaves shimmer as they drove the winding lanes to Doylestown. Manicured lawns and spacious meadows shone in the sun. Proud farms stood tucked under the spreading sycamores and elms. Michener had not lived here since 1925. Since then, this part of Bucks County had become a mecca for celebrities and the literati. In addition to

Oscar Hammerstein, who was currently working on the libretto for *South Pacific*, other residents included George Kaufman, residing at Barley Sheaf Farm in Holicong; Dorothy Parker and husband, Alan Campbell, living at Fox House in Pipersville; and Nobel Prize–winner Pearl Buck, residing at Green Hills Farm in western Bucks County. Just across the Delaware River in Lambertville, New Jersey, lived the cantankerous James Gould Cozzens, who frequently visited Doylestown for inspiration and to drink a cup of coffee with Michener. Although only a four-hour drive from New York, the county still seemed worlds removed from the hubbub of the city.

Vange fell in love with the region, filling Jim's ear with her wishes to build a house and settle here. After a weekend with the Silvermans, Jim told Herman that he was leaving for several weeks but that Vange was coming back to scout acreages. A few days later, Vange Nord moved in with the Silvermans to begin the process of buying a parcel of land. In the meantime, Jim went west to Reno and got a speedy divorce from Patti.

In late July Herman and Vange found a rugged promontory of land near Doylestown called "High Rocks" and bought it for $2,000. Vange told Jim over the phone about her find. "That's where everybody is going to climb up there and kill themselves!" Jim's voice crackled in the receiver. "Better find me another piece of property." Vange was disappointed: she had imagined building a modern, cantilevered house that took advantage of the rocks and water, similar to Frank Lloyd Wright's Fallingwater near Bear Run, Pennsylvania.[5]

For the next three weeks, when not scouring the territory with Herman, Vange lounged in the Silvermans' living room, sipping tea, smoking cigarettes, talking with Ann, and flaunting her sophistication. Headstrong and opinionated, Vange liked to think she was the catalyst for Jim's writing career. She was a writer herself—albeit an unknown and struggling one. She admired Jim's writing ability and envied his success, once claiming in no uncertain terms she was a better writer than he was.

Jim ended up donating "High Rocks" to the Bucks County Parks Department. After more searching, Herman and Vange found a thirty-five-acre, heavily wooded parcel of land located in Pipersville, nearly ten miles from Doylestown. It had beautiful views and was laced with trails, perfect for Jim's daily rambles. They bought it for a $100 an acre. Silverman, who would serve as Jim's general contractor on the house project, began in his mind to see what the spot required. Among other things, Silverman and his crew needed to bulldoze a narrow winding road up to the house, which would require Jim and Vange to buy a jeep to negotiate the driveway in spring mud season and winter snows. With his new house in the planning stages and his divorce from Patti finalized, Jim married Vange Nord, without ceremony or fanfare, in New York City in August 1948.

As the year ebbed and the chill autumn winds stripped the locust trees bare along Fifth Avenue, Jim and Vange enjoyed their last days as residents of New York City. After honeymooning at the Silvermans' in Doylestown, they had burrowed into Jim's brownstone in Greenwich Village, periodically emerging to go to the opera, visit the Metropolitan Museum, and pop into the corner market to buy a late snack. By all outward appearances they were a happy couple. They enjoyed each other's interests, which for the most part included art and music. While Jim was at work at Macmillan, Vange spread out her work on the couple's oval breakfast table and wrote short stories and articles, hoping to grab a byline in *McCall's* or *Ladies' Home Journal.* Often she took her work down to a café on Bleeker Street and wrote at a corner table.

Jim strolled the six blocks to work on Fifth Avenue, following the customary route of bakeries and fruit markets. During his walk, he often pondered his career and his role as a writer. He was continuing to work on his historical novel of Colorado, which would deal with some of the problems and difficulties of settling that corner of the West. It was not his easiest novel. He told Vange some of the details of the new project, but for the most part the beginnings of a novel were always a private matter.

As he gained confidence, Jim began formulating how he wanted to define himself as a writer. He differentiated between the terms "author" and "writer." "I was taught as a child," he observed, "that authors were pompous American men of the last century who wore beards and had three-barreled names, such as Henry Wadsworth Longfellow and Oliver Wendell Holmes. I wanted to be a writer, like Thomas Hardy, Charles Dickens, Gustave Flaubert and Leo Tolstoy."[6] Authors attended parties, signed books, and boasted of their accomplishments over cocktails. For Jim, hammering away at the typewriter with his two index fingers and spending hours in libraries were what being a writer was all about.

At Macmillan he went through the motions of a being an editor, even though his actions clearly showed he was burning out. He traveled frequently in search of new textbooks, particularly to the western United States, including Greeley, Colorado.

It was clear to himself that he was leading a double life of writer and editor, and all it would take was some certainty and a leap of faith for him to renounce the latter. His landlady, Nancy Shores, continued to remind him that the best writers were 100 percent committed ones. His agent, Helen Strauss, added her own assurances.

Newly married and mindful how successful writers had met tragic ends, he was reticent to give up a steady income. As the winter of 1949 advanced and the frigid winds roared off the Hudson River, Jim waited for a sign to confirm that he could survive as a freelance writer. That would happen—with the help of a few characters from Jim's past.

In the winter and early spring of 1949 James Michener's career received two sharp and potent inoculations. The first was Random House's publication of *The Fires of Spring*, and the second was the debut of Rodgers and Hammerstein's much anticipated musical, *South Pacific. The Fires of Spring* was Jim's addition to the revival of American domestic fiction, and in many ways it was the book that most aspiring writers longed to write. Unlike *Tales of the South Pacific*, which was not highly publicized, *Fires* got an enormous boost from the marketing department, leaping onto the best-seller lists and remaining there for several months. It was a book that the public adored and critics chided. Thirty years after its publication, Jim was still receiving laudatory mail about its hero, David Harper.[7] Having won the Pulitzer Prize for his first novel, Michener was in the unenviable position of having to

prove himself even more with his second novel. Critics were eager
to damn or praise it. They were expecting a novel with more revolutionary form and certainly of greater scope than *Tales*. What they
discovered was a naive, homespun work in the grand tradition of Booth
Tarkington, Theodore Dreiser, and Sinclair Lewis. They didn't know
what to make of it.

The autobiographical novel is always a dangerous form for a writer
to contemplate, because it assumes that what he or she finds interesting, readers will find absorbing as well. Readers did find Michener's
story compelling, even though many pointed out, quite correctly,
that it should have been his first novel rather than his second. "I was
willing to write *The Fires of Spring* out of order because I felt that it was
a book that had to be written even though I was in my forties and it
was the kind of book normally written when one is in one's twenties
or thirties. I have never regretted that decision."[8] Adding some embel-
lishments and presenting an easy cadence to his prose, Michener
tells his own story. The book follows David Harper from the age of
eleven through his coming of age in Depression-lean America of the
1930s. Michener's rendering of the poorhouse and the amusement
park is especially convincing, but after those episodes the inability
of the central character to propel the narrative becomes evident.
Michener's own description of his work—that it attempted "to get
at the growth of a very ordinary American boy into the full stream
of American life . . . in the years between the richness of the 1920's
and the despair of the 1930's"—contains some of the inherent problems of the book.[9] What readers found charming, David's innocence
and ordinariness, critics were quick to point out was sentimental and
superficial. Moreover, Jim spent too much time sermonizing about
art and writing.

One after another, reviewers lined up to condemn Jim's second
offering. Of the major voices, Orville Prescott, writing in the *Yale Review*,
remarked: "Mr. Michener is fine with his host of minor characters.
But the passionate women in David's life are less convincing, and David
himself is of little interest. *The Fires of Spring* is somewhat sentimental
and sententious."[10] "*The Fires of Spring* is flawed by sentimentality and
naiveté," echoed C. J. Rolo in the *Atlantic*.[11] "*The Fires of Spring* is full

of grotesques," groaned William Dubois in the *New York Times.* "One suffers as Mr. Michener warms up his opinions of literature, art, and music—and offers them in page-long monologues. One suffers most of all when Love pants on cue, every twenty pages or so . . . [however] for all his haste, Mr. Michener's anger at life is sincere. It is a pity not to let his notes age a bit longer—or, at least, that he did not take the time to dramatize his anger in believable terms."[12] "Most of the writing is brilliant high school stuff," complained J. H. Burns in the *Saturday Review of Literature,* "[filled] with soggy prose and embarrassing dialogue."[13] Writing in the *Christian Science Monitor,* Horace Reynolds observed that "there are commendable things in this novel, Mr. Michener writes with gusto and good sense of story. . . . The stream of American life through which the hero walks, seeking both its meaning and knowledge of himself, is well realized . . . [but] Mr. Michener is addicted to melodrama, violence, and coincidence, and his story does not have the clarity of outline, the control and reserve his character David finds in Henry James."[14] Other reviewers, such as G. D. Macdonald in the *Library Journal,* suggested that "the basic weakness is probably the lack of definition of the central character"—a charge that even supportive critics seemed to agree on.[15]

Some readers, Helen Strauss among them, claimed that *The Fires of Spring* was actually written before *Tales of the South Pacific.* Reading *Tales* and then reading *Fires,* one can readily see how that claim could be made. The idea for Jim's autobiographical novel probably came to him as early as 1941, when he returned to the East Coast from Colorado.[16] He made notes and perhaps sketched out a chapter but abandoned the project when America entered World War II. However, the idea for the novel remained with Michener throughout his stint in the South Pacific, although he made no formal progress on the manuscript. After the war, while wrapping up *Tales of the South Pacific,* he resumed the project, writing the majority of it between early 1946 and late 1947. So in one sense *Fires* was thought of earlier than *Tales,* but in terms of completion and publication, it is rightly considered Michener's second novel.

Michener wanted *The Fires of Spring* to establish him as an American writer concerned with homegrown values and heartland traditions.

He mentioned at one point that he was relinquishing his interest in writing of foreign lands and cultures. Although he reneged on this commitment, he remained a staunch advocate of the values and beliefs he represented in *The Fires of Spring*.

Despite the book's critical failure, Michener was pleased with his accomplishment and with the novel's popularity. *Fires* went on to sell over half a million copies in the next ten years and occupy a reverential position on his bookshelf.

On a brisk March 1949 evening at the Shubert Theater in New Haven, Connecticut, Jim and Vange took their seats and for the next three hours watched as *South Pacific* went through the paces of its first out-of-town tryout. Its New York premiere was still over a month away. Jim watched as the characters he had created—Nellie Forbush, Emile de Becque, Lieutenant Cable, Liat, Bloody Mary, and Luther Billis—moved for the first time on stage. He laughed at the comic scenes and wept at the romantic love songs.

At times he was so overcome he had to excuse himself and head for the lobby. As the show ended, there was dead silence, then a burst of hearty applause. Curtain calls lasted more than half an hour. After the show, he and Vange saw a buoyant Richard Rodgers standing at one exit, Oscar Hammerstein at the other. They were asking theatergoers: "Did you like it?" "Did you like it?" People not only liked it, they raved about it. They pumped Rodgers's hand and showered him with their enthusiasm. Upon exiting the theater and heading home for the night, Jim knew that *Tales of the South Pacific* would endure beyond the printed page.

Originally, the two love relationships—Nellie and Emile, Lieutenant Cable and Liat—were considered equal in prominence. During casting, however, the perfect Emile de Becque emerged in the person of Ezio Pinza, an acclaimed Metropolitan Opera basso. Richard Rodgers remarked, "Pinza came East in June to do a radio show, and we arranged to meet him at lunch at the Plaza. In walked this great, big, attractive looking fellow. We went to his broadcast and heard him sing in front of an audience."[17] Hammerstein loved him on the spot and planned to rewrite the script so that the De Becque–Forbush relationship would be the focus of the musical. In rehearsal, Pinza proved to be a formidable romantic figure. "The show is nothing without him," said Hammerstein in a private moment to Herman Silverman.[18] Pinza became famous for his flirtations with costar Mary Martin as well as with the women in the chorus. "Pinza is in fine shape," Rodgers commented, "and keeps the girls in a fine state of anxiety. They just never know what end to protect." His virility became the subject of much gossip. Playwright Russell Crouse noted, "Pinza has three balls and when he sings they light up."[19]

Hired to star with Pinza was Mary Martin, who had just come off a successful engagement in *Annie Get Your Gun*. Having what was dubbed a "Broadway voice," Martin was scared to death to sing a duet with a star of the Metropolitan Opera, fearing she would be horribly upstaged. But Rodgers sidestepped the issue by never having Pinza and Martin sing at the same time. Martin had no illusions of her beauty. Somewhat gawky in a sweet, adolescent way, she nevertheless could dance, do light comedy, and seduce an audience with her antics. Rodgers loved and admired her. As the plucky Ensign Forbush, Martin brought a youthful exuberance and sexy innocence to Michener's character. With Pinza's impassioned singing and Martin's puckish charm, Rodgers and Hammerstein knew they had a winning combination.

Jim knew it, too. Opera and music lover Michener worshipped Pinza and his talent. Winning the Pulitzer Prize for his first novel was one thing. Having a Met star sing in his original story was an additional bonus. Jim often chatted with Pinza in the wings of the stage, mostly about opera and orchestras. To relieve tension before going onstage, Pinza often broke into a conversation about his bicycle racing as a youth in Italy. The stage manager would bark: "Two minutes Mr. Pinza!" Pinza continued his monologue about bicycles, until the manager chimed in with: "One minute, Mr. Pinza!" Whereupon Pinza would grow silent, say good-bye to Jim, and march onstage to his cue.[20]

By contrast, Mary Martin rarely appeared in the wings or backstage. When asked how she prepared to go on, she replied: "When they call the half hour I go into the john and stay there until Gladys [the maid] comes and says, 'You're on Miss Martin.' Then I lean down, pull up my panties, and go out onstage. Well, that's the way you deal with stage fright."[21] Once in character, however, adrenalin took over. Martin gave everything to a scene. When it was over, according to Jim, she would stagger offstage limp and with her eyes so filled with tears she could hardly recognize anyone.[22]

Martin was also an adept gymnast and dancer. Once, however, during a performance in New Haven, she almost lost the starring role. While singing "A Wonderful Guy," she tried to complete a series of cartwheels across the stage when a spotlight temporarily blinded her. Staggering forward, Martin went hurtling into the orchestra pit, leveling the vocal arranger seated at the piano and knocking the conductor to the floor. She ended up bruised and shaken in a heap next to him. No one, including Martin, was seriously hurt. After several orchestra members helped her to her feet, she straightened her hair, composed herself, and went on with the show.

Although Jim did not have a personal relationship with Richard Rodgers, he did get glimpses of the latter's prodigious talent. After Hammerstein wrote the lyrics for "Bali Ha'i," the show's central theme, he brought them to Joshua Logan's apartment, where several cast members were gathered. Both Hammerstein and Rodgers recognized the importance of "Bali Ha'i" to the musical: it had to capture the sweep, color, and lush beauty of the South Pacific, and it had to do so simply and intensely. Michener had described the mythical island this way: "Like a jewel it could be perceived in one loving glance. It was neat. It had majestic cliffs facing the open sea . . . It was green like something ever youthful, and it seemed to curve itself like a woman into the rough shadows formed by the volcanoes on the greater island of Vanicoro."[23] When Jim got to Logan's apartment, Rodgers, who suffered from back problems, was stretched out on the floor with two pillows propped under his legs. He was talking to Mary Martin seated on the couch. Hammerstein came in and announced he had the lyrics for "Bali Ha'i," but he needed Rodgers to work on the score. Rodgers looked over Hammerstein's words, rose from the floor, and disappeared into an adjoining room. Ten minutes later Rodgers reappeared with the finished version. Rodgers had captured Michener's exotic island using a nucleus of three notes and a rising octave. Jim was astounded at Rodger's feat—and so was everyone else at Logan's apartment that night.

To the plaintive beginning notes of "Bali Ha'i," *South Pacific* opened at the Majestic Theater in New York City on April 7, 1949. Tickets were not only scarce but nearly impossible to secure. Jim and Vange got theirs through Oscar Hammerstein, who doled them out carefully. The timing of the musical could not have been better. *Tales of the South Pacific*, Michener's Pulitzer Prize winner, was still fresh in everyone's mind. For those who had not read the book, the prospect of two deep love stories set against the backdrop of a tropical land-scape proved irresistible. There was also the theme of overcoming racial prejudice, which went over well with the audience. The song "You Have to Be Carefully Taught," once considered susceptible to cutting, actually stimulated interest in the show. Jim liked that aspect of *South Pacific*, that it could tell a romantic story against a setting of smoldering racial friction.

South Pacific continued for 1,925 performances, running from spring 1949 through 1954. In terms of critical reception, awards, and popular appeal, it was probably the most successful Rodgers and Hammerstein musical. It won the Pulitzer Prize (1950), eight Tony awards, and nine Donaldson awards. The Pulitzer was a particularly remarkable achievement since *South Pacific* had to compete with more serious dramatic works. Since the inception of the Pulitzer awards in 1917, only three other musicals have captured the prize in the cate-gory of drama. Michener clung to his 1 percent of the profits, which over the next twenty years or so provided a modest but dependable income of $10,000 per annum.

Throughout the spring, Herman Silverman put the finishing touches on the Micheners' Pipersville home. It was neither a mansion nor a bungalow. More than anything, the home was to be a place of modest country living and quiet concentration. Vange designed it: "A mod-ernistic, one-story frame house with [a] picture window overlooking the valley," wrote Silverman. "The living room floor was flagstone, and all the heat pipes were put under the floor to keep the floor warm . . . there were two bedrooms, one bathroom, a big living room–dining room with a gigantic stone fireplace, kitchen and an office."[24] Jim told Silverman that he would "rather have trees than furniture." Silverman combed the nurseries for a suitable forest of "cheap, big evergreens" to plant close to the house.[25] By early summer the Micheners were ready to move in.

Jim viewed moving back to Bucks County with mixed emotions. On one hand, he was pleased for the sanctuary away from the bustle of New York. This was his home, he realized. On the other, the bitterness of his youth, the treatment of Mabel by the citizens of Doylestown, and the memories of his hardscrabble existence combined to make him wary of a comfortable return. He spent his last days as a resident of New York taking in the Metropolitan Opera or pacing through the Whitney and Metropolitan museums.

Helen Strauss asked Jim to lunch at Sardi's. At the age of forty-two, he had reached the inevitable road that branched in two directions. He debated, indeed agonized over, the decision to quit Macmillan and become a freelance writer. He asked several people about the idea, and all had given him their encouragement. He wanted to hear it from the lips of Strauss, whom he had begun to trust with few reservations. While Jim picked at his food, Strauss laid out her view of Jim's situation. "I told Jim," she wrote, "I was sure that I could get magazine assignments which would compensate him more than his pay as an editor. Having won the Pulitzer Prize, he was a recognized name as far as the literary world was concerned. I asked whether he'd like to revisit the South Pacific and do an article on it."[26]

Michener looked at her incredulously. Would a magazine, in fact, pay him to go there? Strauss assured him that she would try to get the assignment. After lunch, Strauss hurried back to her office in Radio City and telephoned Ted Patrick and Harry Sions of *Holiday* magazine, which was just emerging as a top-drawer periodical. Strauss convinced them that Michener could write a series of articles focusing on the cultures of the South Pacific. Thinking that the articles might one day form a book, Strauss negotiated with *Holiday* to have all rights revert back to Michener. Strauss then telephoned Michener with the details.

Sitting at his desk at Macmillan, Jim listened with the care of a man just receiving news that his wife has had a baby. After work he went home and told Vange, who added her support. The following day he typed out his resignation letter from Macmillan—by far the hardest decision he ever had to make. In the back of his mind were the haunting images of successful writers who destroyed themselves trying to dance with the "bitch goddess" of success: Ross Lockridge, best-selling author of *Raintree County*, who at the age of thirty-four backed his car into his garage, locked the garage doors, and left the engine running; and *Mister Roberts*'s Tom Heggen, also a victim of suicide. Michener also reminded himself that one foolish choice and weak moment of moral judgment could send him right into the gutter— or worse, back to the poorhouse in Doylestown to spend his declining days, toothless and broke, stumbling from wall to wall down an endless hallway.

In the end, he signed his resignation letter and sent it on to George Brett. With the assignment from *Holiday* magazine in hand, he and Vange prepared to head for the South Pacific, the land that made him famous in the first place and the land that was destined to sustain him during the bleak periods to come. Perhaps out of fear, he never looked back.

PART THREE

The World in His Arms
1950–1969

CHAPTER 8

The Occasional Husband

After Michener left Macmillan, he was free to spend his time traveling to various points in Asia and the South Pacific and to write about his experiences. However, he remained vexed by the idea that in flying off to Sydney, Papeete, or Fiji, he was selling out the opportunity to report on America. When he returned from the tropics in the spring of 1950, he resumed work on the manuscript known as "Jefferson," the name of a fictional state in the Rockies. After the war, themes about the American West began to achieve popularity and critical attention. A host of major historians and fiction writers had emerged: Bernard De Voto (*Across the Wide Missouri*), Wallace Stegner (*Beyond the Hundredth Meridian*), A. B. Guthrie (*The Way West*), David Lavender (*Bent's Fort*), Frank Waters (*Masked Gods*), and Paul Horgan (*Great River*). Three of them—DeVoto, Guthrie, and Horgan—would win Pulitzer Prizes for books based on western subjects during Michener's rise to fame. Later, in 1972, his good friend and colleague Wallace Stegner would win the prize for his novel *Angle of Repose*. Even the western movie had come out of its trivial, B-grade phase and achieved respectable stature in the hands of capable directors like Howard Hawks, John Ford, and Fred Zinnemann. With "Jefferson," Michener felt confident he could join the company of senior writers who wrote about the West.

Being in Colorado only periodically in the 1940s had made the West fade slightly in his memory, but the photographs that he had taken in 1936 and 1937 kept his memories alive. "If I had not taken [them] and implanted them on my mind, studying them often when I was miles away from Colorado, I would never have written the novel. It was the persistence of these images that kept the ideas vital."[1] As he plodded along through the opening pages of the novel, he kept the photos lined up sequentially on his desk for reference.

"Jefferson" had been simmering since his days in Greeley in the 1930s. He had worked on it periodically after the war, but in early 1950 he began in earnest to develop the historical perspective, setting, and characters. The "Jefferson" manuscript—the precursor of *Centennial*—was typed on cheap glazed newsprint, which Jim took from a single ream. The ninety or so pages were left unnumbered, and insertions were made in pen. He also drew a map in colored pencils, featuring the towns of "The Plains" and the western portion of the state known as "The Sunset Side." The manuscript began with the sentence: "It began with a cloud no bigger than a man's hand." Containing more than thirty characters, the manuscript was projected to focus on the decades of the 1930s and 1940s in the West.

Quite suddenly, however, in late spring 1950 he abandoned the manuscript entirely. Realizing he did not have the skill or the preparation to weave all the threads of the narrative together, he set the novel aside, where it lay for the next twenty years. "Most of all," Jim observed, "I realized that it would be folly to attempt a novel about the West while living in the East, and it was not possible for me to move back to the Platte River."[2] Other voices were more strident that season, particularly the ones that were to reward him with money and notoriety.

Fiction may have been compelling, but nonfiction was lucrative, particularly when periodicals such as *Holiday* and *Life* lined up to offer him assignments. In late 1951 *Holiday* again sent him across the Pacific, this time to report on conditions in Japan, Siam, and Hawaii. By summer 1952 he was back in New York City, where he sat down to lunch with De Witt Wallace, founder of *Reader's Digest*, and several editors.

Wallace had followed Michener's career since *Tales of the South Pacific*. He and his wife raved about *South Pacific*, especially the provocative song "You Have to Be Carefully Taught."

By the early 1950s, when Jim arrived on the scene, *Reader's Digest* boasted of a circulation of twelve million readers with thirty-seven foreign editions in thirteen languages. Its target audience was the urban and suburban middle class. "The ultra-sophisticated, literary types and intellectuals are not interested and do not read the magazine, although some do," observed one of the editors.[3] Michener's style—uncomplicated, informative, and unadorned—appealed to Wallace, and he thought it would also appeal to his wide readership.

Hobart Lewis, a *Reader's Digest* senior editor, sat next to Wallace at lunch and had the opportunity to size up Michener's demeanor. Lewis asked Jim to elaborate on his experiences in Korea, a subject that had lately gained escalating interest to readers.

For more than two hours Jim recounted his trips to interview front-line troops dug in along a 140-mile stretch of barren Korean scrubland south of the Yalu River. He told them stories of heroism and deprivation. Accustomed to battle reports from Panmunjom and other safe areas, the editors were impressed by Michener's pluck and determination.

When Jim finished, Wallace asked him to write for *Reader's Digest*. "Mr. Michener," said Wallace, "do you have some project that you have [a] burning desire to write about for us?" Michener stared at him. "Mr. Wallace, I have never had a burning desire to do *anything* in my life."[4] Michener's comment took the editors aback.

"Another writer," observed Lewis, "would have come up with a roomful of ideas, and maybe one in ten would have been good. Not Michener. He was a man of few words and, like Wallace, a terrific listener."[5]

Gradually, a mutual respect developed between writer and publisher, a respect that would blossom into a lifelong friendship for Michener and Wallace. "I liked him immensely," remarked Jim, "indeed, I felt toward him as a son feels toward an understanding father. I found him easy to talk with and filled with ideas."[6]

A week after their lunch, Lewis contacted Michener about writing an article on the Korean War for *Reader's Digest*. "We would like to find a way to share with the American people some of things you told us," remarked Lewis. "Would you have time to cast it up in an article?" Lewis left the narrative approach to Michener but included a series of questions that the article should answer: "How long do men stay [on the front line]? What are the eating and sleeping facilities? Are the men equipped with anti-shrapnel vests? . . . How good is the enemy marksmanship with rifles, with artillery?" Lewis offered $2,500 and a $500 kill fee, plus return of the manuscript "if we are for some reason not able to publish the article."[7] Michener accepted the assignment and was on the next plane headed to Seoul.

In mid-July 1952 Michener, clad in fatigues and boots and with a helmet loosely strapped under his chin, began interviewing a unit of marines in a sandbagged bunker south of the thirty-eighth parallel. Frequently Jim sat astride a wooden ammunition box, while jotting careful notes. Surrounding the bunker, blanched hills rose and swelled monotonously toward the horizon. One evening a courier from *Life* magazine in the Tokyo office delivered a package to Jim—the advanced galleys of Hemingway's *The Old Man and the Sea*. The editors sought Michener's comments for publicity purposes. "I assured the emissary that I would read the manuscript," noted Jim, "praying that it would be good, and if it was I would not hesitate to say it boldly."[8]

Although he was working on the *Reader's Digest* article ("The Way It Is in Korea,"), he pored over Hemingway's novella. As the apprentice reviewing the work of the master, he was at first cautious. "From Hemingway's opening words," Jim noted, "through the quiet climaxes to the organ like coda I was enthralled, but I was so bedazzled by the pyrotechnics that I did not trust myself to write my report immediately after finishing."[9]

Intuitively, he knew it was a "masterpiece." Wishing to be "shed of its sorcery," he stuffed the galleys under his bedroll and went for a walk in the Korean night.[10] In his mind, he was placing the novella with the best of Henry James, Edith Wharton, and Joseph Conrad. However, he had to be certain, since *Life* magazine was asking for his opinion to launch the work to an international audience.

When he returned to his quarters, quite convinced that Hemingway had written one of "those incandescent miracles that gifted writers can sometimes produce," he dashed off his laudatory comments to the magazine. He had no other point of reference except his knowledge of Hemingway and the galleys that rested on the rickety table next to him. "No one reading my words," wrote Michener, "could doubt that here was a book worth immediately reading."[11]

That September *The Old Man and the Sea* was published in *Life* with Michener's fulsome words accompanying it. Michener later learned he was one of six hundred reviewers to receive advance galleys. The magazine sold more than five million copies in the first two weeks. The book version later rose to the top of the best-seller lists and returned Hemingway to the top echelon of American literary figures. While Michener had helped champion Hemingway's cause, he was also working on his own novella, *The Bridges at Toko-Ri*, which was developed from an article for *Reader's Digest* ("All for One: A Story from Korea"). After Hemingway's story appeared in *Life*, Helen Strauss asked Jim if he might by chance want to publish his novella with the magazine. She wanted about thirty thousand words (Hemingway's was just over twenty-six thousand) and needed for Jim to meet a deadline of May 1953. After Jim agreed, she conferred with Jay Gold at *Life*, who agreed to publish *The Bridges at Toko-Ri* sometime in July. This time the editors of *Life* chose Herman Wouk, recent recipient of the Pulitzer Prize for *The Caine Mutiny*, to serve as the marketing voice for the novella. Although Bennett Cerf was "furious" over not being consulted about the novella's debut in *Life*, he nevertheless backed the book publication by Random House, which coincided with the magazine serialization.[12]

As 1952 came to a close, James Michener was reasonably assured that his gamble to leave Macmillan and become a freelance writer had paid off. His articles for *Reader's Digest* were met with immediate praise. "Your picture of the way it is in Korea is magnificent," wrote Hobart Lewis. "Nothing like it has come from the front, and it surpasses our expectations."[13] De Witt Wallace echoed Lewis's sentiments:

"There is no one whose work we value more highly."[14] Later Wallace asked Michener for an exclusive working relationship with his magazine, a request that Helen Strauss flatly turned down. A writer of Jim's caliber needed to be "completely free," Strauss maintained.[15] Wallace then made his next move, offering Michener a carte blanche invitation to "go anywhere in the world" and "write anything" he wished to write. *Reader's Digest* would cover all expenses. The magazine would have first shot at his article. If for some reason *Reader's Digest* could not use it, Jim could sell it elsewhere, and he would owe the magazine nothing. It was a tantalizing option: the magazine would pay him between $3,500 and $5,000 for a two-thousand-word article; for longer pieces, the pay ranged from $10,000 to $30,000. Being the opportunist he was, Michener grabbed the offer without hesitation.

For the next twenty years and in a total of sixty-nine articles, Michener contributed his views to *Reader's Digest* on such garden-variety topics as war babies, Mexican matadors, education, Russian art museums, pornography, and the electoral college. Dependable, optimistic, and always serving up a generous portion of middle-class respectability, Michener became a staple in the magazine and a trusted voice in American life.

Early spring in Bucks County meant blossoms, freshets, soft rain, and mud, especially on the Michener property located "on the hill" in Pipersville. Jim's morning began with writing till about noon, when he would have a light lunch and then head out in boots and a barn coat to walk the circuitous trails around the property. His two mutts usually bounded along by his side. Although he had a hundred homes— under the moon and stars or a hotel in Tokyo or Saigon—he found his Pipersville home his spiritual haven. "I need a base," he remarked. "I need a land which I have known all my life. I need neighbors whose careers are familiar, whose wild ascents and descents are fully understood. . . . I especially like the landscape in these parts. The Delaware River is a majestic water, and everyday I drive into New York. . . . I remark on the height of the river, for it fluctuates radically, sometimes being so low in winter you can walk across it." His favorite pastime was to walk his two dogs, choosing a different route each time. "Through the woods I've cut about a mile of paths," he noted, "and those I walk every day of my life at home. Winter or summer, the woods are inviting, and I can never remember walking through them without seeing something new, or some old thing in a new prospect. I think I would diminish if I had to live without nature."[16]

At forty-six he felt his career was in full stride. He had published four books and was a frequent contributor to *Holiday, Saturday Evening Post, Reader's Digest,* and *Life.* The *New York Times* and the *Saturday Review of Literature* eagerly sought his expertise in reviewing books about Asian culture. The musical *South Pacific* was in its fourth successful year on Broadway. Two films—*Return to Paradise,* starring Gary Cooper, and *Until They Sail,* featuring Paul Newman—had been made from stories in *Return to Paradise.* In 1951 and 1952 he earned over $100,000 in royalties—not bad for a vagrant kid from Doylestown. He began investing his earnings with Merrill Lynch, who by late 1952 estimated his portfolio at nearly $110,000.

If his career was on fire, his marriage to Vange was slowly disintegrating. In the early days of their marriage, Vange enjoyed traveling with Jim. His assignments in war zones precluded her accompanying him, however. After 1951 she gradually began staying home in Pipersville, preferring to work on her own writing career to helping Jim with his. Although she sold some articles to magazines, her career never really went anywhere. They slowly drifted apart, Jim into a self-imposed isolation, Vange into a world of silent rage. In between assignments, as Jim showed up with bag in hand, Vange became resentful and progressively argumentative.

In spring 1953 both she and Jim flew home from Tokyo. Hoping to fill the emptiness in their marriage, and also to create a ploy to keep Jim more at home, she discussed adoption with him. Vange thought fatherhood might make him more a family man and bring them closer together. They contacted Pearl Buck's Welcome House, a local agency directed by the famous author that specialized in placing foreign babies in American households. They soon received a two-week-old Asian American baby whom they named Mark. For a while they were overjoyed and doted on the infant. They requested a second baby from Welcome House, and this time they adopted a nineteen-month-old Chinese Caucasian boy they named Brook. Suddenly, Jim and Vange had an instant family, and joy filled their Pipersville home. He opened a $10,000 trust fund in Mark's name and made plans for the family to spend the summer together.

For Michener, a foundling raised by Mabel Michener, having Mark and Brook relieved some of the pain and sadness stemming from his own miserable childhood. He was determined to give them the home and be the father that he never had. But his eventual decision regarding the boys spoke worlds about his character, and neither his background nor his deep determination mattered very much in making it.

Michener's involvement with Asia made him a natural lightning rod for groups seeking his name and leadership abilities. One of these groups was the San Francisco–based Asia Foundation, which had been founded in 1951 under the name "Citizens of Free Asia." The foundation supported the multifaceted efforts geared toward Asia revival. Supposedly nonpolitical, it derived most of its financial resources from private businesses and institutions. Part of the foundation's mission statement was to "make private American support available to individuals and groups in Asia, who are working for the attainment of peace, independence, personal liberty, and social programs."[17] Michener clearly saw the group as a vital organ operating against active Communist aggression in Asia. Only with its support, he believed, could the weaker nations of Asia resist the persistent threat of Communist takeover. As an unofficial spokesman for the group, Jim traveled tirelessly on its behalf.

When Michener was asked to become president of the Fund for Asia in February 1954, no one was more pleased than the Federal Bureau of Investigation (FBI), which used his services to ferret out suspected Communists trying to infiltrate the organization. His other role was to direct and monitor the fund's interests in Asia. "It is not anticipated," remarked Michener in an official statement, "that the Fund for Asia will initiate any programs. What we look forward to is the support of certain programs that will benefit the masses of the Asia peoples." He cited community development projects, scholarships, teaching fellowships, foreign language textbooks, and self-help projects in refugee colonies as the areas needing the most attention. Idealistic and full of integrity, Jim served the fund until he felt his services were no longer needed.[18]

Meanwhile, the Korean War was winding down to an exasperating conclusion. Jim had thrown himself into the conflict mind, body, and soul. Unlike his supporting role in the South Pacific during World War II, he craved the action on center stage. Consequently, he reported from such dangerous locations as the deck of the U.S. carrier *Essex* as it prowled the North Korean shores, from foxholes where men avoided frostbite by singeing their gloved hands with lighters, and from briefing rooms where anxious bomber pilots pored over maps of enemy territory.

At one time he accompanied a bomber crew dispatched to take out bridges deep in Korea. "In those days of research for *Toko Ri*, I would participate in catapult takeoffs and cable-grabbing landings many times. I never knew which was worse, the sudden leap forward to get us aloft or the instantaneous stop when we came back down, but I cherish those experiences as among the most exciting I ever had. When the time came to write the novel, I knew what would be happening in the airplanes and how the pilots would be reacting."[19] Flying deep into enemy territory, the plane carrying Jim happened upon a North Korean supply train. "In sickening dives" his bomber strafed the engine pulling forty or fifty boxcars. "Then in runs down the length of the train," continued Michener, "we tried to damage the individual boxcars, but I could see we accomplished little. Another carrier plane, however, came from a better angle and wreaked havoc."[20]

Upon completing their mission, the pilots returned to the *Essex*, which from above looked "hellishly small."[21] For Jim, one of the great wonders of aviation was to land a jet airplane on the Band-Aid–size strip of a floating aircraft carrier. To his continuing amazement, the pilots performed this ritual routinely.

Michener originally began his novel of Korea in 1951, but it never "got off the ground." In 1952 he wrote a complete outline for the *Toko-Ri* storyline based on the experiences of Norman Broomhead, a young navy ensign who attempted unsuccessfully to land a disabled plane on the deck of an aircraft carrier. That outline was laid aside three times, before Helen Strauss and *Life* magazine asked him for a short novel to run in serial form. Jim sat down and wrote without pause. "The story I told them that day wasn't changed by so much as a comma when I came to put it down," Michener remarked. "When I talked to them, the hard work had been done."[22]

In July 1953, as hostilities in Korea ended, James Michener's *The Bridges at Toko-Ri* appeared in the pages of *Life*. Random House published it concurrently, declaring the book "a masterpiece." Michener had penned an engrossing story that raised several philosophical issues. It was not that war was unfortunate and stupid: it was; it was not that it put innocent people in precarious situations: it did. It was that ordinary men and women could perform valorously in the face of fear and death. Jim's greatest triumph in the novel was to place readers "inside" the war, to have them experience the emotions of men under the stress of battle. Herman Wouk claimed that Jim's depiction was "a battle hymn of the republic in fiction. God Bless Michener for telling his yarn so well. His eyes have seen the glory!"[23]

Michener's taut, patriotic drama went on to receive fulsome praise, with some critics declaring that it was the best of his five books. Writing in the *New York Times*, Robert Payne observed, "Mr. Michener has Kipling's dangerous gift of making engines live," but he added, "[he] is not so fortunate with his human characters. . . . He has not written the novel of Korea we are all waiting for, but he has entered more compassionate depths than ever before."[24] James Kelly in the *Saturday Review* declared: "Mr. Michener turns in his best performance. Always an acute observer of human character, usually a serious-minded and formidably informed reporter, he has been less at home as a fictioneer. But *Bridges at Toko-Ri*, a honed-down story of action, ideas, and civilization's responsibilities, moves forward with the inevitability of literature."[25] Not all the critics were complimentary, however. Writing in the *New Republic*, H. C. Webster observed that Michener's characters were "two-dimensional . . . what they do and feel and say sounds too frequently like the Voice of America than fine art."[26] The *New Yorker*'s reviewer claimed that although Jim's theme was "admirable . . . he contents himself time and time again with situations so trite that we weary of them before they begin to be resolved."[27]

In the end, Jim gave Helen Strauss the majority of the credit for her handling of the project. Calling *Bridges* his "best single piece of writing," Jim told Strauss in a letter: "I suspect that I might never have put it to paper had it not been for your strong urgings in that direction."[28] In fact, after Strauss sold the movie rights, Jim was convinced that Strauss was the essential ingredient in his success. The film version, starring William Holden, Grace Kelly, and Frederic March, debuted in 1954 and was directed by Mark Robson, in his second turn at a Michener story (*Return to Paradise* was the first). With its swift pacing, location photography, and solid direction and acting, it was perhaps the best movie ever made from Michener's material.

After the success of *The Bridges at Toko-Ri*, Michener faced inevitable comparison with Ernest Hemingway. Although Jim might have agreed with Alfred Kazin that Hemingway was "the bronze god of the whole contemporary literary experience," Jim had consciously divorced himself from Hemingway's other qualities—notably the latter's capacity for self-destruction.[29] There were points of similarity between the two writers. For critics eager for someone to pass the baton to, Michener seemed the likely choice. For one thing, Jim had fashioned something known as the Hemingway style. He shared Hemingway's instinct for aggression but lacked his tragic vision. While Hemingway agonized over his words—three hundred a day was a good production—Michener banged them out and shaped them later. Hemingway was frequently bombastic about his knowledge of nature, as Jim was about his Aristotelian command of literature, the arts, geography, and social customs. Both writers were suspicious of other writers whose success might threaten or overshadow theirs.

The critic who knew best their strengths as well as their weaknesses was probably Orville Prescott, the *New York Times* critic and Pulitzer Prize juror from 1945 through 1948. Prescott witnessed the rise of Michener's career at the same time that Hemingway's was falling. As a conservative young man from an upper-middle-class family and an honors graduate of Williams College, Prescott both feared and admired Hemingway's brutish world, where "to face death with virtue is the supreme human virtue." Prescott claimed that Hemingway's early novels—*The Sun Also Rises, A Farewell to Arms,* and *For Whom the Bell Tolls*—represented "a vision of life that is not the result of conscious reflection but of an intense emotional response." Prescott confessed: "Hemingway's world, alas, is undeniably a recognizable part of the modern world. And as time passes and current news becomes past history the segment of the modern world it reflects grows. The growth may be as unhealthy as that of a cancerous tumor and as dangerous, but it cannot be denied. Moral restraints have lost their power to control a large percentage of humanity. The cult of violence gains new converts every day."[30] After the war, however, Prescott noticed, along with other critics, a different Hemingway. Prescott called Hemingway's 1950 novel *Across the River and Into the Trees* a disappointing follow-up to his previous novels and an indication that Hemingway the artist was slipping into decadence. Hemingway, in Prescott's estimation, was not alone. Good fiction was dying, thought Prescott. Among Prescott's group of "squandered talents" were John Steinbeck, John O'Hara, and William Faulkner. Having said this, Prescott still held some hope that these once great artists had time to renew their careers with truly insightful and creative work.[31]

While the writers of the first half of the twentieth century were languishing, a new crop seemed ready to invigorate the novel. Among those Prescott cited were Norman Mailer, A. B. Guthrie, Conrad Richter, John Hersey, James Gould Cozzens, and James Michener. Prescott thought that *Tales of the South Pacific* was one of the top five novels about the Second World War. Prescott claimed the stories in *Tales* "were amazingly good, fresh, simple and expert in their presentation, humorous, engrossing and even moving. They were all distinguished by an unusual combination of thoughtful insight appealing to mature minds and old-fashioned storytelling, which made the most of exotic local color."[32] Whereas Mailer in *The Naked and the Dead* and James Jones in *From Here to Eternity* resorted to "adolescent sensationalism, lack of restraint and a lack of artistic proportion," Michener displayed a balanced maturity and a "profound admiration for courage, patience, kindliness, and humor."[33] Moreover, Michener exhibited

Hemingway's sense of craft and a keen understanding of men and women in periods of severe emotional stress.

For all of their apparent similarities, Michener and Hemingway met only once, in the late 1950s, when Hemingway was reaching both artistic and physical entropy. At Toots Shor's one evening, Michener entered with Leonard Lyons, a *New York Post* columnist, and sat next to an inebriated Hemingway, who "was so self-conscious and rude that he failed to acknowledge that I had joined the party."[34] Soon, however, the conversation got around to bullfighting, with Jim relating how he had traveled with the great Mexican matadors. Hemingway retorted that he knew the major Spanish bullfighters. Michener happened to mention that he had seen his first bullfight in Valencia in the 1930s and that he worshipped the artistry of Domingo Ortega. Hemingway turned to Toots Shor and muttered: "Any man who chooses Domingo as his hero knows something." With the bullring as their common ground, the two talked into the night. "He could not bring himself," noted Jim, "to thank me for what I had said about the *Old Man* [*and the Sea*], nor did I wish to bring up the subject."[35]

During the summer of 1954, the Michener marriage remained in critical limbo. From Vange's perspective, Jim spent too much time away from home, while she played the role of the literary widow, writing and preparing the house for her husband's arrival from God knew where. She felt trapped and alone, frequently using violence to break through Jim's cool reserve. Jim, on the other hand, could not understand why any woman in her right mind would not put up with his career. He reasoned that since he was now a famous writer, a spouse would be privileged to help him with his frequently stressful life. Since he expected, perhaps unconsciously, for his wife to fill the role of the selfless Mabel Michener, it was incomprehensible that a woman might be unsatisfied being married to him. Communication in their relationship was almost negligible; hard feelings were rampant.

The decline and fall of their marriage, according to Jim, began in 1952, when Jim was traveling in Korea. In a bitter letter dated January 18, 1956, he related in "a simple account" the tragic slide of their relationship. In the letter, he accused Vange of drunkenness, adultery, and abuse. Before going into those claims, however, he prefaced his account by saying that he did not wish "to communicate with [her] again in any human way."[36]

In 1952, "after several years of what I thought were completely happy married life," wrote Jim, "you kissed me goodbye in Japan as I headed for Korea. While I was there you asked a man at the Correspondent's Club to go to bed with you. . . . When I returned from Korea you told me this and we had a dismal scene, the upshot of which was that I said I still loved you and you said you wanted to be a good wife." While Jim was back in Korea, Vange sent him a letter from Tokyo asking for a divorce, saying in no uncertain terms: "You're a fraud. Your interest in Asia is a fraud. Everything you do is a fraud." When Jim finished his assignment, he returned to Tokyo and found Vange "in pretty dreadful shape." Vange was drunk, disorderly, and needed hospitalization. "I did my best to bring you around," continued Jim, "but in the end you ran off to Korea and traveled about with various men. While I was working at sea, you were thrown out of the Correspondent's Club."[37]

Returning to Bucks County, the two tried to patch up their marriage. They adopted first Mark, then Brook. Vange proved to be "an exceptionally fine mother." Things, however, got worse. "In rages of temper you would stand by our bed and howl all night for certain kinds of sexual performances. When I tried to sleep you threw boiling hot coffee in my face. When the inside of my head exploded with pressure and I was under a doctor's care, you stood over me all one night and screamed: 'I don't care if you die! Go ahead and die!'" And then Michener made an explosive charge: "You used to take our second son, Brook, into the bathroom, stand naked over him, and dangle your breasts down before him so that he could play with them, and when he wouldn't you became outraged with him."[38]

Within three months of bringing Brook home from the orphanage and before the final adoption occurred, Vange returned the child to Welcome House. Jim blamed Vange for the decision. Mark remained with the Micheners. Her earlier thought that a family life might keep Jim at home seemed, at this point, absurd. Jim was traveling more than ever, and she was reduced to being a single parent and caretaker of the estate. In February 1954 she had taken enough, and she told Jim she was ready to file for divorce, citing "indignities to person." Their legal battle dragged on through the year. As a settlement, Jim offered Vange the Pipersville house, savings worth over $300,000, and a $40,000 trust fund for Mark. Vange, however, wanted more. She cited an insurance policy and Jim's royalties from *South Pacific.* Jim was livid at the thought. "By the grace of God," he reported, "I overlooked two things: a lousy little bit of insurance, worth in cash $11,000, and future income from *South Pacific.*" According to Jim, Vange screamed all night: "I'm going to have the insurance and *South Pacific,* too!'"[39]

Jim agreed to let Mark stay with Vange after the breakup. "When I taught at the Hill School and the George School I learned that children of broken homes are best if they remain with one parent, and in spite of your incredible behavior with me, you have always been an ideal mother for Mark." Vange had always charged that Jim lacked feelings for children. He made it clear in the letter that "the home on the hill would always be ready for him" should Mark need it. "I fully expect you to reject Mark one of these days when he interferes with what you want to do."[40]

In truth, both Jim and Vange were emotionally unequipped to deal with responsibilities of raising one adopted child, let alone two. The strain in their marriage exacerbated this deficiency. Jim had been raised without a father, and despite his best intentions, he condemned his son to the same existence. Although he said he loved children, he loved them most from a distance. He took no active part in Mark's development, expecting that Vange should take that role.

The divorce was finalized in January 1955. Vange had already moved to the town of Swarthmore, near Philadelphia, with Mark. In the settlement, Vange won $250,000 and custody of Mark. Jim raised a feeble protest at the hearing, saying that he was just as capable of parenting Mark, but both he and his attorney realized that, given his occupation, he was not in the most stable position to take care of a youngster. He was relieved, therefore, when Vange won custody and he could temporarily wash his hands of the situation.

Japan, a country that had figured prominently in Michener's travels, now became the subject of his next novel, *Sayonara*, published in 1954 and, in a poignant irony, dedicated "to Mark." It was easy for Jim to love Japan. With its modest culture, splendid gardens, and artistic tradition, Japan arrested his epicurean tastes. But were Americans prepared to accept a country they once regarded as a bitter enemy? Having little resentment himself toward the Japanese, he predicted that Americans, after nearly a decade of peace, were ready to begin the healing process. "Here one sees with absolute clarity," he observed about Japan, "the fact that all men live upon the land and what it can produce. Here, wherever you look, you see humble people wrestling with their tiny fragment of soil and catch some glimmer of the grandeur of man."[41]

Surprising to Michener was that most hostilities in the American occupation of Japan occurred between U.S. servicemen and young Japanese women. Frequently and disturbingly, such relationships led to murder and suicide because of the taboos against interracial marriages. This racial tension formed the plot of *Sayonara*: an American air force major tries to dissuade a young enlisted man from marrying a local Japanese woman. In the process, he meets and falls in love with a Japanese dancer, who changes his attitude about interracial marriages. "The central portion of the book," reported Jim to movie mogul David O. Selznick, "is a deeply emotional love affair between the major and Takarazuka girl. They move in with [an] enlisted man and his wife, and the story becomes one of discovery and appreciation for the strange Japanese way of life. . . . The story ends on a definite down beat, for the enlisted man and his wife commit suicide— as so many Americans have done under these related circumstances."[42]

Michener's manuscript encountered production difficulties. "*Sayonara* from beginning to end was trouble," lamented Helen Strauss. "After I read the first draft and both Jim and I agreed it needed revisions, he asked me to send it to his editor at Random House, Saxe Commins, with the word that he was eager to have his opinion and wanted to do whatever writing was necessary." In the early 1950s Commins had a sacrosanct reputation at Random House. After he read the manuscript, he proclaimed it ready for the printer, without any corrections or alterations. Strauss was concerned that without any revisions the manuscript would not reach its potential; she thought that Commins was either "on in years" or too distracted by other work to make an informed decision. Commins had even encouraged changing the title to *Japanese Idyll,* a move that did not please Michener. Strauss confronted Bennett Cerf about Commins's inaction, precipitating a "palace revolution" in the offices of Random House. "Bennett figuratively hit the ceiling," remarked Strauss. She threatened to have Jim's contract canceled if the book did not get the editorial help it needed. "Most writers," claimed Strauss, "need editorial help and frequently a good book can become a much better one if the author and editor work together."[43]

In the end, a new editor, Albert Erskine, was assigned to the *Sayonara* project. Strauss maintained that "it was the best thing I did for Jim's career," for it meant that Michener could always work in tandem with a meticulous editor. With a distinctive southern drawl and an elegant pipe clenched between his teeth, Erskine quickly developed a rapport with Michener, eventually understanding the prolific author so well that, if necessary, he could have written the endings to many of Jim's novels.

CHAPTER 9

The Writer at Large

Culture was not the only thing Japanese to which Michener was attracted. After the success of *Sayonara*, *Life* magazine assigned him to report on the success and failure of Japanese American marriages. In Chicago to attend a luncheon organized by the magazine, he met one of the invited guests, Mari Yoriko Sabusawa, a radiant, thirty-four-year-old Japanese American editor of the American Library Association's *Bulletin*. Mari (accent on the first syllable) was direct and headstrong, and as someone who had been assisting Japanese war brides in America, she took Michener aside and informed him that not all mixed marriages ended as tragically as the one in *Sayonara*. Over a ten-day period, Mari helped Jim with the research for the *Life* article; in the process, he fell in love with her.

The daughter of a cantaloupe farmer, Mari Sabusawa was a second-generation Japanese American born in Las Animas, Colorado, in 1920. Her father had emigrated from Japan to Colorado in the early part of the century, hoping to make a decent living raising melons in the land along the Arkansas River. By 1935, however, he decided to move his family to Southern California, which was then undergoing a population boom. After the attack on Pearl Harbor and America's entry into the war, the Sabusawa family, along with more than a hundred thousand people of Japanese ancestry, were rounded up and sent to internment camps in California. For four months, the twenty-one-year-old Mari and her family shared a horse stable at the Santa Anita racetrack with fifteen other people. Conditions were appalling. Stripped of their possessions and their dignity, the Sabusawa family survived on biscuits and water. Later, they were sent to the barbed-wire-enclosed relocation center in Granada, Colorado. Located in a dry sagebrush valley, the camp featured guard towers and spotlights; armed soldiers, their bayonets fixed, patrolled the perimeter. To maintain a sense of community and to foster hope, many families cultivated a garden outside their quarters. On the radio, they heard reports of the war being waged in the Pacific and listened to the music of Benny Goodman and Glenn Miller.

In mid-1942 Mari was placed in an experimental program sponsored by the National Japanese-American Student Relocation Council, which enrolled young Japanese American students in American colleges. She was selected to attend Antioch College in Yellow Springs, Ohio, where for the next three years she studied political science and international relations. As part of the college's cooperative program, she moved to Washington, D.C., to help analyze Japanese communications for the Foreign Broadcast Intelligence Service. In her role as intern, she received a top-secret clearance.

After the war, Sabusawa was accepted as a graduate student in the sociology program at the University of Chicago. She went on to work for the American Council on Race Relations, which led to her becoming an editor with the American Library Association. She met Michener shortly thereafter.

In stature, Mari was barely five feet tall and weighed a hundred pounds. Jim loved her boundless enthusiasm and gentle warmth. In Jim, Mari saw an understated gentleman, a distinguished man of letters, a dedicated worker, and someone who displayed a great deal of affection for Japanese culture. A short time after their meeting, Jim told Mari that he was off on assignment in Asia for the next ten months. He also mentioned that if their love was meant to be, it would need time and distance.

With Vange and Mark moved out, the big house at Pipersville seemed suddenly tomblike. It was November 1954; an early storm had wheeled through, leaving the air frosty and with a speckling of snow on the ground. Down the slope of Jim's property, the leafless elms were etched against the bleak sky. Beethoven and Haydn played on the turntable. Michener's growing art collection was prominently displayed throughout the house. At his desk, Jim wrote correspondence and prepared for a ten-month journey to the Pacific, Asia, and Afghanistan. For his next book project, he planned to work with A. Grove Day, a professor at the University of Hawaii and an expert on Polynesian culture. On November 15, he wrote Day, who was living as a Fulbright lecturer in Australia: "I would enjoy collaborating with you on a book to be called something like *Wild Men in Paradise.* It would consist of about eight long, accurate, provocative, and poetic biographical essays on some of the worthies of the Pacific."[1] Michener named ten ideal personalities, mostly outlaws and scoundrels who made their reputations in the South Pacific.

As he prepared for yet another trek to the Pacific, his agent, publisher, and friends were convinced that Jim had temporarily lost touch with America in his writing. But why? Certainly his breakup with Vange was crucial and hurtful; De Witt Wallace and *Reader's Digest* were also a continual invitation to adventure. It seemed that just when he got settled, another foreign assignment from *Life* or *Holiday* jolted him from his concentration. Ultimately, Michener was a free spirit, conditioned in his youth to hit the road whenever life got too difficult or too threatening. And in late 1954, there was sufficient pain and loneliness in his life for him to flee the country voluntarily. His trip to Hawaii, Southeast Asia, and Afghanistan would inspire three of his next four novels (*Rascals in Paradise, Hawaii,* and *Caravans*).

In February 1955 James Michener lounged with A. Grove Day and Bennett Cerf and his wife on the sun deck of the Royal Hawaiian Hotel on Waikiki Beach. On a bright, cloudless day with tourists swarming over the beach, the three sipped their drinks and talked shop. The mercurial Cerf, wearing a Panama hat, wanted to make a deal with the two authors—who perhaps had visions of becoming the next Charles Nordhoff and James Norman Hall, authors of *Mutiny on the Bounty*—as they discussed their joint project. Cerf hated the title "Wild

Men in Paradise," although it was much closer to the content of the book than his own euphemistic title, "Rascals in Paradise." "Wild Men" sounded barbaric, thought Cerf, and readers might be put off by it. In the end, Cerf and Random House got what they wanted. He signed Michener and Day on the spot to complete *Rascals in Paradise* by the following year. After signing a contract, Jim left for Tokyo and then on to Kabul, Afghanistan. By mail over the next year and a half, Jim and Grove Day chose the historical characters and shaped the book that became Jim's first collaboration with another author.

Arriving in Afghanistan to write several articles, Jim found a country that challenged all of his principles of a liberal democracy. Indeed, here was a land medieval in its political system, fierce in its justice, repressive in its social customs, bleak and arid in its landscape, and alternately blistering hot and bone-chilling cold in its climate—and he loved it. "This is a magnificent place for a writer," he wrote in a letter to Herman Silverman.

> The other day two policemen got into a fight over their mutual love for a young dancing boy and one stabbed the other to death. The government thereupon turned the murderer over to the father of the slain man. This old man tied the murderer to the ground, then with a rusty scimitar cut his throat while about a hundred approving spectators watched in the public square . . . a photographer who was present asked the old man with the knife to "work from the other side of the throat so the sun will be better." . . . I almost heaved my cookies.[2]

For over two months Jim traveled through the cities, deserts, and mountains of Afghanistan, making copious notes and generally being nosy without appearing so. He kept a pocket notebook, three by four inches in size, in which he recorded the smallest details of his visit. He cared little for grammar and sentence structure in his notes. Often one word in bold letters was scribbled across the pages. The next page would have a few fragments, with words underlined for emphasis. He drew a crude map of Kabul showing the relative distances between the embassies and other important government buildings, paved and unpaved roads, and any landmarks that might help jog his memory in the future.

He made two important treks into Afghanistan's interior: the first was a jeep caravan that headed southwest to Kandahar and the cities near the Pakistan border; the second, also using a caravan of jeeps, took him northwest to the Russian border and the cities of Mazur-i-Sharif and Tashkurghan. On the first journey, begun June 6, 1955, he saw with fascination how the Afghans dealt with their harsh, desert environment.

As he had in Colorado with Floyd Merrill, he studied the Afghan farmers' irrigation systems. "Digging such an irrigation system is most dangerous," he observed, "and men who work at this job are given extra pay, extra clothes, extra food and extra women. When they die from suffocation or falling rock, their clothes and women are passed on to some new digger, and the precious water continues to flow."[3]

Traveling deep into "the desert of death," the temperature hovering at close to 110 degrees Fahrenheit, Michener's jeep caravan cut its own path across the simmering sands: "It was an unmatched experience to see tiny jeeps climb and drop and sweep and swerve across limitless dunes, knowing that an hour after their passing, there would be no sign that they had ever touched the desert."[4] When the caravan stopped, Michener put on his wide-brimmed hat, climbed out of the jeep, and stared around him.

"I liked the desert best at blazing noon," he recalled, "when for twenty miles in each direction I could see absolutely no living thing: not a mouse, nor a blade of grass, nor a weed, nor even a dried bone to remind me of something that had once lived. This fantastic desert was the emptiest earth I had ever seen, rivaling the heaving ocean or the arctic wastes." At night the caravan bivouacked under the blaze of stars. Jim remarked: "Sometimes a gazelle would pass in the moonlight, and always in the distance we could hear the terrifying shriek of jackals, sounding like tormented humans . . . the night-girded Afghan night was a place of immortal beauty."[5]

Traveling throughout Southeast Asia had made Jim acquainted with Islam, but trekking through Afghanistan and witnessing the holy sites gave him a fresh appreciation of it. In "Islam: The Misunderstood Religion," which appeared in *Reader's Digest* in May 1955, Jim asserted that "the United States will in the future meet many problems in the Muslim world." His goal in the article was to set down, as plainly as possible, the history and beliefs of Islam, so that American Christians would have a basis of understanding. "Islam is a very manly religion," Jim noted, "and required strong writing. It was a mystical religion and deserved poetic understanding. It was a religion of the desert, strong in illustrations from nature, and this ought to be recorded. It was also a militaristic religion in that it spoke of men battling for a cause. And it was a religion which preached brotherhood and social change, and the commentator ought to point out that the former principle operated today while the latter did not."[6]

Michener wanted to a write a major novel about Islam. His attraction to Afghanistan now made the idea urgent and compelling. He at first thought he would center his book in Constantinople in 50 B.C. and stretch into the years of Constantine and Helene; the novel would follow the years of the crusades of the Middle Ages and end in the battle of Gallipoli in the First World War. The novel never got further than the planning stages.

It was too vast, too unwieldy. Instead, Michener settled on writing about the nation of Afghanistan in the years following the Second World War. That novel, *Caravans,* would take seven years to reach fruition. In between, he would work on an earlier version, "The Sharif of Koristan," which came directly from his time spent in Kabul.

On July 10 Michener flew from Kabul to Saigon, where he spent several weeks walking the byways and researching an article. He stayed at the Majestic Hotel, an aging relic of French colonialism. Saigon was a hotbed of strife. After the French were defeated the previous year at Dien Bien Phu, Vietnam was "temporarily" divided into North and South sections at the seventeenth parallel. Elections were to be held to select a single unified government, but that never happened. The region soon broke into civil war, with the Communists in the north trying to wrest the nation from the anti-Communists in the south.

On July 20 Michener was working in his hotel room when a full-scale riot broke out in the streets below him. He recorded the events of the day:

I was hiding in my room on the third floor when the revolutionaries came storming down the hallway, throwing people out the window. After killing the man in the room next to me they crashed into mine. For a reason I could never explain, I stood in the middle of the room clutching my typewriter and shouting: "You can't throw me out! Press!" And for reasons I'm sure they couldn't explain, they stopped a few inches from me, smiled and rampaged elsewhere.[7]

The army soon arrived and prevented any further destruction of the hotel. In a letter to Herman Silverman, Michener commented: "As I write this, quite shaken up, a little boy stands guard at my door and says, 'An American friend.'" Jim went on: "Brother Herman if I sound casual about this, I ain't. Only my determination not to let the gang in after the door went down saved things here and if one of those wild men with the clubs had said 'Boo' I'd have fainted."[8]

For the next hour or so, to the sounds of machine-gun and small arms fire, the army rounded up the rioters in the street outside the hotel. Debris and broken glass littered the concrete. Clouds of tear gas drifted down the street. Flames poured from a gutted car tipped on its side. The soldiers soon herded the rioters into trucks and drove off. "This is my one riot, I hope," claimed Michener. "I couldn't stand another."[9]

Jim returned to America in early September, barely enough time to write three articles, work on *Rascals in Paradise*, prepare a speech for the Fund for Asia meeting in October, and make a return journey to Chicago to ask Mari Sabusawa to marry him. He did not tell any of his close friends about his upcoming marriage, including Herman Silverman, who drove him to the airport and had to find out that Jim was married by reading the newspapers. On October 23, 1955, the couple was married in the University of Chicago chapel, with the Reverend Jitsuo Morkawa of Chicago's First Baptist Church performing the ceremony. Both Jim and Mari wanted a wedding with the accent on internationalism—and they got what they wanted.

After their wedding, the couple left immediately for their honeymoon: an around-the-world journey, financed by *Reader's Digest*, that would take them to Sydney, Bombay, New Delhi, Bangkok, Singapore, Hong Kong, and Japan. Jim had planned a three-month honeymoon. However, delays and distractions extended their trip to nearly eight months. Arriving in Australia in early November, Michener was pleased to find the Australians, whose hatred of the Japanese still lingered, were receptive to his new bride: "My lady has been a sensation in Australia where they hate the Japanese, and with some reason. . . . She has been on the front pages of the Australian press for about two weeks and seems always to have exactly the right thing to say."[10]

After they spent January in India and February traveling in Asia, the couple left Japan and headed across the Pacific aboard the ship *Pioneer Dale*. On April 25, they arrived in Honolulu harbor. Jim met Grove Day to compare chapters on *Rascals in Paradise*; at the time, they had half the book written. Jim also indicated to a reporter from the *Honolulu Star-Reporter* that he was planning a "big" book on Hawaii but that it would have to wait until some of his other projects were finished.[11]

Jim and Mari arrived in Pipersville in late June 1956, after having driven from the West Coast via Chicago. Mari for the first time unpacked her bags in her new home and prepared to be the wife of an internationally famous author and itinerant squire of Bucks County.

Mari had the distinction of being, along with Jim, one of the few Democrats in the county. She had worked for Adlai Stevenson's campaign before their marriage and wept when he lost the 1956 election. Mari shaped much of Jim's liberal views and was one of the major forces in his becoming a confirmed Democrat. Jim voted Republican in the 1952 election but voted Democratic in 1956. Although Mari supported her husband's career graciously and without reservation, she frequently debated Jim on key issues, particularly those involving minorities and underrepresented groups. She offered no professional or personal threat to his career. From her first days in Pennsylvania, she respected him. If they had a difference of opinion, they were open about it and settled it soon thereafter. One of the hallmarks of their marriage was that they rarely bore ill will toward each other. "Mari was the opposite of Jim," said Herman Silverman. "She was warm and outgoing. But they respected each other's differences."[12]

Their differences at first caused tension. Jim was accustomed to using the word "Jap" in Mari's company. She let Jim get away with it a couple of times, and then she threatened to knock his teeth out with a ketchup bottle if he said it again. He got the point. Although anti-Japanese sentiment was still prevalent in some parts of the country, it was not in Bucks County; most citizens greeted her warmly. Later, in Hawaii, however, that would not be the case.

From the outset of their marriage, Jim and Mari decided that, when practical, they would always travel together. Frequent and prolonged separation was one of the crucial issues of his first two marriages, and he did not want to repeat that with Mari. For his career, that first meant discussing his projects with Mari, which had its decided ramifications. For instance, Michener always considered writing a book about California, but because of Mari and her family's mistreatment there during the war, she would not have anything to do with the place. Consequently, Jim never wrote his book on California or even vacationed or traveled much within the state.

Mari became an avid reader of Jim's reviews. While he ignored what they said, she pounced on any reviewer who happened to say unkind words about her husband. According to Jim, Mari used to create doll effigies of critics and stick hatpins in them as punishment for a poor review of one of Michener's books. In some cases, this was lighthearted fun; in others, it was deadly serious.

When it came to Vange, Jim's ex-wife, Mari maintained an unusually strong resentment. After their divorce, Vange, much to Jim's surprise, moved with Mark to the Swarthmore area. Considering that Vange had no family or friends in the vicinity, it was an odd decision indeed. "No one knew why Vange came to Swarthmore, but she wanted to be accepted," admitted Terry Shane, whose husband was an administrator at Swarthmore College. "I saw her occasionally at parties, but people tended to ignore her. No one at the college would have anything to do with her. After a while she gave up Mark and moved away."[13]

Rumors were rife in town that Vange abused Mark and that she resented having to care for him alone. Michener's secretary, Evelyn Shoemaker, even claimed that Vange never "really loved Mark."[14]

When word reached Jim and Mari that Vange was threatening to return Mark to Welcome House, they were both furious and concerned. According to Mari, Vange had used Mark to drag Jim through a vicious custody battle and demand a huge alimony payment from him. Mari confessed that this was a strong indictment against a woman she had never met, but, as she told Pearl Buck, "we have to deal with a woman who has not only selfish motives and evil intentions, but malice in her heart."[15]

The crisis over Mark reached its head in the summer and fall of 1956. In August a television assignment from NBC took Jim to Asia, where for five weeks he traveled with a camera crew through Java, Bali, Malaya, Cambodia, Vietnam, Thailand, and Burma. Mari, who preferred a more leisurely form of travel, took a cruise to Europe, ending up in Amsterdam. After completing his ninety-minute television show, "Assignment—Southeast Asia," Michener flew to Amsterdam to spend some free time with Mari and take in the multitude of fine museums. While there, they received a startling cable from Pearl Buck indicating that Vange had returned Mark to Welcome House and waived all her rights to his custody. Unless Jim wanted him, Mark would be an orphan. Jim and Mari spent several anxious hours talking over what they should do. Jim wanted a son, that was true, and Mari would support him if he decided to include Mark in their family. Jim, however, had to face the sober reality of his lifestyle—he was constantly traveling, and his writing routine did not include the many needs of a four-year-old. Mari, too, had never expressed interest in being a mother.

By the time the Micheners had to give Pearl Buck their decision about Mark, another event of international proportions intervened. The Hungarian revolution was escalating in central Europe, and Hobart Lewis of *Reader's Digest* had asked Michener if he would leave Amsterdam and fly to Austria to cover the conflict for the magazine. At the time, Michener had no interest in writing about the events in Hungary. He had written several articles for *Reader's Digest* and *Holiday*, and clearly his interests were in finishing his *Rascals in Paradise* project with Grove Day. However, one night in Paris, he and Mari happened to encounter some French students protesting in front of a Communist newspaper office. For a moment, Jim was riveted on their impassioned movements. "Impressed by the new bitterness and violence" toward Russian domination of Europe, he decided on the spot that he would take Lewis's assignment to cover the Hungarian revolution.[16] The next day he was on a plane to Vienna to cover the uprising in Hungary.

It was left to Mari to write Pearl Buck that the Micheners thought it in Mark's best interest that Welcome House find him a loving and stable home. "This is very painful for Jim," noted Mari in her letter, "knowing as I do how he feels for the boy and the boy's happiness."[17] Eventually, Buck, who revered Michener, did her best at placing Mark in a suitable home in Ohio. He grew up to be a well-adjusted boy with few traces of his difficult early childhood. Jim never saw him or corresponded with him or his parents. Jim's initial reason for this estrangement was that we wanted absolutely no pretext for Vange to enter his life again. But after her influence faded, he had really no explanation as to why he had given up his legally adopted son. Jim walked out of Mark's life, never to return.

After Vange returned Mark to Welcome House, she temporarily left the country and fled to Europe, where she led a gypsy life on Jim's alimony settlement. After a few years, she moved to the Philadelphia area and settled into a quiet suburban life. She never remarried or attempted to contact Jim after their divorce.

On October 23, 1956, a student rally in downtown Budapest ignited a mass demonstration against the Soviet-controlled government. After the police retaliated, the mob sacked the Communist Party's newspaper office and tore down symbols of Russian authority. Protesters waved revolutionary banners and sang patriotic songs, their music rising above the din of street warfare. The uprising continued and intensified throughout the day. The following morning the government called out the army to suppress the revolt, but the presence of the troops only enraged the crowds. Demonstrators mobbed the streets, opening the prisons, ransacking the police station, and hanging members of the secret police.

The news of the revolution in Hungary flashed throughout the world, garnering immediate sympathy for the country that was locked in a David-versus-Goliath struggle. In the days following October 23, it appeared that the demonstrators were on the verge of winning a miraculous victory in the streets of Budapest. In Washington the events were met with excitement and gloom. The Eisenhower administration supported the long-term independence of Iron Curtain countries, but it was unwilling to risk global war over the crisis in Hungary. With his hands tied militarily, all Eisenhower could do was to offer fleeing refugees a haven in America.

In the last days of October and first days of November, it appeared that the revolution had at least temporarily succeeded. On October 31 *Pravda* issued a statement that promised greater equality between the Soviet Union and the countries of the Eastern European bloc. It further claimed that the Soviet government "is prepared to enter into the appropriate negotiations with the government of the Hungarian People's Republic and other members of the Warsaw Treaty on the question of the presence of Soviet troops on the territory of Hungary."[18] The statement shocked outside observers.

In a complete reversal of that position, however, Soviet tanks and troops entered Budapest in the chill morning hours of November 4. The massive show of force, which included four thousand tanks and over 140,000 infantry, was intended once and for all to crush the rebellion and reassert Soviet domination in Hungary. Unruly crowds tried to stymie the Russian advance in the streets. Demonstrators brandished kitchen knives and threw Molotov cocktails but proved no match for the heavily armed Soviet forces. After intense street fighting, eighty thousand residents of Budapest lay dead amid the rubble. Many others fled for the Austrian border, where at a town named Andau a rickety wooden bridge allowed them to pass to safety in the West. There were other escape routes to Austria, most notably at Nickelsdorf and Sopran, but Jim would make Andau famous.

Michener arrived in Vienna just prior to the Russian invasion. He stayed at the Hotel Bristol, which by early November had become a beehive of international correspondents sending dispatches to the four corners of the globe. It also housed a number of Russian spies, Poles fleeing oppression, and a cadre of American Red Cross workers. Vienna was one hundred miles from Budapest and nearly forty miles from the Austrian border, where waves of refugees were seeking asylum. Vienna was probably the closest point that most journalists dared get to the action in Hungary. Within days, Mari joined her husband in Vienna.

Among the assorted types at the Bristol, Jim met a thirty-nine-year-old whiskey-voiced combat photographer named Georgette "Dickie" Chapelle. On assignment from Time-Life, Chapelle preferred missions that led her into the thick of the action. In a male-dominated profession, she reasoned that only through forceful derring-do on the battlefield could she hope to compete. Draped in Leicas and Nikons, clothed in olive drab fatigues, and with a cigarette sprouting from her lips, she eagerly tagged along with a famous author who was capturing the events in Hungary. Although some of her peers thought her reckless and "self-destructive," Michener called Dickie the bravest person—man or woman—he ever met.[19]

Throughout November, as refugees continued to pour from Hungary, Jim and Dickie made repeated runs to the Austrian-Hungarian border. After an evening meal in Vienna, they would leave about 9:30, drive along unlit, sinuous mountain roads, and arrive in Andau at midnight. Eluding the Soviet guards, they would stalk across the bridge into Russian-held territory, greet hundreds of refugees, and spirit them to safety on the Austrian side. By 4:00 in the morning, as the number of refugees diminished, they would drive as many as they could to Vienna, where Mari waited with hot chocolate, sandwiches, and cold beer. As Jim and Dickie's rescue mission continued, he interviewed constantly—men, women, children, teachers, musicians, professors, mechanics, and shopkeepers. During the stint, he used two interpreters—the first quit because of fatigue. Jim filled his pocket journal with notes and impressions. Dickie's cameras kept clicking away. Stories of neglect, abuse, and torture were common. One man told Michener how he survived in the horrendous conditions of

Recsk prison, where he lived for three years in a small room with eighty other men and was forced to smash, day after day, tons of granite into rubble. He worked from 4:30 in the morning until nightfall. If he fell short of his quota for the day, the guards made him stand in cold water up to his knees during the night. If the guards were in a particularly sadistic mood the next morning, they made him carry a hundred-pound rock up and down a ladder fifteen to twenty times. These were the milder attempts at torture and humiliation. At other times, the secret police who ran the prison had more creative and brutal punishments for the prisoners.

Michener went through a painstaking process in verifying the refugees' accounts. "I cross checked the interviews with two teams of Hungarian experts," he explained. "When any discrepancies showed up I had still a third group look them over. I had detailed maps of Budapest and hundreds of pictures of specific buildings and streets. I made the people point out the exact spot where the incidents they related took place, and by comparing one report with another, I was able to weed out inaccuracies."[20]

Jim was both outraged by the refugees' stories and honored that he could help them. He remained surprised by the youth of the refugees: "In my time I have observed many emigrations: pathetic Indians struggling out of Pakistan, half-dead Korean women leaving Communist-held North Korea, Pacific Island natives fleeing the Japanese, but I have never seen so many young people fleeing oppression." "The soul of the nation," commented Michener, was being drained from Hungary, and committed volunteers like Jim and Dickie were doing whatever they could to relieve the misery of the refugees. Perhaps because he was so moved by the refugees' courage and determination, he decided that his account needed to be longer and more in depth than he had planned. Plus, he wanted the largest platform to voice his anti-Communist views, which in summarized form ran: "Any nation which permits itself to be drawn into Communism's orbit is certain to lose everything it values, including its freedom."[21]

Jim also devised a scheme to assist many Hungarian religious leaders. An American offer to admit refuges was based on certain quotas that favored the more predominant religious denominations in Hungary. Based on the most recent census, Catholics were the largest group, Protestants were second, and Jews were third. As it turned out, a disproportionate number of Jews fled, and Jim was faced with the problem of what to do with them. He hit upon the idea of masquerading Jews as Catholics and Protestants. "We taught Hungarian Jews to be Baptists and Methodists whose quotas were never filled," remarked Jim of the escapade. "I explained that it was pretty easy to be Baptist if you kept your mouth shut, and even easier to be a Methodist, because you didn't have to worry if the examiner asked, 'Where were you baptized?' I told the bearded rabbi, 'Shave and we'll make you a Baptist.' He did and we did."[22]

Meanwhile, Chapelle was becoming more daring and independent in her movements. On December 4, while Michener was away from the hotel, she failed to show up for a lunch date with Mari. Fearing the worst, Mari led a behind-the-scenes investigation into her whereabouts. She discovered that Dickie had crossed the border and had been arrested by Russian guards and thrown in jail for six months as a spy. Jim regretted his inattention to her disappearance. "I was absent at the border," he remarked, "and so could possibly have been excused for my apparent callousness, but had I been on the ball I might have deduced that something was wrong. I didn't. Others knew that she was in trouble and did nothing about it. One news media [sic] was completely indifferent. Its personnel said such immoral and detached things that I have never felt free to name the organization involved. I deeply resented their behavior toward a hard working woman reporter-photographer."[23] Dickie's actions were not in vain, however. Her photographs from the border served to generate enormous support for the refugees, helping to inspire Time to name the Hungarian Freedom Fighters as its "Man of the Year."

After her release from prison, Chapelle returned to America and spent time recuperating at the Micheners' Pipersville home. "During this period she was our guest," wrote Michener, "and we did everything possible to rehabilitate her, my wife being especially attentive to any of her needs . . . my wife and I both loved her. . . . We considered her one hell of a woman, the first of her breed, someone to be protected."[24] Afterward, Dickie continued to seek out dangerous missions around the globe. She was killed by a land mine in Vietnam in 1965 while on patrol with marines. "She was an early edition," observed Jim, "and for her premature behavior she had to pay a heavy price in scorn, rejection, ridicule and resentment . . . she was a forerunner, encompassing all that terrifies men in the women's movement, but also encompassing the fundamental virtues of that movement."[25]

Reasoning that Jim's account of the Hungarian revolution should have the widest possible audience, Hobe Lewis cabled Michener suggesting that Random House publish it in book-length form and that *Reader's Digest* serialize it over several months beginning the following March. Jim concurred. For six solid weeks, twenty hours a day, first in Vienna and later in Bucks County, Jim toiled on the account of the Hungarian revolt that became known as *The Bridge at Andau,* an often horrifying tour de force of sustained drama.

Jim delivered all but one chapter of the manuscript in late December 1956. Albert Erskine and Bert Krantz, acting on Bennett Cerf's orders to rush the book into print, spent a cheerless weekend in Random House's offices editing and readying the manuscript for the printer. "[The book] is so timely and important that it would be unthinkable for us, as publishers, than to do otherwise than present it to the public as fast as we can get in print," Cerf remarked to A. Grove Day.[26] Cerf decided to delay the publication of Michener and Day's *Rascals in Paradise,* scheduled for an early 1957 release, until June. *The Bridge at Andau* would be published in February, four weeks after Jim submitted the last chapter, which at the time was a record delivery date for a major publisher.

CHAPTER 10

Islands in the Sun

A s he celebrated his fiftieth birthday on February 3, 1957, Jim wondered if he should continue to be the roving correspondent, able to fly to an international hotspot on a moment's notice, or to settle down, as he hoped, in his home in Pipersville to pen the epic novel he had longed to write. More than two months in Austria and Hungary writing, traveling back and forth to the border, and assisting refugees to safety left him clearly exhausted. After a brief rest, his attention turned to his forthcoming book, *The Bridge at Andau*. Notwithstanding the book's historical importance, Michener was uncertain that such a graphic and anguished account would sell well. "People want something lighter and more diverting," he claimed.[1]

Random House published *The Bridge at Andau* the last week of February; *Reader's Digest* planned two condensed installments, one in March and the other in May. The *Digest*'s European editions had to add sixteen pages at a cost of $65,000, prompting Hobe Lewis to admit that it was "well worth it."[2] The book edition sold briskly; stirred by the recent events in Hungary, critics were eager to review Michener's account.

The strength of Jim's book lay in his reporting skills and his use of fictional techniques to tell the story. The central character in the opening chapter, Josef Toth, is a composite of three young refugees Jim met and interviewed on the border. Fearing reprisals against their families back in Hungary, they urged Michener not to use their real names. In other chapters, with the person's permission, he was free to use real names for historical accuracy. By using representative figures for the great tide of refugees, he achieved a poignant dramatic focus. This handful of soiled, everyday heroes, he asserted, confronted the Russian tanks and submachine guns. In his book they would serve to inspire the rest of the world.

The Bridge at Andau won the Overseas Press Award, but some critics, Orville Prescott among them, thought that Michener's penchant for political causes, though it produced memorable reporting, affected his development as a fiction writer. "The evidence is piling up," wrote Prescott, "that as Mr. Michener becomes more expert as a journalist he is becoming less effective as a writer of fiction. There is no harm in that. We need journalists as good as Michener. But those who were excited by the appearance of Tales of the South Pacific cannot help being disappointed."[3] For ten years, after the January 1947 publication of Tales of the South Pacific, Michener had briefly dallied with American themes (The Fires of Spring) then bolted for Southeast Asia, where he spent a majority of his time writing of the postwar cultures. Voice of Asia, Return to Paradise, The Bridges of Toko-Ri, and Sayonara were all products of this romance with the East. In his writing, Jim was first and foremost a teacher who educated his readers on geography, manners, social conditions, and ethnic differences, and he had no intention of veering from that course with his next book.

As spring advanced, Michener's Bucks County home offered him temporary sanctuary, long enough for him to saunter over the snow-encrusted trails, scrape the mud from his boots, lounge in his office, listen to opera, and consider future plans. "The need to write is so pressing for me," Michener remarked, "and the act itself so delectable an experience that with little pause I move eagerly to the next assignment; the ideas are impatient to leap from the prison of my mind."[4] Among the more ambitious projects vying for his attention were his novel of Islam; a novel of Scotland; his aborted novel of Colorado, which looked like it was doomed to remain unfinished; a book tentatively titled "The Americans," dealing with travelers in Asia; and a fictional project that had been gaining momentum over the last few years that traced the history of Hawaii. The Hawaii project seemed the most likely candidate that March. On his desk were books with titles such as *Insects of Hawaii* and *Ancient Tahiti* and a book that traced the migrations of Polynesian peoples.

During Michener's numerous trips to Asia, Hawaii had acted as an important crossroads. He began writing about it seriously as early as 1950, when he wrote a major piece for *Flair* magazine. In 1953 he appealed to Americans to consider statehood for Hawaii, an idea that was to gather some momentum in the country but be stymied by certain members of Congress. Writing in *Readers' Digest* in August 1953, he insisted that "every American who can possibly do so ought to visit Hawaii. It is a rare experience: physical beauty, exotic flowers, a new way of life and a social experiment of world importance." In late 1953 he talked over the idea of a large novel about Hawaii with Albert Erskine, who was both intrigued and skeptical. In April 1956 he indicated to a Honolulu newspaper that he intended someday to make Hawaii his permanent home. "This is the greatest place on earth," he maintained.[5]

For several years Jim had wanted to write an epic novel, one that would be read a hundred years after his death. If he was going to write a panoramic book, he had to know the geography, history, and culture of the area. And no writer knew the Pacific Rim as well as Michener. Hawaii was additionally tempting because of its ties to America and its impending statehood. For his conception of the novel that ultimately became *Hawaii*, he drank deeply of writers like Dickens and Balzac, whose spacious novels nurtured him through an impoverished childhood. For further inspiration he drew on the memory of an innocuous novel of Java, *Max Havelaar*, by Eduard Douwes Dekker. "I was astounded," noted Jim, "by the freedom with which he incorporated in his novel material of the most revolutionary character: price lists, data on the cultivation of sugarcane, long disquisitions on life in Indonesia and political analysis." Jim realized that Dekker's "chaotic material" created "an ambience that was overpowering."[6]

Michener further understood that that he, too, could incorporate such material but only if he did it with skill and artistry. Armed with this belief, he delved into the very sources of Polynesian life and began to construct the outline of the novel.

In early October 1957 Jim was as shocked as most other people by Russia's launch of *Sputnik*. In his article "While Others Sleep" for *Reader's Digest*, he maintained that only with the mighty presence of the Strategic Air Command (SAC) could America deter the Russian threat of world dominance. *Sputnik* shook his confidence not only in that program but also in America's technological supremacy. However, Michener learned about the launch after the fact; the same day that *Sputnik* was shot into orbit, he was traveling with eleven airmen from Guam to Tokyo on board an air force C-47. It was perfect flying weather: the sky was a pearl blue, the wind was light and variable, and the sea rolled in a light chop. Suddenly an engine sputtered and flamed out. Michener, strapped in with his back to the front of the airplane, glanced out the window. The starboard engine trailed smoke. As the crew made preparations for a crash dive, Michener discussed with the others what they should do after they hit the water. Cutting its engines and dropping from the sky, the C-47 glided for several moments over the sea, finally slamming into a wave. With its belly sheared off, the plane miraculously stayed afloat long enough for the passengers to jump into the water and begin inflating the life raft. As Jim thrashed in the water, the crew and passengers pulled themselves one by one into the raft. Jim tried and failed. "For Christ sakes, old man, get in!" someone shouted at him. "Swing your ass up and over!" Again he failed. An enlisted man jumped in the water and heaved Michener into the middle of the raft, where he landed in a tangle of legs and arms.[7]

For several seconds the plane floated nearby, and then it disappeared beneath the waves. The raft slowly drifted from the crash site, leaving a trail of boots, bags, personal effects, and papers—including Michener's working notes for *Hawaii*—strewn on the sea. The raft floated for eighteen hours. A Japanese fishing boat, responding to a navy SOS, arrived on the scene toward nightfall of the second day, rescued them, and brought them to Japan.

At home in Pipersville, Michener reminisced about his aborted plane ride and celebrated his and Mari's second wedding anniversary on October 23. Within two years Mari had become his confidante, travel agent, valet, and personal bodyguard. While his secretary, Evelyn Shoemaker, handled the routine appointments, Mari coaxed Jim into attending the important ones, especially when there was an urgent political or social interest behind them. They continued to support the Democratic Party in Bucks County and showed up for Democratic fund-raisers. At one gathering, Adlai Stevenson, who had twice lost in his bid for the presidency, quipped that the Micheners and the Silvermans were probably the only Democrats in the county, but it at least "was a foothold. We can build on that."[8]

Jim and Mari developed a fondness for pet names. They started calling each other Cookie. Jim's friends remained mystified by the origin of the term. Mari doted on Jim, especially after his ditching in the Pacific.

He reconstructed the outline for *Hawaii* and began an intensive reading schedule on Polynesia. As they planned for their move to Hawaii, Mari secretly worried that her Japanese ancestry would cause problems for Jim and his book. The average white person distrusted "Asian-looking" people, and although Hawaii had made great strides in integration, it was not quite the melting pot that it claimed to be.

Notwithstanding Mari's reluctance, there were important reasons why a novel on Hawaii made sense. Jim heard from Helen Strauss that *South Pacific* would be made into a movie and be filmed in the islands. His old buddy Josh Logan, who helped shape the stage musical, was signed to direct. Additionally, most Americans thought of Hawaii as their closest thing to a tropical paradise. As tensions in the world mounted during the cold war, the idea of Hawaii became a restful diversion for many Americans. Moreover, Hawaii was the gateway to Asia, and reasoned an idealistic Michener, if America was going to build a peaceful accord in the Pacific, it would begin in the islands.

In March 1958 the Micheners packed up a crate of necessities— books, notepads, typewriters, and personal effects—and prepared for a long sojourn in Hawaii. Jim rented an apartment in Waikiki.

In April, after a brief stay in San Francisco, they landed in Honolulu, where they met A. Grove Day, Michener's erudite guide through paradise.

Jim arrived in Hawaii with his priorities set. First, he was a writer; second, he was a political agitator; and third, he was a beach bum who enjoyed sauntering along Waikiki Beach in his aloha shirt doing absolutely nothing. On May 1 he began his part as a novelist by attacking his book on Hawaii. He moved his desk to a bare wall in his apartment and began the initial draft. Jim loved beginning a book, when he could type his thoughts with near abandon. His partnership with the typewriter was similar to that between Jackson Pollock and his drip paintings. Sitting in his shorts, his fingers hammering at the arctic whiteness of the page, Jim felt a sensual, near sexual, euphoria.

He took to his new surroundings immediately, but that was vintage Michener. "I can work anywhere, in any climate, under any conditions," he noted, "providing I have a large enough desk on which to keep my papers organized. On some seven occasions I have solved this problem by buying at a lumber yard an unfinished door which I have propped up on bricks or two-drawer filing cabinets."[9]

In its preliminary form, *Hawaii* was divided into five parts: "(1) The coming of the Polynesians to Hawaii, (2) the coming of the haoles to Maui; (3) the coming of the Chinese to Oahu; (4) the coming of the Japanese to Kauai; (5) and the coming of the Filipinos generally."[10] This rough outline, which he formulated over several years, became the blueprint for the novel. After devouring more than a hundred books on Hawaii, he typed the first forty pages in a white heat. He tried to get the plot down first and then polish the prose later. Jim used the cut-and-paste method. If he needed to insert a portion of manuscript, he typed out the section of prose, cut it out with scissors, and pasted the section into its proper place. Whole manuscripts were "bandaged" in this fashion.

After he had written a sizable amount of words, he placed a phone call one evening to Clarice B. Taylor, a noted Hawaiian scholar and the woman who would serve as his chief technical adviser on the project. A gracious woman in her sixties, Taylor was surprised to hear the famous author's voice on the phone and was perhaps more shocked when Michener asked her to lunch the following Monday. "Grove Day told me to call," Jim said. "Well, I'll be damned," Taylor said to herself. On Monday they met at the Halekulani Hotel, where Jim sketched his novel for her. "I was skeptical," remarked Taylor afterward. "No one had ever written such a story. I kept this skepticism to myself for after all the man's name was Michener and Michener was a magic name."[11]

For the next month, Jim and Taylor pored over the Hawaii project. When Jim wanted books to verify his information, Taylor told him bluntly: "The things you want are not in books . . . all this material you want has to come out of my head. A book cannot tell you how a Polynesian acts or how he talks." Consequently, Taylor became an essential source, sharing everything she knew of customs, language, family names, and nuances of Hawaiian culture.

Their partnership was not without its friction. When Jim first showed what he had written to Taylor, she was aghast. "His people did not talk like Polynesians," she recalled. "How am I going to tell a man named Michener that he was all wet?" After she got up the nerve, she pointed out his errors. "I want it to be right," Michener insisted.

Taylor responded: "Then you don't mind rewriting and correcting this entire story?"

"No," said Jim. "I'll correct on the galley proofs if necessary." Together they tore the first pages apart. Beginning from scratch, Jim once again barnstormed through the manuscript—this time with Clarice Taylor looking over his shoulder.[12]

They labored over authentic names found in the various cultures that settled Hawaii. Michener asked Taylor for a list of two hundred Hawaiian names and a five-generation genealogy. After discarding several names, mainly because they were not pronounceable, they settled on thirty to fifty names for the characters in the book. Each name for Jim had to have a clear-cut meaning. Some were as melodic as Bali Ha'i from *Tales of the South Pacific*. One was Iliki, which meant "the sea spray in a chief's face." "The Polynesian and New England names were an easy problem in comparison to the difficulties we encountered with the Chinese names," noted Taylor. Although Michener was well versed in Chinese culture, he made a mistake on certain names. "You can't have a woman named for her ancestral grandmother!" fumed Taylor. "The Chinese simply do not name their children in memory of dead persons. . . . You can't have your boys carry these names. Only the family name is carried on. Each generation of boys must also have a similar middle name—according to a couplet selected by the person who names the children." "Yes, of course," responded Jim. "I knew that about the couplet. Why didn't I remember?"[13] Michener ended up rewriting the section three times before getting it right.

Other fine points were important in the narrative. During their discussions, Michener wondered why missionary husbands in the nineteenth century insisted on delivering their own children. "Why," Jim questioned, "didn't they use the capable Hawaiian midwives?"[14]

Taylor answered: "Don't you know that no ethnic group would ever trust its wives to another ethnic group? White men would not trust their wives to the best-trained Hawaiian. That was also true to the Chinese. The Japanese brought their own midwives as did the Filipinos."[15] Taylor suggested he read Ethel Damon's *Koamalu*, the story of Mary Rice, who in 1844 and while eight-months pregnant walked forty miles just so that a missionary's wife could deliver her baby. She eventually had a healthy baby, but there were numerous instances of women dying at the hands of untrained missionaries. In Michener's novel the distrust of cultures surfaces tragically: a young missionary leads his pregnant wife to the house of Abner Hale, the New England missionary-hero in the story. Refusing all other help, especially from the native Hawaiians, they entrust the woman's care to Hale, who has little experience but nonetheless agrees to help deliver the baby. While the "heathen" midwives gather outside his residence and offer folk remedies that have worked for centuries, Hale refuses their entreaties. Embarrassed and uncomfortable at seeing a woman without clothes, he is unsure of himself during the birth. The young wife ends up bleeding to death. As Hale and the woman's husband console each other, they both agree it "is the will of God."[16]

During the writing of the novel, Taylor remained skeptical that Jim could successfully intermingle the four primary racial stocks of Hawaii—the Polynesians, Japanese, Chinese, and Caucasians—and produce a readable narrative. Jim continued to allay her concerns and to press on. Although he was attracted by the black beaches, the stunning blue skies, and the palm trees leaning over the sea, he was primarily interested in how these peoples came together on the islands, mingled, and formed a harmonious society. As in any culture, there was latent discrimination among the groups, but the fact remained that a Japanese man could become chief of police, a Chinese woman could become a great educator, and a Filipino boy could dream of attending the university. The need to represent social equality drove Michener through the manuscript.

When he wasn't consulting with Taylor, Jim either spent his days at the Hawaiian-Mission Historical Library or with his think tank of local Hawaiian scholars. Among the specialties that Michener sought advice about were island history (Atherton Richards and Randolph Crossley), volcanoes (Gordon Macdonald), botany (Harold St. John), pineapples (Beatrice Krauss), and Chinese culture (Chinn Ho and Sai Chow Doo).

Between May 1958 and February 1959, from 7:30 in the morning until noon, seven days a week, Jim toiled on *Hawaii*. As with his work in the South Pacific, he felt he was not only following in the tradition of other writers of Hawaii—Stevenson, London, Maugham—but also breaking new literary ground. The size and scope of *Hawaii*—and later, its success—irritated some of the resident literati, most notably John P. Marquand, who rose to fame with his Pulitzer Prize winner, *The Late George Apley,* in 1937 and later with the Mr. Moto series of books. Marquand resented Michener's sudden stardom, calling him a "journalistic show-off and self promoter who with no credentials or literary qualifications to speak of, had appropriated as his fictional bailiwick a quarter of the globe."[17] Marquand's and Michener's knowledge of the Pacific was impressive; however, Michener was certainly more prolific. In the end, Jim shrugged off Marquand's bitter comments, ultimately believing that self-promotion was neither a literary nor a Quaker sin.

In writing his first epic novel, the Genesis-through-Revelation, Alpha-through-Omega opus that became his signature, two powerful psychological forces were at work, forces so deeply seated that they would shape how he approached most of his future projects. Many readers were quick to ask: why did Michener spend so much effort in creating lengthy preambles, mostly concerned with the scientific development of particular places? Perhaps the reason is buried in Jim's childhood. Being a foundling, without knowledge of his ancestors, he yearned for connections in his life. Later, his inability to have children further compounded his sense of isolation. Genetically "marooned" in real life, he sought through his art to provide a sense of form and completeness, of one generation firmly connected to the next, of a great chain of events naturally proceeding from the distant past to the present.

When he came to Hawaii, and later Israel and Colorado, Michener resorted to telling the whole story with an opening such as "millions and millions of years ago." It was the world according to Jim. Not having a genealogical past, he yearned to create his own bible of creation and the begetting of generations. His art served to compensate for the inadequacy he felt on being alone on earth. The psychologist Alfred Adler advanced this compensatory theory of creativity, believing that humans create because of some physical defect or sense of inferiority. Such a theory may explain why Jim began and continued the tradition of the multigenerational, panoramic novel. Michener's readers were often divided into two groups: those who enjoyed the initial hundred pages of scientific and geologic information and those who skipped it and proceeded right to the storyline. Michener was often amused by this dichotomy.

As the number of manuscript pages mounted, Jim had the idea that a simple direct title such as *Hawaii* might capture an audience, but he let Albert Erskine and Bennett Cerf make the final decision. He had used a one-word title once before (*Sayonara*) and was pleased with its economy. After the title of *Hawaii* was finalized, Michener decided that one-word titles would become his trademark. When Helen Strauss heard the title, she at first thought that a book named *Hawaii* sounded too much like a travelogue. After reading Jim's brief proposal, however, she knew she had a winner. Armed with this belief, she walked into Bennett Cerf's office prepared to wage a "heretic assault on the tenets of publishing." Strauss wanted 62 percent of the paperback royalties for her client; Random House would then get a third. Because Jim was such a valuable author for Random House, she did not think the traditional split of fifty-fifty should apply to him. "You are going to put us out of business!" cried Cerf. Nevertheless, Strauss got what she wanted and left a befuddled Cerf in her wake.[18]

In February 1959, after extensive rewriting and totaling nearly five hundred thousand words, *Hawaii* was ready to send. Random House soon projected a November 1959 publishing date. Drained and exhausted, Jim put the bulky package in the mail at the Waikiki main post office and went for a long walk on the beach.

During his time in Hawaii, Jim cast about in search of a politically liberal Galahad to which he could give his heart and soul. In June 1959 Jim found him. On a balmy Honolulu night, Jim attended a Democratic fund-raiser honoring the visiting senator from Massachusetts, John F. Kennedy. In his speech Kennedy quoted from some of the key documents in American history, while a rapt Michener listened in the crowd. Afterward, Kennedy took Michener aside and told him: "I hoped you would be here. I've always liked your *Fires of Spring*." Later that night Jim went home and ruminated about his evening. He thought that Kennedy was a breath of fresh air in politics and someone who bore watching. "[He] is unusually appealing," admitted Michener. "He knows what to say to people. But I'm not sure I want to support him for President. Not yet." In the meantime, he and Mari attended Democratic parties, spoke out for candidates, and awaited the upcoming elections.[19]

After the Democrats were soundly defeated in the local Hawaiian elections in 1959, Jim spiraled into a funk. Some of his liberal friends blamed him for not speaking out more loudly for the Democratic cause. One remarked: "Don't you feel a little sick at your stomach when you think that your television speeches could have won the election for the Democrats?"[20] Other Democrats thought he was too soft and too conciliatory toward the GOP. On the other hand, some of his Republican associates thought he was "temporarily deranged" for abandoning them in the final months before the election. "More unpleasant," Jim noted, "were the other friends who explained to the community that I had supported Democrats only because my wife happened to be Japanese-American, for in Hawaii many of the younger Japanese were Democrats." After the Democratic loss, Jim wrote a five-part autopsy of the election for the *Honolulu Star-Bulletin*, blaming, among other things, the Democrats' sluggish start and poor organization.[21]

Feeling ostracized politically was just the beginning of Michener's woes in Hawaii. His novel *Hawaii* was due to be published in November, and some who had read the advance galleys predicted a firestorm when it finally appeared. Several readers objected to the way Michener took license with Hawaii's history and culture; others, such as Clarice Taylor, suggested that many would "scream" when they read Jim's work. "The screams," continued Taylor, "in certain quarters will arise because so many of us in Hawaii are accustomed to pretty stories about ourselves and our ancestors, stories which make plaster saints out of our leading businessmen and particularly our laborers. This is not for Michener, who hews to the truth."[22]

Also troubling to Michener was the overt bigotry toward Mari. Although people in the islands professed ethnic tolerance, Jim and Mari found otherwise. "On the day to day operating level," observed Jim, "at which my wife and I had to live, we met with more racial discrimination in Hawaii than we did in eastern Pennsylvania." Jim cited a time when they went to buy a home in Kahala and were met with restrictive covenants precluding Japanese residents. "The three finest clubs in Hawaii," Jim added, "admit no Orientals to membership."[23] The treatment of Mari perhaps hurt him more than the political loss and the novel's reception in the islands.

After encountering several instances of discrimination directed at Mari, he made the key decision that he was going to leave Hawaii and return to his home in Pipersville. Moreover, he would put his convictions to work by assisting in any way he could with the 1960 presidential election. He felt "no bitterness" toward the people of Hawaii, only "a deep commitment" to his next course of action.[24]

A month before *Hawaii* appeared, *Life* magazine published a preview of the novel: the forty-page opening, "From the Boundless Deep" (published under the title "Birth of Hawaii"). It was the section that Jim fretted about the most. Although Albert Erskine and others at Random House praised it, without dialogue or characters, the section was a gamble. "No beginning writer would have dared it," said Michener. When Jim was writing it, a friend asked him: "How can you expect a reader to plow through thirty-seven pages of no dialogue, no people, and no plot?"[25] Others voiced similar opinions. Nevertheless, the opening chapter was a testament to Michener's writing ability and demonstrated how the artist could breathe life into the most dehydrated subjects.

Except for the opening chapter and a few later scenes, there is nothing remarkable about *Hawaii.* Michener dispenses large quantities of information in vivid language. His characters, as William Hogan observed in the *San Francisco Chronicle,* are more prototypes than real people. The final chapter, "The Golden Men," is perhaps the weakest. It does not solve the novel's central conflict and has Caucasians stealing the positions of political power. Although Michener knew the sound and look of the tropics, there are few memorable scenes. He achieved, however, a masterful, coherent whole, a seamless connection of history and people and culture that both instructs and entertains. His style, which changed little in the next thirty years, fulfilled its goal without much innovation or fanfare. Rather than being supple and provocative, its pace remained as orderly as the tread of a well-drilled army marching inexorably into action.

In addition to being his most ambitious project since *The Fires of Spring, Hawaii* also was his most crucial. He wanted to prove to himself, to the critics, and to other writers that he was capable of writing the multigenerational novel. He had not really had a novel in print since 1954 with *Sayonara.* He intended to make Hawaii itself the central character: culturally dynamic and ruggedly beautiful, the newest gem in America's crown.

Random House, still swooning that autumn over the success of Leon Uris's *Exodus,* prepared for another windfall. Albert Erskine was especially upbeat about the book's prospects, shipping four thousand advance copies to the islands. Bennett Cerf predicted: "I think *Hawaii* will be selling in one edition or another for the next hundred years." The first shipment of books sold briskly—at a faster rate than Random House and the Hawaiian booksellers predicted. It was fortunate that a second shipment arrived just in time for the Christmas shopping season. By January 1960 *Hawaii* leaped into the number-five position and then to number one on the best-seller lists. "The daily figures are nothing short of fantastic," Cerf mentioned to Jim in a letter. "I've never seen anything like it in all these years we have been in the business."[26] Within two months the book had sold nearly two hundred thousand copies and showed no sign of flagging going into the winter months.

At William Morris, Helen Strauss began the bidding for the movie rights at $600,000. "All of the studios," wrote Strauss, "were interested in the book. A few cringed at the price and terms." Eventually, after some fierce bidding, the Mirisch Company, with financing by United Artists, bought the rights for the "astronomical" price of $750,000. Fred Zinnemann, the Oscar-winning director of *High Noon* and *From Here to Eternity*, was hired to direct. As time went on, however, and the project bogged down in studio budget fights, Zinnemann backed out, allowing George Roy Hill to step in. Dalton Trumbo, the once-blacklisted writer and one of the "Hollywood Ten" during the McCarthy era, eventually replaced Daniel Taradash as the screenwriter. Taradash had his own brush with discrimination in Hawaii. When Taradash made plans to visit Hawaii and stay at the luxurious Hana Maui Hotel, the management wrote back implying that if Taradash was a Jew, he would not be welcome there. After several starts, interruptions, and the shuffling of personnel, the critically panned movie *Hawaii* premiered in 1966 and starred Max Von Sydow and Julie Andrews.

More important to Jim than book sales and movie deals, however, was the book's reception by critics. Many reviewers, accustomed to Michener's more recent ventures as a journalist, acquired a deeper respect for him as a novelist. Writing in the *New York Herald Tribune*, John K. Hutchins noted: "Into *Hawaii* the Pacific's most well-known celebrant has poured what for many a chronicler would be a lifetime of data gathering, of observing and imagining."[27] Maxwell Geismar in the *New York Times Book Review* declared: "A brilliant panoramic novel from its volcanic origins to its recent statehood. It is a complex and fascinating subject, and it is rendered here with a wealth of scholarship, of literary imagination, and of narrative skill, so that the large and diverse story is continually interesting."[28] Fanny Butcher in the *Chicago Sunday Tribune* was even more complimentary: "One of the most enlightening books ever written, either of fact or fiction, about the integration of divergent peoples into a composite society. . . . What makes the novel unforgettable is not only the deep understanding of national dreams and ways of life, not only the exciting panoramas of events, but the human beings who were the motivators and movers in the creation of today's Hawaii."[29] Horace Sutton in the *Saturday Review* rounded out the laudatory comments: "The subject is so well covered that it may be a long time before anyone essays another major work on the islands. . . . A masterful job of research, an absorbing performance of storytelling, and a monumental account of the islands from geologic building to sociological emergence as the newest and perhaps the most interesting of the United States."[30]

Overall, the reviews were the best that Michener had ever received. Most observers recognized that a "new" Michener had emerged. He was not just the "book-a-year wonder" but also an adroit artist capable of packing enormous amounts of historical, geologic, and geographic information into a compelling narrative. There were others, however, who thought Michener had fallen short of his goal in *Hawaii.* The *Catholic World* called Michener's work "dramatized journalism."[31] Writing in the *Spectator,* Ronald Bryden cited Michener's "corn-flake-package characters."[32] A critic in *Kirkus Reviews* remarked the book "falls from its own weight."[33]

The forecasted uproar in the islands over some of the book's contents occurred, but only sporadically. Most of the people who objected made the mistake of reading the book as history rather than as a novel. One reader in Sunset Beach claimed that he grew "sorry for Michener. He seemed to be a sort of verbal Picasso—a man of talent, who not being able find any eternal truths in his struggle for expression, finally retreated into caricature. To infer, even in stated fiction, that Hawaiian history can be traced by moving from sordid affair to sordid affair, labels the writer as little more than a product of our times."[34] Writing in the *Honolulu Advertiser,* William Huntsberry observed,

"The reader will want to associate fictional characters with historical personages because he recognizes their affinities. He will want to fight to keep his own prejudices while he is seeing them destroyed. . . . Michener pulls no punches. He sees the whole picture, the pleasant and the unpleasant, the ugly and the beautiful. And it is only by seeing the whole in relation to the mass of parts that one can get the full effect of the author's intention."[35]

Other reactions, however, were not so positive. One indignant reader wrote to the *New York Times* portraying Michener as a scoundrel for disguising a novel in the form of a history. "I tell you I grieve for that book," she cried. "It could have been a grand story for young students and readers everywhere but I cannot recommend it to anyone. What was his motive in calling the book *Hawaii* leaving the impression it is a historical book?" If he wanted to write a novel, the letter continued, why didn't he invent a suitable tropic name?[36] To many readers in Hawaii, the blend of fact and fiction, as seen in the works of Norman Mailer and Irving Stone, was something of an anomaly. In this case, it was an offensive one.

If Hawaii had turned its back on James Michener, the author's affection for the islands remained "unbounded." He could take consolation in the fact that both Jack London and Robert Louis Stevenson encountered similar fates. London and his stories of Hawaii were criticized for leaving the impression with readers that his stories were more fact than fiction. When Stevenson left Hawaii for the last time, the newspapers carried articles condemning his depictions and wishing that cannibals on the next island he visited would eat him.[37]

The success of *Hawaii* exceeded Jim's wildest expectations. "With [the book] I finally found great faith in myself as a writer. This was critical. Every writer looks for a moment, and I was happy to have had mine."[38] Although he was not anxious to write another epic novel, he was at last in a position to go anywhere in the world and take as much time as he liked in order to do it.

Upon returning to Bucks County in October 1959, Jim relinquished his grip on Asian and Pacific culture. He took up residence on the hill in Pipersville, intent on helping the country achieve a new intellectual and artistic vision. Despite some of the ill feelings toward Hawaii, he remained a lover of the islands and its culture. Frequently, through-out the decades of the 1960s, 1970s, and 1980s, he was invited back to some ceremony in Polynesia, Melanesia, or Micronesia honoring a cause he believed in. The period of the 1950s could properly be termed Michener's "Asia decade," for he traveled and studied throughout the region, educating in the process a whole generation of Americans. *Hawaii* was the culmination of that effort. He became associated with the Pacific as much as Zane Grey became associated with the western novel or Agatha Christie with the mystery.

In November 1959, once again ensconced in his office at Pipers-ville, the Pacific cultures seemed remote indeed. He felt he needed to be home in Pennsylvania again. He sensed a new spirit about to emerge in the land, and he wanted to be a part of it. He was disil-lusioned with the track America seemed to be on: "I had watched for ten years how our national image had been debased by ourselves and our enemies. From a distance we did often seem to be a fat and foolish nation. We seemed to be against the great changes that were sweeping the world. During the McCarthy period we were outspokenly con-temptuous of the intellect. . . . From abroad we seemed to be a faltering nation, insecure even in those great principles upon which we were founded, and I felt something had to be done to rectify this national image." After days of brooding about what this might look like for his life, he concluded: "The fundamental thing is that we have got to have a wholly new administration. It mustn't be saddled with old policies and policy-makers. Therefore it's got to be Democratic. This country really needs a Democratic administration."[39]

CHAPTER 11

A Different Drummer

The Micheners hunkered down in Bucks County after returning from Hawaii. In November Jim made a list of the most likely contenders for the Democratic presidential nomination in 1960. John F. Kennedy did not announce his candidacy until January, so he was not included among Jim's front-runners. When Kennedy announced on January 3, Michener wrote the senator a letter offering his services in the campaign. For the next ten months, Jim committed his time, energy, and intellect in getting Kennedy elected. In July, after Kennedy was nominated to the Democratic ticket, Jim became the chairman of the Bucks County Citizens for Kennedy Committee, a position that required him to generate support in a largely Republican stronghold. In October he joined several other prominent supporters, including actors Jeff Chandler and Angie Dickinson and historian Arthur Schlesinger, Jr., in a barnstorming tour of Republican enclaves in the West and Midwest. Alas, of the states in which he and his group campaigned, all went Republican in the election. "In fact," Jim reported, "I can think of no area where I worked in which my efforts modified any important segment of the vote and there exists good reason for calling me the Typhoid Mary of the 1960 campaign. Where I went disaster struck."[1] His involvement in the Kennedy campaign resulted in his anecdotal memoir *Report of the County Chairman*, his ninth book for Random House and one that purported to be "a factual record of the campaign" at the precinct level. Many critics found it humorous and engrossing, although Sydney Hyman of *Saturday Review* commented that the book left the impression that Michener, not Kennedy, was running for president.

As he worked in the Kennedy campaign, Michener also considered several book projects. He had always wanted to write a novel of Scotland, but his memory of it was perhaps too vague to conjure a serious novel. "I have never known why I failed to write my Scottish novel," he reflected. "I knew the land, I knew the people, I knew the history, but the magic moment never came."[2] He mused about a novel centering on the siege of Leningrad, but this never gained any momentum until later. Instead, he turned to Mexico. Memories of his expeditions to Mexico during the 1930s were still vivid. In truth, even while traveling throughout Asia, he thought fondly of bullfights and mariachi bands in the colorful squares of remote Mexican towns. On and off through the presidential campaign, he worked on his novel of Mexico, traveling periodically to Mexico City and environs to conduct research.

Jim and Mari attended the inauguration of John F. Kennedy on January 21, 1961, and were part of an attentive audience that heard his inspiring words. As Kennedy built his administration, he asked Jim to become ambassador to Korea. However, since Mari was Japanese and tension remained between the two nations, Jim turned down the offer. Jim requested other key ambassador positions, namely Afghanistan or Indonesia. Both were promised to other people. Jim did accept the codirectorship of Kennedy's Food for Peace program, which the president created early in his administration. The program eventually failed, but Jim remained honored about his role.

In mid-March Michener flew to Spain to research some of the early parts of his Mexican novel. Life was good for Michener. The proceeds from *Hawaii* were helping assemble an impressive collection of original American art, including works by William Glackens, Arthur Dove, John Marin, and Reginald Marsh. He was continually in demand as a writer, although his pace as a freelancer had slowed considerably since the halcyon days of the 1950s. He wrote several key articles for periodicals, including one titled "My Other Books" for *Harper's*, in which he corrected readers' false notions that he wrote such works as *From Here to Eternity* and *Kon-Tiki*. For *Saturday Review* he penned "Should Artists Boycott New York?" For Hobe Lewis at *Reader's Digest* he wrote "Mexico's Mild-Mannered Matador," which was based on his recent explorations of Mexico City.

From Madrid he traveled first to the university town of Salamanca. Driving in a rental car, he headed through the lush intoxicating hillsides of Old Castile. Upon reaching Salamanca, which would serve as an origin point for his characters, he strolled through the central square, soaking up the town's medieval atmosphere. Driving south to Seville, he read in the Spanish papers of the disastrous Bay of Pigs invasion in Cuba. In Seville, he happened to meet the famous American matador John Fulton, a Philadelphian by birth who had come to Spain via Mexico to fulfill a lifelong ambition. "I have a very warm spot in my heart for John Fulton," Michener later remarked. "Any guy from South Philadelphia six feet one inch tall who decides at age twenty to become a matador de toros is so totally unhinged that there must be something glorious about him. With guts like that, you don't need charm or insight, but John had them both too."[3] Through Fulton, Jim met the American photographer Robert Vavra, who specialized in photographs of horses. Accompanied by Fulton and Vavra, Michener toured the bull ranches around Seville, watching how the young bulls were raised for the future matches in town. "The character of the young bull," Jim observed, "will stem mainly—and some claim totally—from his mother. If she is brave, he will be. If she proves cowardly, so will he, so it is exciting to attend a *tienta* at a rural ranch which breeds fighting bulls, for some of the young cows to be tested will prove to be absolute tornadoes, not only willing but positively eager to attack anything that moves, while their blood sisters will be totally lacking in character."[4]

In Seville the three would "haunt the corrals studying the animals for the Sunday fight, then prowling the sorting area on Sunday morning trying to estimate which of the six bulls would do well that afternoon and which would prove either obstinate or cowardly. With such tutelage I became a modest expert on taurine behavior."[5]

On March 30, satisfied that he had conducted enough research to begin the novel of Mexico, he crossed the Guadalquivir River, bought a few cheap notebooks at the stationery, and began to fill the pages with ideas for the chapters. He worked on fleshing out the novel for several weeks, but it wasn't until he had returned to Mexico in late April that he got the idea for the beginning of the novel—often the most difficult part of the process. As he was driving along the back roads of Guanajuato—the city that became Toledo in the novel—he happened to see two Indian women walking by the side of the road headed to the market in town. "They were so poetic in their movements," Jim wrote, "so inherently a part of the land that I cried aloud: 'That's it! Two women on their way to town carrying the things they have to sell.'"[6] And so the novel began. After several rewrites and drafts and over a period of thirty years, the opening of the novel never changed.

By late summer and fall Jim had typed ten chapters, visiting Spain once again to consult with Fulton and Vavra on the bullfighting sections that would come later in the book. In Mexico City, with ten complete chapters on his desk, he typed a two-page synopsis of chapters 8 through 17 for review by his editors at Random House. At that point the title of his novel was "Festival"; later it would become known as *Mexico.*

In New York, Bennett Cerf perused Jim's latest novel with extreme interest. *Hawaii* was a smashing success, and Cerf expected great things of Michener. When Jim visited Random House to discuss the manuscript, Cerf drew his attention to a segment in chapter 12 that he thought might diminish the work. In the novel, Jim had a Hollywood actor and actress travel to Mexico to attend a Saturday bullfight. Cerf thought it should be cut. "Jim," Cerf remarked, "I think you already have a strong novel, one that's sure to be a big success. Why do you feel you have to schmaltz it up with Hollywood types like Tony Curtis and Janet Leigh?"[7]

"Stunned" by Bennett's remark, Jim began to doubt the validity of his project. Had the comment come from a friend or colleague, it might not have had the devastating effect that it did from Random House's chief executive. Gradually, his belief in the novel began to erode, so that by the time he returned to Pipersville, he questioned the entire structure of the novel. "In a kind of stupor," he recalled, "I put the manuscript aside, interring it among my papers as a dead item. I wrote not another word."[8] He collected the parts of the manuscript—finished chapters, partial ones, synopses, and accompanying maps and notes—and boxed them up for shipment. After he had finished any book, he routinely sent his work to the Library of Congress, where it remained for study by interested scholars and researchers. So it was with "Festival," or that was the plan. In truth, the manuscript never made it out of Jim's Pipersville home. Jim left the boxed project on a table, thinking it would go out with the morning mail. The box, however, was somehow misplaced, ending up in a remote corner of a storage area, where it remained undisturbed for the next thirty years.

With his Mexico project behind him, Jim reflected on the process of its demise. He realized that an ongoing project was tenuous indeed, held together by "a gossamer filament." "It is as fragile as the spinal column," he asserted, "just as susceptible to permanent damage, and just as necessary to continued activity. It is nebulous, of different weight and composition in all men and women, and must be shielded carefully if one hopes to survive as an artist." After his encounter with Cerf, in which he saw the novel crumble before his eyes, he resigned himself never again to consult with anyone about his plans. "I would allow no one to read anything I'd written before it was complete. . . . And it is a demonstrable fact that on many occasions neither my agent nor my publisher has known what I was working on until I delivered a completed manuscript into their hands." He would circulate parts of a manuscript to experts for their opinions, but he would never submit to adverse criticism of the overall idea of a work while it was in progress. "The death of my Mexican novel thus became the birth of a philosophy that has sustained me."[9]

When the Bucks County Democratic Committee urged Michener to run for Congress in the 1962 election, he considered the idea carefully. Running in a heavily Republican area and convincing Mari that it would not disrupt their marriage were two major concerns. She threatened to work for the Republican Party if Jim ran, and if that failed, she claimed that she would run away to Hawaii. Jim attributed her reluctance to her fear of their being continually separated from each other; however, he spent a whole week convincing her that this did not have to be the case. After overcoming her objections and getting the support of Lehigh and Bucks counties, he tossed his hat in the ring. In November 1962, however, after months of vigorous campaigning and travel, he was soundly defeated by his GOP opponent.

Michener counted his loss among the most difficult of his life. "It galls me that I lost. I would have tried to be a good Congressman, and I would have found great fulfillment in such service, and I would have gladly surrendered my books if I could have been of real service in Washington."[10] Surrendered his books? His friends thought differently. Herman Silverman, who knew the things that made Michener tick, asserted, "He was not a good politician because he did not need the job. He didn't belong in Congress. Jim is a born writer and a loner. He said he was going to Washington for the rest of his life, but I didn't believe it. He would have been bored after two or three years."[11]

With the campaign and election over, Jim ruefully turned to his writing desk. His novel of Mexico was, presumably, dead and buried. He rummaged his desk drawer for truncated works that might yield undiscovered strengths. Turning his attention to a ninety-three-page manuscript about Afghanistan titled "The Sharif of Koristan," he began formulating how he might finish the novel. The novel was begun as early as the summer of 1956, the year after he spent an eventful June in the Middle East. Most of the final version was completed between June 4 and September 1, 1957. "The Sharif of Koristan" was set in the mid-1950s, when Afghanistan was the center for American and Russian agents vying for influence in the desert kingdom. The book also featured a SAC component, which Michener had difficulty weaving into the plot. When *Hawaii* came along in 1957, Jim conveniently shelved the book. However, before giving up on the novel, he jotted an interesting note on the last pages of the manuscript: "Maybe drop SAC approach. . . . Could be solely Afghanistan-driven."[12]

"The Sharif of Koristan" remained an unfinished manuscript, but the idea for a novel of Afghanistan remained vivid in Jim's mind. Between November 1962 and March 1963, he wrote the novel that became known as *Caravans*, which was based entirely on Jim's recollections, maps, and notes from the 1955 journeys in and around Kabul. The SAC approach was dropped in favor of a mid-1940s storyline. Except in setting, it bore little resemblance to the earlier manuscript.

Afghanistan appealed to Michener's untamed spirit. He liked the trackless desert, the fierce independence of the warlords, the mud villages, and the sere beauty of the hills. Afghanistan was a wild, violent, "don't give a damn" kind of place, precisely the spot in which he could turn loose his campaign-battered heart.

He was also fascinated by the Islamic religion. Since the mid-1950s, Michener had been a student of it, but his goal of writing a major novel about Islam never materialized. *Caravans*, a third the size of *Hawaii*, was meant as an adventurous romp and not a serious investigation of Islamic culture. While he worked on *Caravans*, he made plans for the spring of 1963 to travel to Istanbul and write a longer novel of Islamic history. But as things happened, the lure of Israel and the subsequent work on *The Source* intervened.

In the early months of 1963, Jim was quite content to finish *Caravans* and work on the corrections with Albert Erskine, who played a significant role in focusing and shaping the rough edges of the story. With every book, Erskine's role had become increasingly essential.

Michener called Erskine "a brilliant man intellectually and a perceptive one artistically. He points with devilish accuracy at points where I have gone wrong, at interior contradictions, at sloppy motivations for specific acts. Erskine is an educated man with one hell of a good eye, which is all important." Moreover, Jim added, they both liked Chinese and Italian takeout.[13] If the situations and characters in *Caravans* were contrived, the depictions of postwar Afghanistan were the staples of the book. Wolves prowled the city streets. Crowds stoned adulterers in the public squares. Executions (which Michener had witnessed in 1955) were also public social events. Vicious sandstorms swallowed jeeps, trucks, and unsuspecting travelers. Warlords ruled the desert sands. Among these scenes, Michener wove his narrative:

a young blond-haired Jew named Mark Miller is recruited by the American embassy to find and rescue Ellen Jaspar, a social dropout and recent Bryn Mawr graduate who has run off with an Afghan engineer. Miller's search for Jaspar takes him to the remote hinterland of Afghanistan.

Once again, racial and ethnic prejudice forms a major theme, as one of the principal characters, Dr. Stiglitz, a Nazi war criminal who experimented on Jews during the war, encounters the morally conscious Miller, giving Michener the opportunity to comment on a wide range of ethical issues. Additionally, Jim's descriptions are particularly sharp and concise, revealing the influence of Japanese woodblock prints and writing for the *Reader's Digest*: "Kabul was superb in winter, particularly when the late afternoon sun rushed toward some rendezvous in Persia, to the west; for then the normal drabness of the miserable mud homes was masked in snow, and the solitary figures with carbines who moved across the empty fields outside of town bore an epic quality which captivated the eye. No stranger, at such a moment, could forget he was in Asia."[14]

Like most Americans, Helen Strauss had difficulty finding Afghanistan on a world map. But this was only one reason why she had problems with the book. She ended up disliking the project, "notable only for some vivid descriptions of the scenery and customs." Expecting something as muscular as *Hawaii*, she was disappointed in the setting, characters, and scope of the work. "It was a bad property for films," she admitted, "but all the studios wanted to buy it."[15] She eventually sold the screen rights to MGM for $500,000 and no percentage of the profits.

When the book appeared in summer 1963, the critical opinion was mixed. *Time* magazine, under the headline "Bull Market," dismissed it as a quaint travelogue. "*Caravans* shows more research than imagination," the review ran. "Michener studs his narrative with Afghan legends and interminably breathless descriptions of sere and bleak Afghan landscape. All he succeeds in doing is making Afghanistan seem like Hawaii West."[16] Harry Cargas, writing in *America*, provided a more informed position: "Perhaps the finest characterization of all is that of Afghanistan itself. Michener obviously loves this part of the world. . . . What is more, he has the ability to communicate this love. The traces left in Afghanistan by men like Alexander the Great and Genghis Khan are built into the plot effortlessly and convincingly."[17]

Despite the critical mix of opinion, which was largely based on expectations following *Hawaii,* Michener called his book "a minor classic." He had taken a distant corner of the Islamic world, largely unknown to Americans, and created a forceful and engaging narrative. To this day, *Caravans* remains a vivid description of the Islamic world and a fascinating record of a vanished era in Afghan culture.

In spring 1963 Jim began to anticipate writing his major novel of Islam. For Jim, there were two important geohistorical pivot points in the world. In the Pacific Rim and Asia, it was Hawaii; in the occidental world it was Istanbul/Constantinople/Byzantium. Like Hawaii, Istanbul was a critical crossroads of religions and cultures. Early in the 1950s Michener had identified Istanbul as the center of his novel of Islam, and he was prepared to spend a long time there to research the book. In early April he flew to Israel with columnist Leonard Lyons and comedian Harpo Marx, hoping to do some research in Haifa and Akko before heading to Turkey. In Haifa, Israel's major port city, he, Marx, and an Israeli archaeologist poked through Athlit Castle, an abandoned outpost near the Bay of Haifa once used by Crusaders in the twelfth and thirteenth centuries.

Athlit Castle, with its ragged stone tower looming over the wild Bay of Haifa, was perhaps best described in 1902 by English traveler and scholar Geraldine Bell, who was in her twenties when she saw it for the first time: "It is all on a scale of magnificence: the huge walls, the enormous masses of fallen vaulting, the great splendour of the sea and the gorgeous defiance of the fort—not crumbled you understand, broken by great force or standing by great force, with the rush and swirl of the sea below it and the roar of the sea echoing through its vaults, and as loud—the echo of battle, Phoenician, Jewish, Christian, all holding out here to the last."[18]

Descending into the dungeon, Michener stood transfixed as he drank in the moldering ruins. "As I stood in the dungeon of that ancient fortress," he recalled, "with the shadowy forms of warriors long dead moving in the dust, I suddenly conceived my entire novel *The Source.* Feverishly, in a small notebook I always carry, I outlined the seventeen chapters, taking no more than minutes to do so, and they remained just as I wrote them down, and in their exact order. . . . I had spent ten years studying Islam, and without being aware of the fact, I was at the same time educating myself in its sister religion, Judaism."[19]

Jim's decision to author a novel of Israel also precluded any work he might write on the Muslim world, for a good word spoken about the former was interpreted as a negative word about the latter. Therefore, *The Source* would be "interpreted as being pro-Jewish and therefore anti-Arab. . . . It was not intended to be that way."[20]

As quickly as he could get a flight out of Israel, he returned home and informed Mari that they were going to spend an extended time in Haifa. By late April the two of them were on their way to London and Italy, the first stops on their itinerary to the Holy Land. In early May 1963 James Michener, writer of means, champion of the underdog, hater of injustice, and student of both obscure and popular history, took up residence at the Dan Carmel Hotel in Haifa to write the story of the Jews and their heroic struggle.

Mabel Michener circa 1910

James Michener as a
child growing up in
Doylestown, Pennsylvania

Jim was a basketball star at
Doylestown High School.

Jim during his years at
Swarthmore College

Michener in the navy
before being sent for duty
in the South Pacific during
World War II

The newly crowned, Pulitzer
Prize–winning author

Mari and Jim on their wedding day, October 1955

Michener (right) with cartographer Jean Paul Tremblay, who drew the maps for many of Michener's books

"The Random House team": Bert Krantz (left), Albert Erskine (top), Michener (right)

Michener, standing in baseball cap, during the 1969 running of the bulls in Pamplona. Photo by Prince.

Researching *Centennial* in Colorado, 1973. Photo by Tessa Dalton.

In New Guinea in 1977 while filming *James Michener's World* for PBS

Jim and Mari with Nancy Parker at the Woodson Research Center, Rice University Library

Revising *Chesapeake* in 1977. Photo by Russ Kennedy.

Mari Michener and actor David Janssen on the set of the made-for-TV movie *Centennial*, 1978

Jim trying to corral an armadillo in Texas, 1984. Photo by Michael Mauney.

At the Alamo with San Antonio mayor Henry Cisneros. Photo by Michael Mauney.

With sharp-eyed editor Albert Erskine

In Havana researching *Caribbean* with Cuban poet Pablo Fernandez. Photo by John Kings.

CHAPTER 12

"Noiseless, Patient Spider"

Most people in northern Israel would call the Dan Carmel Hotel, if not swank, certainly upscale. Rising thirteen floors over the ancient town of Haifa, it had a commanding view of the Bay of Haifa and, farther north, the city of Akko. But the bookish resident of the twelfth floor cared little for exciting vistas when he was working, except perhaps to rise from his desk, pad over to the window, and, with his hands plugging his pockets, stare briefly at the houses spilling down to the harbor, the waves wrinkling the bay, or the bright green strip of the Bahia Gardens shining under the palm trees. For Michener, engrossed in another project, it was business as usual.

During the summer and autumn of 1963, while Haifa simmered below, Jim turned out the manuscript pages for *The Source*. His seven-foot-long desk, crammed with books and journals, faced the window. He knew from the beginning that *The Source* would be his most formidable challenge as a writer. Consequently, he attacked it with typical Michener fervor. He consulted a list of experts in archaeology, culture, and history. He worked from 7:30 in the morning until 1:00 in the afternoon, seven days a week. He would then put in comparable time in the afternoon or evening doing more research. He would go for a stroll in the streets of Haifa or take the bus over to Akko and see the Crusader ruins or walk through the Al-Jazzar mosque. Often, however, he would just fall asleep on the sofa in his room. He was willing to admit that he was a Gentile attempting to write a history of the Jews. He knew that other people were more qualified to write of Jewish history, but then again, no one seemed willing to spend two years attempting to write the book that Michener visualized.

For the novel, Michener created an imaginary site known as Tell Makor ("Tell" meaning "mound" in Hebrew, "Makor" "the source") and situated it in the mountains ten miles east of Akko and fifteen miles northeast of Haifa. A group of modern archaeologists assemble on the site to begin excavating the many layers of civilizations that have inhabited the area. The team consists of an Irish American Catholic, John Cullinane; an Arab, Jemial Tabari; and an Israeli Jew, Ilan Eliav. "They go through fifteen layers of these civilizations," explained Michener, "digging up items which appear in the first chapter of the novel. They have philosophical discussions, minor adventures; they have picnics together. It's somewhat in the mood, one might say, of Jane Austen—just a group of people."[1] There is a further complexity to the novel, however: "When the archaeologists have uncovered fifteen layers of civilization by the end of the first chapter, a series of fifteen flashbacks in reverse order begins. These are the glimpses of man, of what has happened to man in the Holy Land, and it comprises the bulk of the novel—nearly half a million words. The flashbacks look at society in terms of profound problems, built upon incidents implied by what the archeologists uncover." Michener likened the structure to a Cesar Franck symphony: "A theme at the beginning, a return to the themes at the end, and discursions and excursions during the body, with the theme repeated. . . . It's a complicated and sometimes beautiful and sometimes difficult ebb and flow of history." This complex structure would have proved disastrous for a writer of lesser talent than Michener. Even Jim admitted that he would not "recommend it to another novelist, nor would I have the courage to use it again myself, but in *The Source*, it worked."[2]

The structure of the novel was ingenious, for it allowed the reader to see the clashes of religious and historical differences through the conversations of the main characters. Moreover, the reader could experience the sweep of history through the successive eras, each one revealed by another exposed layer in the soil. At one point, after many layers of history have been unearthed, Cullinane asks his friends if the Jews had a moral right to occupy Israel. Surprisingly, the Arab archaeologist admits that "any organized people which has demonstrated a cohesiveness and common purpose has a right to its ancestral lands." After some further debate about the "moral right" to occupy certain lands, the Jew concludes that "Israel's ultimate justification must be moral, but not in the way that nations have used that word in the past. Anyone can attain [custodianship] with a police force and some agricultural specialists. But Israel's custodianship of people, of human rights, is going to be spectacular."[3] It was a debate and a line of investigation Michener had used in *Hawaii* and would again ponder in such later novels as *Centennial* and *The Covenant*.

In sifting through fifteen layers of ancient through modern civilizations, Michener wanted to probe the very idea of Jewish identity. How did the Jews survive against all odds? How did they endure centuries of persecution, flight, exile, and systematic murder? What were the roots of Arab-Israeli hatred, of Muslim-Jewish hostility? Explicitly or often implicitly, Michener answered these questions in his 909-page novel, the only novel to combine his love of history, geography, linguistics, religion, politics, and antiquities. Michener maintained that Jewish survival depended on four factors: a close bond with the past, community, faith, and a sense of destiny.

While writing certain episodes, Jim researched throughout Israel. He visited Tiberias, Nazareth, and Cana in the north; Hadera and Tel Aviv on the Mediterranean coast; and Beersheba and Dimona in the south. If anyone criticized the book, he believed, the critic would have to focus on the structure of the narrative and not on his accurate and exhaustive research. This proved to be true. While critics scorned the characters and parts of the dialogue, they tended to praise the depth of his scholarship.

Reporters followed him around Israel, anxious for any hint of a storyline. All Michener would report was that he was "writing about a mixed marriage, an American who comes to live in a kibbutz, a romance between an Arab and a Jew, and the irrigation of a field."[4]

Fearing that any criticism might scuttle his project, as happened with his novel of Mexico, he said very little to Helen Strauss and Albert Erskine.

In late November Jim and Mari were invited by Jewish friends to their Friday seder. Jim noticed that the group was unusually somber and kept staring intently at Jim and Mari. Later, one of them took Michener aside and said: "We have very disturbing news. Your president was murdered two hours ago."[5] The Micheners hurried back to their hotel; Mari began to sob on the way. The two talked for an hour, after which Mari went to bed and Jim sat alone in the dark overlooking the lights of Haifa. He brooded for several moments, then jotted in his notes some immediate impressions about who might have killed Kennedy. He thought it was a conspiracy of right-wing groups that had it out for the president. He also thought it might be the Central Intelligence Agency (CIA) or members of Jimmy Hoffa's Teamsters Union, although after later reading the Warren Commission Report, he retracted his earlier opinions. As news of the assassination in Dallas broke around the world, Jim listened to updates on the radio broadcast from Egypt.

Decidedly shaken by the assassination, his faith temporarily shattered in the American dream, Jim resolved to stay in Israel much longer than he first anticipated. He intended to bury his anguish in work on *The Source*, which he thought might be completed by early summer 1964. To that end, he threw himself into the novel's completion, working harder than ever and at a pace that worried even Mari.

Michener's grief was deep and prolonged. He had loved John Kennedy since 1960 and over the years had developed an unusually strong attachment to him. Jim was amazed, as most Americans were, by how quickly Kennedy was transformed into a universal icon. Although his legislative gains were modest, Kennedy achieved almost overnight stardom; people seemed willing to judge him not on his accomplishments but on what they thought he represented. Ironically, in death Kennedy achieved more than he did in life. In the postassassination atmosphere in Washington of grief and suspicion, his successor, Lyndon Johnson, was able to slide through Congress almost all of Kennedy's New Frontier proposals.

After Kennedy's assassination, Michener withdrew temporarily from an active role in politics. When Johnny Welsh, the director of the Democratic Party in Bucks County, asked him to run again for Congress in the eighth district, Jim turned him down. He opened Welsh's letter, dashed off a reply, and tossed Welsh's letter in the wastebasket.

Michener finished the first draft of *The Source* in April 1964. By the end of May, working at the King David Hotel in Jerusalem, he completed the second draft, which he delivered personally to Helen Strauss in Istanbul. Strauss, who was kept in the dark on the project, carried the manuscript back to New York via Paris. The mere weight of it once caused her to lose her balance and fall to the sidewalk. *The Source* was to be the last property she handled for Michener. She moved to the agency office in California and worked at selling scripts to Hollywood. A young Owen Laster was selected to handle Jim's work, and he remained in that role throughout the remainder of Michener's long career.

In Istanbul he also met Hobe Lewis, who was waiting to assign Michener several articles for *Reader's Digest*. Lewis thought Michener look drained. Michener respectfully told Lewis that he had no intention of traveling around the globe writing stories for the *Digest* and that he preferred to focus on one or two articles a year about subjects of his choosing. Michener mentioned that he would be interested in writing about three important museums: the Hermitage in Leningrad, the National Gallery in Washington, and the Prado in Madrid. They also discussed Michener's next book project. Lewis raised the idea of a book on Christianity, a suggestion that seemed to excite Michener, for he outlined the novel that autumn.

After returning from a European trip that took Jim and Mari to Italy, France, Norway, and Russia, he finished his article, "The Hermitage: Russia's Art Palace," for the March 1965 issue of *Reader's Digest*. "It is like no other art museum," Michener claimed in the piece. "It contains about 2,500 rooms, two and a half million art objects including fourteen thousand paintings. Merely to walk through each of the rooms requires a hike of twenty-five miles."[6]

Visiting Russia also resurrected the idea of a novel of Leningrad, one of a number of projects that Michener had filed away in his mind. After settling matters in Jerusalem and Haifa, he said good-bye to his friends in Israel. In addition to being physically exhausted, Michener was emotionally spent. Israel was very close to his heart; the suffering of the Jews moved him deeply. "When I was done writing *The Source*, I had put on paper everything I believed, all the profound emotions that swept through me when I hiked across the Galilee, and there was simply nothing left. . . . I wrote *The Source* because Hitler's behavior in 1933–1945 toward the Jews was morally outrageous and left a scar on me and on the rest of the world. The scar is still there."[7]

Michener returned to the States in October 1964 to begin, in concert with Erskine, the final rewriting of *The Source*. Erskine was pleased after reviewing the second draft, admitting to Jim, "the construction is so clever and the balance of narrative material with other elements so neatly done that I believe readers who wouldn't have thought they would be interested, will be in spite of themselves. It is really a magnificent job."[8] Working in Pipersville and New York City with Erskine and Bert Krantz at Random House, Michener labored on the revisions of *The Source* through February 1965. As he neared the end of the task, he feared that he had come up short: "The text reads very well . . . heavy and at places awkward or too compressed, but very powerful. Working on it every waking hour as I do, I frequently feel that it is hopelessly complicated and that no one will take the trouble to read it."[9] His scholarly reader was Elie Mizrachi, a citizen of Israel, who assured him that the narrative and the content were smoothly and accurately integrated. During the extensive revision process, it was customary for Jim to doubt his first and second impressions. He once said that he was an average writer but an excellent reviser. All too often, however, as he went through the tenth or eleventh revision of a chapter, the writing lost its freshness. He often compared himself to another Random House author, John O'Hara, who turned in a polished manuscript "ready for the printer," in the estimation of Bennett Cerf.

Bolstered by an extensive marketing campaign, *The Source* was published in May 1965. Despite the lifeless title ("Tell Makor" would have been better), it is Michener's most accomplished book, followed closely by *Tales of the South Pacific, Centennial, Hawaii, Iberia, The Fires of Spring, The Covenant, Caravans, Chesapeake,* and *The Bridges at Toko-Ri.* In *The Source* Michener achieved nearly everything he had set out to do as a writer. He mirrored the complexity of the nineteenth-century novel; he threaded together a chain of historical events in a unified narrative; he brought history and archaeology to life; and he maintained a masterly control of his material. The universe Michener created in the novel holds together extremely well. The modern-day archaeological discussion about art and history is interesting and provocative. The period descriptions are sharply realistic. The maps and inset illustrations of the unearthed artifacts, drawn by Jean-Paul Tremblay, add to the veracity of Michener's imagined world. Michener felt that he accomplished some of his best writing in *The Source.* At times the narrative plods as slowly as an archaeological dig, but the reader is rewarded with a wealth of rich historical detail. Although the characterizations are sketchy and not fully realized, the pacing of the historical scenes is swift and colorful. In particular, Michener cited the first-person narrative of the subjugation of Jews under King Herod in 4 B.C.E. and the chapter titled "A Day in the Life of a Desert Rider," set in 635 B.C.E., as two of his greatest triumphs in the novel. *The Source* shot to the top of the best-seller lists and remained there for nearly a year and a half, becoming the highest-grossing novel of 1965. As Helen Strauss warned, however, the critics were ready to target him.

The criticism fell into two camps: *Time, Newsweek,* and the *New York Times,* aware that Michener was going to make a windfall on the book and movie deals, felt inclined to be punitive. Robert Payne in the *New York Times* focused on Michener's poor handling of characters. *Time* and *Newsweek* followed suit. The most fulsome press came from important but lesser-known publications. Jewish American scholars were unexpectedly praiseworthy of *The Source.* Writing in the *Chicago Jewish Forum,* Eric Freidland remarked: "For all the inadequacy of the discussion of the Talmud, Michener is distinguished by remarkable scholarship and invests his book with dramatic detail. . . . *The Source* is a fascinating story of the vast sweep of Jewish history. It communicates the irony of our experience that has always made Palestine an oasis of man's dreams and frustrations. Technically, the book is limited and yet is an archeological detective story."[10] In the *Congress Bi-Weekly*, Samuel Irving Bellman observed: "*The Source* does not 'define the sensibility of an age,' as the greatest novels are supposed to do. But it does provide an invaluable examination of the circumstances surrounding the origin and development of Judaism, and it enhances this with an extended consideration of the parallel developments of Christianity and Islam and relations between adherents of the three faiths."[11] Leslie Fiedler, in remarking on the book, also summed up Michener's twenty-year writing career: "Some writers are read because they have a voice like that of an old friend. Michener doesn't have that. His is as close to a neutral or non-style as you can get." Yet this detachment worked, according to Fiedler. "He puts a book together in a perfectly lucid, undisturbing way, so that even potential troublesome issues don't seem so. . . . *The Source* is about the Middle East, one of the most difficult parts of the world, but he has forgotten all the ambiguities. His approach is that if you knew all the facts, everything would straighten out, so it's soothing and reassuring to read him."[12]

There was also a positive response in Israel and the Arab world. After the *Hawaii* debacle, Michener wanted good relations with Jewish and Arab scholars and readers. Several prominent Jewish religious leaders congratulated him on bringing Jewish history into public view. Although some Arabs objected to his patronizing the Israeli cause, most gave his work quiet assent.

On September 9, 1965, Michener was playing a doubles match in Pipersville with tennis partner Mary Place. He had developed a fairly good backhand, while Place's forte was her famous drop shot over the net from midcourt. Michener considered himself in fine physical shape. He did not smoke or drink alcohol except for a rare glass of wine or a beer. He walked regularly, played tennis when he could, and carried only a few extra pounds in his midriff. At one time he had a bad case of gout in his big toe but took Benemid daily to remedy the pain. At fifty-eight, he worked hard, played hard, and generally only fretted about how he would structure his next novel. He finished his set with Place, toweled his face and arms, and headed to the house for an evening of work and relaxation. At 4:00 in the morning he bolted upright with a bad case of indigestion. Calling his doctor, who advised him to drink water mixed with bicarbonate of soda, he drained the glass and stared at himself in the bathroom mirror. Looking ghostly pale, he dragged his hands over the hollows of his cheeks and staggered back to bed. By 5:30 the pain was intense, and he once again alerted his doctor. The doctor arrived, took his pulse, and called for an ambulance.

At Doylestown Hospital, Michener was treated for a major myocardial infarction. In the next few hours he responded to treatment and by the afternoon was able to see visitors. His heart specialist, Paul Dudley White, whom Michener had met at a conference in Leningrad, was summoned from Boston to supervise his care. White characterized Michener as a mesomorph—a person "with a heavy chest structure, arms attached somewhat like an ape, forward leaning, big-boned, a throwback to primitive man. Most superior athletes are mesomorphs, many powerful political leaders. Tense men who pay the price with sudden heart attacks."[13] White explained that Jim had suffered a major heart attack, but since he had made it through the first day he had an excellent chance for a full recovery. To accomplish that, however, Jim would have to reduce his writing and traveling regimen, eliminate certain foods from his diet, and exercise more. Grateful that he had another opportunity at life, he complied. After six weeks lying in a hospital bed, Michener returned home to Pipersville. Resting in an easy chair in his study, he took stock of his life. His arms felt like tissue paper, but worse was the feeling that he had lost intellectual sharpness and rigor. He went to his desk, sifting through his new notebooks about Leningrad. He could not remember the narrative he had in mind or, worst of all, the overall concept for the novel. His mind was blank. He settled into the chair, horrified that his life had taken a sudden turn for the worse. He tried giving himself a pep talk: "Come on, Kid, don't lose it here."[14] Nothing seemed to help.

For a week Michener stalked around home, fearing that he would never again write a major novel. Regretfully, he closed his notebooks on his Russian novel. It was certainly too ambitious at this point even to consider completing. He threw his pen down on the desk. Leaving his study, he went out into the garden. "Damn writing altogether!" he muttered. "If I can't write I can still walk the dogs!"[15] In the next few days he took his dogs down the trails of the house on the hill and tended the evergreens that had begun to surround the garden.

Although following a strict Spartan schedule and diet never bothered Michener, the months of recuperation in which he seldom wrote anything of value began to wear on him. The more inactivity he encountered, the more irrational fear, persistent since childhood, began to creep back in. Despite being one of the world's most successful writers, he feared that long-term care, or another setback in his health, might drain whatever savings he had. The image of the Doylestown poorhouse was seared in his imagination and remained vivid.

In spite of his misgivings, he stuck by his rehabilitation program. The Silvermans stopped by to encourage him; Albert Erskine, Hobe Lewis, and a score of friends sent their hopes for a speedy recovery. Mari babied him and monitored his health. His music soothed him but did not make him happy. Like a veteran lion, staring hungrily across the barren plain, he waited for his next opportunity.

CHAPTER 13

A Traveler in Spain

The summer of 1966 saw discontent and violence in the nation's cities. Racial strife and protests against the war in Vietnam increased, along with the soaring temperatures. In July rioting broke out in Chicago's West Side after a fire hydrant being used by African American children to keep cool in the hundred-degree temperatures was turned off. Further rioting erupted in Baltimore, Oakland, Omaha, San Francisco, Brooklyn, and Jacksonville.

Meanwhile, in Washington, D.C., President Lyndon Johnson dealt with a war in Vietnam that nobody particularly wanted. In January he had announced resumption of bombing raids of North Vietnam. In June the military commenced bombing of Haiphong and Hanoi. The number of troops in Vietnam reached 285,000, with more arriving daily. Thousands of protesters in many American cities took their anger to the streets. For Michener, both the civil rights movement and the antiwar movement caused him deep sorrow. He had championed equality of the races—all races—but the current turmoil and destruction of cities bothered him. As for the war in Vietnam, he believed at first that an unsupported South Vietnam would soon fall to Communists; however, with mounting casualties and outrage across the country, his resolve had begun to buckle. He no longer had a fervent desire to see Yankee democracy in Southeast Asia at the cost of so many young American lives in an interminable war. "First in Korea," he remarked, "and again in Vietnam we tried to force a war that the entire nation did not support. We thought we could get away with a nickel and dime war. We should have learned in Korea. I became distraught about Vietnam because I could see it was a terrible mistake."[1]

His health had improved considerably. In Pipersville, Michener felt well enough to begin packing his bags for an extended stay in Spain. His doctor checked him thoroughly and pronounced him fit. With his project of Russia forgotten, he outlined in April 1966 a collection of essays dealing with the cities, countryside, and history of Spain. The project actually germinated as early as spring 1965, when he renewed acquaintances with John Fulton and photographer Robert Vavra while in Spain for *Reader's Digest*. Michener and Vavra sketched out a modest book, with Michener supplying the text to Vavra's photographs. At the time, Jim imagined writing a book "with no thought of a wide readership, only that it had to be the best possible evocation of a land I had grown to love."[2] Thus, with only a cursory idea of what he wanted to accomplish, he and Mari flew to Madrid.

The book, which he eventually titled *Iberia* (a misnomer, since Portugal is hardly mentioned), was Michener's experiment in the traditional lengthy travel narrative made famous by the British writer H. V. Morton and others. As a young man at St. Andrews University in Scotland, Michener toted around a dog-eared copy of Morton's *In Search of Scotland* (1929) and *The Soul of Scotland* (1930). Morton's books became staples of the genre. Written with skill, charm, keen descriptive abilities, and a knowledge of history, Morton's books set the lofty standard of the twentieth-century travel narrative, a form that Michener wanted to master using his journeys in Spain. Morton had written *A Stranger in Spain* in 1955, which Michener enjoyed. But Michener wished to go Morton one better. Whereas Morton was lyrical and often nostalgic, Michener would be didactic and analytical, particularly when discussing the effects of Franco's regime on the country. Other books that influenced Michener when writing *Iberia* were V. S. Pritchett's *The Spanish Temper*, Somerset Maugham's *Don*

Fernando, George Brenan's *The Spanish Labyrinth,* and Hugh Thomas's *The Spanish Civil War.*

There was certainly no science to Michener's travels in Spain. He drew up a list of the cities and regions he wanted to visit and then let happenstance take over. In a sense, Michener had always been a travel writer, eager to jot down a regional oddity or describe a face in the crowd. With his knowledge of history, art, and geography and his wary eye for detail, he was a natural travel writer. Armed with an omnivorous intellect, he planned to pore over Spain like a tourist poring over a foreign menu.

And so Michener, still feeling weak in the legs, hit the road. He had dropped twenty pounds since his heart attack, and getting around Spain would be his first major challenge. It was a broiling day in Madrid when he and Mari got off the plane. Using Madrid as his home base, he and Vavra traveled about in a rental car through Franco's Spain, a country he often referred to as his "second home." From July 1966 through January 1967 he circumnavigated the Iberian Peninsula: Tudela, Pamplona, Burgos, Santiago de Compostela, Salamanca, Badajoz, Avila, Guadalupe, Seville, Cordoba, Cadiz, Granada, Malaga, Toledo, Valencia, and Barcelona. Along the way there were little hamlets just waking up from thousand-year sleeps. Robert Vavra worked independently. His photographs at times depicted scenes from Michener's text; often they did not. Both Michener and Vavra agreed upon the terms of the partnership: "Vavra will go over Spain guided by his own eye, completely indifferent as to what Michener may write or think or prefer. Shoot a hundred of the very finest pictures he can find and make them his interpretation of Spain. If he can succeed in this, the pictures will fit properly into any text. But Vavra must avoid trying to guess what someone else wants. Make others see what he has seen."[3] For the most part, their collaboration worked. However, it also led to some egregious omissions in the book. Most notable was the lack of photos to accompany Michener's lengthy discussions of important works of Spanish art in the Prado, such as El Greco's magnificent *Burial of Count Orgaz* and Velazquez's complex *Las Meninas.* With no pictures to illustrate his observations, the reader had difficulty following Michener's analysis.

From the outset, Michener posed several questions he sought to answer about Spain: Why was Spain "emotionally confined" to the Iberian Peninsula? After 1492 why did Spain expel its "undesirable" ethnic groups? With its love of personal freedom, why has Spain persistently turned toward dictators and monarchs? Why has Spain's artistic tradition declined so markedly? How can the average Spaniard, who is outgoing and so in love with the trivia of daily existence, be at the same time so withdrawn and "inwardly mystical"? "What makes Spain so different," he concluded, "is that here these speculations are positively unavoidable. . . . I knew that Spain was a special land, and I have spent many subsequent trips trying to unravel its peculiarities. I have not succeeded, and in this failure I am not unhappy, for Spain is a mystery and I am not at all convinced that those who live within the peninsula and were born there understand it much better than I."[4]

One of his first stops was Pamplona during the feria of San Fermin in July. The running of the bulls attracted a vast assortment of people from all over the world: clerks from Newcastle, teachers from Lyon, and hotel cooks from Indonesia, as well Hollywood types like Darryl F. Zanuck and Orson Welles. People jostled in the streets. The bars were jammed with Americans, Dutch, Germans, and South Africans babbling in several languages and usually "stone drunk by five in the afternoon."[5] Michener had assembled his own band of festive companions. In addition to Vavra, John Fulton had flown in from Mexico; Hemingway's friend Juanito Quintana had joined them, as had Kenneth Vanderford, a tall, barrel-chested, bearded Hemingway look-alike who was an expert on Spain and taught at Ripon College in Wisconsin. At the Caballo Blanco one evening, the group sat down together and over drinks discussed the myths and inaccuracies of Hemingway's legacy in Spain. Since Jim was always fascinated about the private artist and public legend, he encouraged his friends to spill the beans about Hemingway. They discussed everything from his suicide to A. E. Hotchner's latest book, *Papa Hemingway*, which Quintana thought distorted some of the truth about the author. Mari and James Michener disagreed in their views about Hotchner's account. Before publication by Random House, Bennett Cerf had asked each for their candid assessment. Mari told Cerf that the book "was an unwarranted and inaccurate invasion of privacy." She also wanted the courts to suppress its publication. On the other hand, Jim thought "Hemingway was a public figure and relevant facts about him should not be withheld from the public." Michener voted to have the book published, which Random House eventually did.[6]

With his creased, tanned face, Quintana seemed a fitting subject for Velasquez. That evening he was unusually voluble. At one point in the conversation, Michener leaned over and asked Quintana: "How did [Hemingway] treat you?" "Always a marvelous friend," replied Quintana. "Once he said, 'Juanito, you're never to worry about money. You've been my constant friend and I'm going to take care of you.'" "Did he?" "No," said Quintana. "Ernesto paid me every peseta he ever owed me, but only what he owed. Never sent me a penny from America."[7]

Michener always considered Pamplona "authentic." "At the great carnivals, you can buy a mask for twenty cents and fake it," he remarked,

> but if you're a young man at Pamplona you can't. You can claim you did this or that but some guy is going to be there with a camera. . . . Pamplona is noisy as hell. The fights aren't very good. You can't get a decent room. On July fourteenth the place is simply overrun with enthusiastic Frenchmen who explain everything to you, because they live close to Spain and you don't. There's a great deal wrong with Pamplona, but once you have been an authentic part of this ambience you are hooked.[8]

His heart and legs feeling sturdy enough, Michener wanted to feel the excitement of the running of the bulls. Choosing a vantage point, a corner on the Cuesta de Santo Domingo, a safe distance from the main thrust of the bulls, he watched as the seven o'clock gun sent the bulls thundering past him down the street. Hooves pounded the ancient brickwork, as brave men darted for cover under anything that might protect them—window ledges, sides of buildings, curbs. Some of the men lay still in the gutter, feigning death. A few of the bulls marauded for several moments, pausing to swing their horns at men, taunting them to strike. Men were falling on both sides of the narrow street, some severely injured, others dead. Jim's heart was pounding "like a cement mixer." As the bulls made the turn into another section of Pamplona, Jim felt they "carried his fear with them."[9] "Why would a man who had been so close to death by a heart attack a short time before subject himself to such a risk?" he later recalled in a letter to Vavra. "I think it is because that one must not take death too seriously. I sensed that if I were going to survive the serious attack I suffered I could [do] it only in one of two ways: I could be a pampered cripple who retired from life, or I could return to where I was before and take every risk I had ever taken. Pamplona was the test, and when the bulls thundered past and I felt only a surge of normal excitement I knew I was free to resume whatever life I had enjoyed in the past."[10]

Compared to his experiences in Pamplona, the rest of his time in Spain was relatively serene, which was perfect for his health and also suited his inquiring intellect. He strolled along the streets of Seville, perhaps his favorite city in Spain, seeking out its cultural richness. "Sevilla is a feminine city," he observed in *Iberia*, "as compared with Madrid and Barcelona, but if one finds here the ingratiating femininity of grillwork on balconies and grace in small public squares, one finds also the forbidding femininity of a testy old dowager set in her preferences and self-satisfied in her behavior. It is not an accident that Sevilla has always been most loyal to movements that in the rest of Spain are in decline."[11] In Toledo, home of El Greco, he discussed a crucial battle in the Spanish Civil War. In the university city of Salamanca, he explored an Augustinian convent dating from the 1400s. In Avila, home of the mystic Saint Theresa, he listened to the choral music of Tomás Luis de Victoria and speculated on the dearth of Spanish music. While in Barcelona, Jim and Mari attended the famous Liceo opera house. "Although we had attended opera in some of the fine houses of the world, and sometimes under rather gala conditions, we had never witnessed anything like this. The dress was impeccable, the excitement intense, and there must have been a couple of hundred thousand of us in the street, watching the entry of the Catalans into the Liceo."[12]

Whether clad in tuxedo or shorts, Michener the teacher, the erudite art critic, the political pundit, and the irreclaimable nomad boldly emerged in the travel narrative. He proved to be an amiable traveling companion, able to discourse on architecture, local corridas, regional food, and anything he considered authentically Spanish.

In Madrid, Jim sought answers to the difficult political questions facing Spaniards. What difficulties were there in ruling Spain? he asked of people. "You must start, Michener," an unidentified official remarked, "with the fact that the Spaniards are utter bastards to govern. We are Texans cubed. . . . In the hundred years prior to [Franco] we had 109 changes of government, twenty-six revolutions, and three major civil wars. Would you agree that an attitude toward government that produces such results needs overhauling?" The man further observed that people should view Spain "as a three-legged stool. Church, army, landed families. If any one of the three topples they will all go down. . . . In the press you can say things against the Church and maybe you will get away with it . . . but you are absolutely forbidden to say anything against the army. They rule." Michener mentioned that the new industrialists might challenge that authority. "If the industrialists made one false move they would be wiped out overnight and their business expropriated," another man answered. "What happens after Franco dies or is deposed?" asked Michener. "The choice is between a dictatorship of some kind or another or a restoration of the monarchy," the man replied. "I believe it will be the monarchy. After all, our constitution states that we are a monarchy and Franco has openly announced that he serves merely as caretaker for that monarchy. There would be an advantage to us in having a king again, because it would make us popular in England and the United States, both of whom love royalty."[13]

Some critics of the book charged Michener with treating Franco with kid gloves. "He writes with greater critical awareness of earlier dictators than he does of Franco," wrote James Nelson Goodsell, "and at times he seems an apologist for some of the Spanish leader's actions."[14] Jim's words did cause alarm in Madrid. Later, when the book was nearing publication, the Spanish government felt so offended by Michener's claims that it threatened to ban the book outright or at least to have only a censored version available in the country. Michener consented to the Spanish version, if he and the censor could agree on the revisions. The censored version was eventually published, with Michener's approval, although he hushed up his role in it. "My position on this is simple," he noted. "The original still stands, available everywhere and in various languages, so that if anyone sincerely wants to know what I wrote about a certain topic he can find out. In such a situation, censorship affects only a portion and is itself dangerous because a concerned mind can compare the original and the official version and tell a great deal about the latter."[15] Despite the Spanish regime's criticism of the work, and in a gesture that amazed Jim, the Spanish Literary Society awarded him a gold medal for the book (in 1980), citing it as one of the most significant books on modern Spanish culture.

Michener was perhaps at his best when discerning regional differences and rivalries. In the early seventeenth century during the reign of King Philip IV, the peninsula was divided into three distinct "crowns": the crown of Portugal in the west, Castile in the middle, and Aragon, including Catalonia, in the east. The crown of Castile was the wealthiest due to riches flowing into its ports from the New World. Over the years, as Spain became more unified, the regions retained much of their original identities. The people of Aragon and Catalonia, for instance, considered themselves as Catalans first and Spaniards second. The battle for supremacy was singularly acute between Barcelona and Madrid. Barcelona, viewed by residents of Madrid as an anti-Franco city during the civil war, was always open for ridicule and regarded as second-rate. "All business and no soul," said one Madrid resident. The Barcelona architect Gaudí was often singled out as a representative of architecture that perverted the classical Spanish style. "What can you make of those towers?" one Madrid citizen asked. "At their base, Gothic. Midway up, pure Art Nouveau. At the top, Picasso cubist. It's junk architecture and it's lucky for us it was left unfinished. Perhaps a real architect can move in now and bring the mess to some conclusion."[16]

Michener ended his "pilgrimage," as he considered it, through Spain at Santiago de Compostela, the traditional burial site of Saint James.

He explained that since his heart attack in 1965, he had lain idly in "fitful slumber" wondering if he would ever again see the monuments and sacred places of his youth. "I thought then that if I ever were to leave that room, which I sometimes doubted, . . . I should like to see Compostela again."[17] For centuries, pilgrims from all over Europe and the world have made journeys to Compostela, many of them following the route from Paris, Tours, Poitiers, and across northern Spain. Beginning at a spot in the Spanish Pyrenees, Michener surveyed the Way of Saint James that led through the medieval towns of Estella, Burgos, and Ponferrada toward Compostela. "Here, in all ages," Jim noted, "pilgrims from various parts of Europe used to convene to form bands for the long march to Compostela, some nine hundred miles away. Kings and beggars, queens and cutthroats, butchers and knights, poets and philosophers all met here, and for a wild variety of reasons." He cited some of the famous travelers on the route: Charlemagne, King Alfonso II, Louis VII of France, Saint Francis of Assisi, James III of Scotland and England, and Giovanni Roncalli, later Pope John XXIII.[18]

As Michener made his way along the pilgrimage route, he stopped at various towns to savor their history and their contribution to contemporary Spanish life. He found the ubiquitous Romanesque cathedrals beautifully suited to these modest hamlets. "It is a church that relates to the soil," Michener said of one such church at Eunate. "Its arches are low and rounded as if they preferred to cling to the earth; its pillars are heavy and rooted to the earth. . . . It has a tower, but not a tall one; it is built with eight sides, for some reason that no one now remembers, and is surrounded by a curious unroofed cloister of austerely beautiful construction."[19]

As he traveled through northern Spain, Michener reflected on his love of Romanesque architecture, which he preferred over the soaring vaults of the Gothic and the flamboyant lines of the baroque. In its solid and simple designs he found an architecture that mirrored the humble chapels of rural Pennsylvania and the steadfast ideals of his Quaker heritage. "Of all the beautiful things I have seen in Spain, I suppose I liked best the Romanesque churches of the north. To me they were a form of poetry both epic and elegiac; the rows of human beings carved in the doorways were people I have known; the use of space and simple forms produced an impression as modern as tomorrow; and if on my various trips to Spain I found only these quiet and monumental buildings, I would have been amply rewarded."[20]

After witnessing many festivals and interviewing countless Spaniards, Michener arrived in Compostela in late July during the religious celebration honoring Saint James. In the cathedral the great festival was in full swing. Dodging the solemn procession, he made his way down the nave and up the narrow flight of stairs behind the main altar. From his vantage point looking down on the nave, he could see the entire colorful ceremony as it unfolded. "It was a dazzling moment," Michener recalled, "as rich in pageantry and filled with the spirit of Spain as any that I had witnessed, and there I hid in the darkness as if an interloper with no proper role in the ceremonial except that I had completed my vow of pilgrimage and stood at last with my arms about the stone-cold shoulder of Santiago, my patron saint and Spain's."[21]

Michener's Spanish journey may have ended at Compostela, but in many ways it was just the beginning of another aspect of his career. In January 1967 he sent a rough twelve-chapter manuscript to Erskine at Random House, with the idea that Erskine could get a general grasp of the book while Michener finished a more polished version. "It certainly tells you more about Spain than you want to know," he wrote Erskine. "I would describe it as a 19th century travel book in the same tradition, filled with personal opinions and told in a very leisurely and narrative manner."[22]

While Erskine worked from his end, Michener, still working in Spain, called in Kenneth Vanderford, in Michener's words "the nit-pickingest son of a bitch in the Spanish-speaking world." For a solid month they sat down together and "hacked away at every crazy idea we had." They agreed on major items and disagreed on minor ones. One of the latter concerned how to translate "O Santo d'os Croques," the name of a famous statue at Santiago de Compostela. Michener asked Vanderford: "Is this to be translated Saint of the bumps (who has bumps on his head) or Saint whom you bump (your head against his for good luck)?" Vanderford insisted that the Spanish language was such that the construction "saint of the bumps" meant that the bumps must have belonged to the saint and must be part of his essence. Eventually, Jim tracked down a poem that translated "Santo d'o Croques" as a "saint they bump their heads against." An indignant Vanderford then claimed that both the translator of the poem and Michener were "horses' asses."[23]

From 8:00 in the morning till 11:00 at night, with brief respites for an afternoon bullfight and a discussion over a beer at night, they went at the manuscript. Vanderford had seventy-five pages of comments and questions for Michener to review. After each item had been resolved, either in Jim's or Ken's favor, Michener typed out a clean copy and sent it on to Erskine.

When *Iberia* was published in late April 1968, it was quickly acknowledged in some quarters as a brilliant travelogue in the grand tradition and in others as a mishmash of history. *Time* called him "the infatuated traveler."[24] Alan Pryce-Jones in the *Washington Post Book World* titled his review "To Spain with Love and Puzzlement."[25] In the *New York Times Book Review*, Robert Payne took issue with Michener's disjointed narrative. Michener, who rarely responded to criticism, told Robert Vavra that the Payne review stung him. In particular, Jim was bothered that Payne, who had also written about Spain, would trammel on Jim's ground. "I think that whenever a man sees a conflict of interest he ought to disqualify himself on the question at hand," Jim stated, "I have worked diligently in politics to enforce this rule. . . . Feeling as I do about Payne, I could not conceivably agree to write a review of one of his innumerable books covering the same ground I have covered; the principle of self-disqualification would not allow me to do so. I am disappointed that he would not apply the same principle."[26] However, writing in the *Saturday Review*, Benjamin Welles called *Iberia* "one of the richest and most satisfying books about Spain in living memory."[27] The *Philadelphia Inquirer* remarked that "all of varied Michener's talents as reporter, researcher, and story teller extraordinary are brought to bear in this delightful odyssey."[28] Edmund Fuller in the *Wall Street Journal* called it the "best book Mr. Michener has done on any subject."[29] Overall, the criticism rang with superlatives, helping *Iberia* to vault to the top of the best-seller lists and place Michener among the luminaries in American letters.

Iberia is Michener's best nonfiction book, and it came at a time when he needed a major work to restore him to physical and mental health. *Iberia* accomplished both of these things. Rarely had a travel book been so comprehensive, insightful, and readable. It also signaled that a cycle of work was coming to an end. In late 1959 he had contemplated a book of Mexico that he discarded after an innocent comment derailed the project. In 1962, after losing a congressional election, he wrote *Caravans*. In 1963, intent on writing about Islam, he chose instead to focus on Jewish history in *The Source*. With *Iberia* and *The Drifters* (1971), he completed a cycle of works dealing with foreign— mostly arid—lands. Throughout his career, wherever he went, in America and abroad, people urged him to write about their countries. He considered their opinions with great care, but often he was not prepared to take on someone's suggested topic.

Traveling and writing in Spain gave Michener confidence to finally try to write a novel of Russia, a project that had been on-and-off for several years. Russia continued to be a key player in Jim's wide perspective. He was intrigued by its thriving art and culture under a brutal, repressive government. Moreover, he liked to think of himself as a commentator on the strengths and weaknesses of the Soviet system. He saw that system at work behind Russian lines during the Hungarian uprising in 1956. In 1963, at the request of the Kennedy administration, he attended a semisecret conference in Leningrad, during which he called for the liberation of three former Baltic republics—Estonia, Latvia, and Lithuania—much to the dismay of the Soviet delegation in attendance. In 1964 he traveled through Russia's provinces in Asia, noting their fragile and volatile relationship with the homeland. After his visit, he determined that any foreign war could ignite a revolution in these provinces. His interest in Russia kept hopes alive of someday completing a novel of Leningrad, in which he planned to cover the nine-hundred-day siege of the city by the Germans during the Second World War. After *Iberia* that project became even more of a possibility. He felt his health was restored, although he tired more easily. He was ready for the travel and research it would take, and could begin work as soon as he had taken a brief rest. However, beyond his knowledge, events were conspiring to once and for all remove Russia from his list.

Back in Pennsylvania in December 1967, the sixty-year-old Michener began a three-month stint in Harrisburg helping to redraft the state constitution. As the representative from Bucks County, Michener's role was to offer alternatives, shape policy, and assist in modernizing and overhauling the Pennsylvania justice system. Minor though his role was, he reveled in the aphrodisiac of political power, once admitting that serving in the constitutional convention was "the best thing" he had accomplished in his life. "And yet every damned thing I wanted I lost," Jim said frankly. "In my entire political life I have lost infinitely more than I have won. . . , I have tried to stand for reasonably good things, and I have learned to take defeat gracefully. I hate to lose. . . . But I have little respect for those who withhold their effort for a good cause because victory is not assured."[30]

Sounding more and more like a candidate preening himself for the next election, Jim briefly entertained the idea of a run for the U.S. Senate in the 1968 election. But toiling in the trenches of Harrisburg, seeing inept delegates rise to glory and brilliant ones shot down in their tracks, he decided against entering any more political campaigns. He would support the Democrats in the upcoming presidential election, he would speak out for racial harmony, and he would always be a voice for social change, but as far as being a candidate, he was finished with the whole wretched but exhilarating world of politics.

CHAPTER 14

Shine, Perishing Republic

In the summer of 1968 Jim was afraid the country was teetering on anarchy. Signs were visible everywhere. Martin Luther King, Jr., had been assassinated in April, Robert Kennedy in early June. And even though peace talks began in May, the war in Vietnam had escalated beyond anyone's imagination. Universities were suddenly hotbeds of revolution, with militant antiwar protesters taking over administration buildings. The government seemed unwilling or incapable of stemming the turmoil. In August, after the Republicans nominated Richard Nixon to the ticket, the Democrats convened at their national convention in Chicago, where more violence erupted into pitched battles between demonstrators and police.

On the night that Hubert Humphrey received the Democratic presidential nomination at the convention, Richard Nixon, watching the proceedings on television, observed: "It seemed as if the Democrats' convention was confirming every indictment of their leadership that I had made in my campaign speeches. Television magnified the agony of Chicago into a national spectacle. I knew that the impact of Humphrey's nomination would now be seriously undermined. He would have to spend his entire campaign trying to patch up the divisions in his party."[1] Nixon's words proved correct. After the conventions, the Republican candidate held a commanding thirteen-point lead in the national polls. Nixon, who had dropped out of public life after losing his bid to become California's governor in 1962, had resurfaced to claim his party's nomination and clearly was the front-runner going into autumn campaign months. Although he loathed the GOP platform, Michener continued to respect Nixon until the Watergate debacle several years later. Michener would have preferred Democratic hopeful Eugene McCarthy but ultimately rejected his candidacy because of McCarthy's stand on Vietnam. After Bobby Kennedy's death, Michener felt a vacuum in American politics trying to be filled by older, more traditional politicians. Eventually, he sided with the party's nomination of Humphrey and wrote "Hubert Humphrey: Portrait of a President" for the Democratic National Committee's *Fact Book*.

Three years after his heart attack, Jim felt progressively stronger and had returned to playing a set of tennis and walking every chance he could. *Iberia* was out and selling well. After considering several permanent locations for his collection of American art, valued at $17 million, he finally chose the University of Texas, a decision that offended most residents of Bucks County. According to Herman Silverman, Jim never paid more than $5,000 for any painting. As the fortunes of the art market would have it, even the modest paintings had appreciated handsomely by the time of Jim's donation.

Michener's decision to house his works at the University of Texas came at the end of a painstaking, deliberative selection process. "I had originally intended that the collection should go to some city museum, and I spent the better part of five years quietly visiting a large number of such museums without disclosing my concern but making such comparisons as I could," he explained. "I suppose all serious collectors do this, and I'm sure they enjoy the job."[2] Gradually, he narrowed the field but opted for a university with both a museum and an art school. He zeroed in on the University of Texas because of its museum and art school, the excellence of its faculty, and the extensive holdings of its library. "I was also satisfied that Texas would know what to do with the sometimes difficult paintings my wife and I had collected and the collection would find an intellectual as well as physical home."[3]

At sixty-two years of age and after writing twenty-one books, copious articles, and various other works, James Michener was an odd bird in the literary world. He rarely accepted invitations to parties where the literati gathered. Many rising and already established stars in the literary world—Norman Mailer, Gore Vidal, Truman Capote, Tom Wolfe—had made their public personas much more interesting than their recessive writers' personalities. But Jim, comfortable in his own skin, refused to engage in this charade. Reluctant to be in the limelight, often self-absorbed, and grouchy when a guest stayed too long, he welcomed his solitary time in his office at the typewriter. His work partly gave him the assurance that he would not go broke, or worse, be forgotten by a generation of readers. Often it was difficult to tell which was the greater motivational factor.

From time to time a great idea for a book came to him when he was researching another. Such was the case for *The Drifters*, Michener's novel of aimless youth searching for meaning in Spain and Africa in the late 1960s. Many Spaniards in his travels talked about the Mediterranean town of Torremolinos, a Babylon of sin and leisure on the Costa del Sol, where young drifters collected by the throngs. Jim's imagination was piqued, but he continued his journey and the writing of *Iberia*. In Pamplona one day in 1967, while he was sitting drinking coffee in a café, three young Australian women implored Michener to take up a collection to fly home a friend, an Englishwoman in Tangiers who was strung out on drugs. "They're screwing her seven and eight times a day," one of the women said. "They invite their friends in. But they don't give her enough to eat."[4] The urgency in the women's voices prompted Michener to reach in his wallet and offer them money for the woman's plane trip back to England. "As I listened to the Australian girls' story the whole novel was born while they were talking," Michener remarked. Later, Jim and Kenneth Vanderford flew to Tangiers to check on the young woman and found that she had died from an overdose of drugs the week earlier. Shaken by the event, he waited in vain for some writer to step forward and tell the story of the youth movement in America and Europe and of the dreadful sinkholes in which the young found themselves.

In February 1969, moved by the ardor of the movement and the story related by the Australians, Jim decided that he would be that writer. In March he and Mari moved to Torremolinos on Spain's southeast coast to begin the novel. Situated in the coastal hills between Malaga and Gibraltar, the tourist town of Torremolinos faces the azure expanse of the Mediterranean Sea, wearing few of the traces of its notorious past. It looks wealthy and scrubbed now. High-rise hotels and posh restaurants line the crowded streets, catering to an international trade. Tourists with cameras swagger up and down hunting for bargains in the numerous boutiques. In the late 1960s and early 1970s, however, it was a haven for the European and American drug culture and was known dubiously as "the Lourdes of LSD" and "Sweden on the Sand." The smell of marijuana was as prevalent as the scent of *el pescaito frito*, a favorite local dish, wafting from beach bars or restaurant kitchens.

Michener quickly immersed himself in the underground culture of Torremolinos. Donning a pair of old trousers and a tourist shirt and sandals, he hung out in bars, urging his companions to tell him their stories. He revealed his identity. *Iberia* by then was in everyone's tote bag, so most were quite eager to hang out with a famous author. He drank beer with them but stopped short of smoking marijuana. In the small apartments, where sleeping arrangements were often cafeteria style, Michener at one time or another sacked out on the floor in a sleeping bag. The lifestyle transported him back to his youthful days riding the rails through America or hiking across Scotland.

Michener had planned an important chapter in *The Drifters* that was set in Pamplona. In July he arrived there for the running of the bulls during the festival of San Fermin. As Michener explained in an article for *Esquire* magazine, people came to Pamplona for vastly different reasons. For actor and director Orson Welles, it "was a privilege. A man would be a damn fool to pass it up." Michener's matador friend John Fulton found he "loved to be with those animals. It's something to feel them thunder past." For a proud Frenchman, running with the bulls on July 14 was in celebration of Bastille Day. Cynics, Michener observed in his article, came up with their own explanations as to why grown men would participate in such a ludicrous ritual. "The Snide New York Journalist" remarked, "A bunch of jaded old men trying to recapture their youth"; "The Clever Woman Writer" insisted, "You must look at it as a group of impotent men who have discovered a sex substitute"; and "The English Cynic" claimed, "It's a chance for irresponsible young men from England, Germany, Scandinavia, and America to come to an exotic place and show off." According to Michener, however, these theories were incorrect. "Throughout history," he wrote, "a certain kind of man wanted to test himself against the most demanding experiences of his culture. Such a motive is idiotic, jejune, unrewarding and senseless, but frequently you find it is the best men who insist upon taking the risks. In our age you can climb Mount Everest, fly to the moon, or run with the bulls at Pamplona. The last is the cheapest, the most available, and you can do it with most exhilarating companions." An additional reason for returning to Pamplona that season "was more prosaic. . . . For some years I had been planning a complicated novel [*The Drifters*] about six young people . . . who drift about Europe and Africa. I had lived with these prototypes in many different parts of the world, had argued with them over drugs, and witnessed their tragedies and triumphs." Michener remarked that he had seen Pamplona before, but only through the eyes of a nonfiction writer. "Knowing a subject from the non-fiction point of view," he observed, "bears little relation to knowing it well enough to use it in fiction. I knew Pamplona, but not as a novelist."[5]

On July 11 Jim took the bold step of running with the bulls in the streets of Pamplona. As he explained in *Esquire*, it was a tragic, bloody day for those around him. A Portuguese photographer, located on a balcony above the Cuesta de Santo Domingo, snapped pictures of the scene, verifying Jim's compelling account for *Esquire*. The sequential photos reveal the horror of the event. At 7:00 in the morning the bulls storm out of the gate. Jim recedes into an alcove, six inches deep, as a raging bull breaks loose from the herd and moves toward him. For some reason, the bull begins "cleaning the wall," raking his left horn along the wall and puncturing whatever he hits. Several men try to lunge out of his path. Jim is only several yards away, his hands grasped together over his stomach, watching the bull rampage along the sidewalk. The bull gores one man in the stomach, rips the shirt of another. The bull, his left horn tipped in blood, now looks for more victims. Other bulls join the melee. Bodies lie in a great chain along the street in front of Jim, some dead, some unconscious, others feigning death. A man reels and dies at Jim's feet; someone grabs another injured victim and hurries him away from the scene of carnage. A man next to Jim tries to force himself behind Michener to use him as a shield against the maddened bulls. Jim stands his ground, his feet planted squarely up to the building. Gradually, the action stops. The bulls move away down the street, leaving a trail of blood and inert bodies. One dead man has been knocked out of his shoes by the force of a charging bull. Jim has not moved a muscle since the action began. As the bulls disappear, a hospital crew moves in to attend the victims. It is all over in a matter of minutes. "I don't know whether I will be able to capture in words and transmit to others what I learned," Jim wrote. "But of this I'm sure. Many men have tried to explain the sensation of running with the bulls through the streets of Pamplona, and some have caught the essence. . . . I'll probably fail, because much happens that the mind does not catch, but at least I did my homework."[6]

Returning to Torremolinos in August, Michener typed the rough draft of *The Drifters* (original title "The Wanderers"). By the late winter of 1970, he was back in Pipersville polishing the manuscript and preparing it for a spring 1971 publication date.

Leaving Spain was always difficult for Michener. Like Michener himself, it was full of contradictions. Fiercely devoted to its art and its history, Spain above all possessed an authentic culture. It was "a rugged, to-hell-with-you country" that, in Jim's estimation, "made no concession to the artist."[7] Spain was also cheap, was easy to get around in, and had a pleasant climate. For several years thereafter, he surrendered to the lure of Spain, even calling it his favorite country numerous times. After Jim returned to America, Vavra often tried to get him back, noting in a handwritten postscript on the side of a typed note: "What do you want me to do about bullfight tickets? We're going to set way up high, top section shade, first row balcony. Let me know if you want to join us."[8]

In late 1969 Michener felt that his international reputation was secure. He had lived through and in some cases helped to create a successful decade. Despite having lost a critical congressional election, endured the assassinations of three personal friends, and suffered a major heart attack, he had also written some of his best work, namely *Caravans, The Source,* and *Iberia.* During the 1960s, Michener furthered his concept of the large-scale novel, which was largely built on his earlier success of *Hawaii.* It was a time when he wrestled with political life, and the artist finally won.

Michener had made friends wherever he went throughout the world. Certain spots would always be dear to him: Israel, Spain, Afghanistan, the South Pacific, Hawaii, Japan, and Malaysia. But in many ways he felt that his work overseas was done, and there was a body of writing to be accomplished in America. Friends and colleagues urged him to write about the United States. Floyd Merrill wanted him to write a book of the West that would be as ambitious as *Hawaii.* Helen Strauss, now busy in Hollywood with a number of movie projects, urged him to write about California. Hobe Lewis, with a view to the country's bicentennial celebration in 1976, offered his own suggestion, a major book about America: "Into such a novel," Lewis remarked, "you could weave all the important national strains that go to make up the American character and experience. . . . I know it is a monumental undertaking . . . but you are the only person in the country who could do it, and I think it is exactly the right time for such a book to be written."[9] Considering these influential opinions, Michener admitted it was time to go home: "I guess I've come full circle. So many of the world's changes emanate from this country. The action is here."[10] He really had no idea where the road into America would take him. He had a few vague notions of themes he wished to pursue, but all he really knew was that he wanted to return to American soil and commit himself to writing about its people.

In spring 1970 he toyed with the idea of revising the "Jefferson" project, which he had abandoned in 1950. By early April, he had outlined the major parts of his novel of the West, one tentatively titled "Centennial." In mid-May he and Mari headed for Colorado to begin research on the project. Interrupting his research and writing schedule, however, was the tragic episode at Kent State University on May 4, 1970, in which a contingent of National Guardsmen fired into a crowd of student protesters, killing four and wounding nine others. The Kent State incident remains one of the most significant and controversial events in American history. At the time, it was regarded by some as a senseless and unwarranted use of military power against unarmed civilians. Others saw it as an appropriate response by the guardsmen to an angry mob of student anarchists. Everyone, it seemed, chose one side or the other.

On the urging of Hobe Lewis, Michener set aside the *Centennial* project and arrived on the scene to investigate the tragedy, reporting from a motel near campus. Working anonymously, he hung out in the local bars, eavesdropping on conversations among the patrons. He watched as shotgun-bearing motorists of Kent, Ohio, patrolled the streets, itching for provocation. Mostly, however, he conducted numerous interviews from his motel room. Researching and writing concurrently, he readied his account for a March 1971 deadline in *Reader's Digest*. Later, Michener's massive tome of the incident, *Kent State: What Happened and Why*, was published by Random House and was greeted with widespread praise from critics. Most dissenters, including two Kent State professors, criticized Michener's method of note taking for interviews. Jim used no notepads or tape recorders. Once a person left his motel room, he raced for his typewriter and, from memory, pecked out the testimony. This method, his critics claimed, led to some egregious errors in reporting. Nevertheless, Michener remained pleased about the outcome of his Kent State investigation, maintaining that he, with the aid of several researchers, accomplished as much as the FBI did with five hundred agents.

During that tumultuous summer of 1970, when the moral lid appeared to be coming off civilization, Frank Shakespeare, director of the United States Information Agency (USIA), asked Michener to lunch in New York. At Michener's request, Hobe Lewis joined them. Michener described Shakespeare, a former CBS television executive, as a man whose "personal politics made Genghis Khan and Bill Buckley seem like free-wheeling liberals."[11] Michener's good friend Lewis was as influential in conservative politics as he was in publishing. Lewis was a close friend of Richard Nixon's, who often stayed with Lewis when he passed through New York. At their luncheon meeting, the three discussed unofficial agency matters.

That autumn a beleaguered Richard Nixon launched a search for liberal intellectuals to join his administration. Chief of Staff H. R. Haldeman noted in his diary: "As of now we have no real ferment of new ideas and no real tough intellectual challenge of present ideas or programs. Main problem is most intellectuals are not on our side."[12] Nixon directed John Ehrlichman, assistant to the president for domestic affairs, to contact agency directors and begin remedying the situation. Among those Ehrlichman contacted was Frank Shakespeare at the USIA, who needed to fill important vacancies on the Advisory Council for Information, the six-member panel that acted as overseer of the USIA. Shakespeare offered a position to Michener, who accepted. Hobe Lewis filled the other vacancy.[13]

According to its charter, the USIA's mission was "responsibility for the U.S. Government's overseas information and cultural programs, among them being the Voice of America, Radio Free Europe, and the Fulbright scholarships program." In representing American interests abroad and as the major propaganda arm of the government, the agency endeavored to strengthen understanding of and support for U.S. policies through a carefully structured communications program. Most of the radio broadcasts were aimed at Communist countries and Third World countries being wooed by the United States.

After President Nixon authorized their selections, Michener and Lewis joined other Advisory Council members: William F. Buckley, the conservative columnist, who became a good friend of Michener's, even though Buckley "was one of the young men most influential in helping swing the nation far to the right, a sinful performance for which I suppose God will forgive him."[14] The USIA's chairman was Frank Stanton, president of CBS Television. According to Michener, Stanton "utilized the highest percentage of whatever natural intelligence he was given at birth. . . . He was soft-spoken, incredibly swift in comprehending ideas and masterly in putting them into execution."[15] "Under Stanton's guidance," Jim observed, "our board did its best to give our agency good counsel in its fight against Communism. We suffered some disastrous mishandling of certain problems that we hastened to correct . . . but never in my work for the USIA did I doubt the value of what we were attempting abroad. . . . I was proud to be a soldier in such honorable warfare."[16]

Michener's appointment automatically required a background check by the FBI for a top-secret clearance. Michener's relationship with the bureau was always tenuous. On the one hand, he liked to think of himself as an unofficial government ambassador involved in a cloak-and-dagger mission in a foreign country. At the FBI's request, he agreed to help root out suspected Communists in the Fund for Asia. On the other hand, he enjoyed the role of an agitator and a gadfly, under the constant scrutiny of the FBI. During the McCarthy era in the 1950s, he was continually trying to help friends accused of subversion. In a tongue-in-cheek article for *Esquire*, "What the FBI Has On Me," Jim described himself in his imaginary file

as a white Caucasian male who conforms to every index that would indicate possible subversion: graduated from Swarthmore, which is bad enough, married a girl from Antioch, which is worse, and did graduate work at Harvard, which is worst of all . . . reads liberal magazines, engages in bird-watching, eats health foods, favors fluoridation. Marriage is interracial, has many black friends, some of whom visit his home, and during the McCarthy period appeared constantly as a character reference for personal friends charged with subversive tendencies. Argued vigorously on their behalf and when questioned was apt to say: "This man is nothing but a liberal who subscribed to the *Nation* and *The New Republic*." When interrogated as to what he meant by the term liberal he would reply, "Someone who reads the *Nation* and *The New Republic*."[17]

Michener admitted that his phone was probably wiretapped but also stated that such a practice was "obligatory" in certain cases. "Because I was dealing with top secret material, the government is entitled to check up on the people it puts into high-level positions. . . . I think wiretapping under certain circumstances and closely supervised is permissible." As for wiretapping private citizens, however, he remained steadfast. "When an administration is irritated by certain newspapermen who aren't writing the kinds of stories they want, and it wiretaps them, then I think we have an entirely different relationship because that is really an attack on the freedom of the press, and that's a pretty invidious attack."[18]

In November 1970 the White House announced Jim's appointment to the council. In his role Jim became even closer to the president's inner circle. Whatever Michener thought of Nixon's policies, he revered the man. Both were Quakers who endured difficult childhoods. Both had become successful through hard work, guile, and a set of fortuitous circumstances. Michener respected Nixon's handling of foreign policy, even though in late 1970 Nixon was being criticized by the press. "In one meeting with President Nixon," Jim recalled, "topics came up that he could not possibly have anticipated, and he proved himself amazingly well informed and completely accurate, even in small details. He was crisp, quick, well organized and able to absorb jokes at his own expense."[19] A Democrat in Nixon's inner circle was something of a rarity, but Nixon insisted he balance the panel with members of both parties. Moreover, he admired Michener's experience in Asia and Russia and his success in literature. The timing of Michener's appointment was ironic in that Jim was researching and writing about Kent State at a time when any criticism of the administration in the book might have sabotaged his work on the council.

By 1971 Richard Nixon faced growing resentment at home as well as hostility abroad. Domestically, Nixon wanted an expanded role for the USIA and the council, including more emphasis on the monitoring of communications within the country. Nixon wanted people like Michener, who was a noted social commentator, to brief him on the mood and tenor of the country, to point out areas where the administration was lacking, and to offer suggestions for improvement. Specifically, Michener advised the president and the council on student unrest, the aims of Students for a Democratic Society (SDS), the economy, and the Vietnam War.

Internationally, Nixon sought détente between America and its two principal adversaries, Russia and China. Jim knew both countries well, although his knowledge of China and Asia was particularly strong. At top-secret meetings with the Advisory Council and with the president, Michener demonstrated his understanding of both Russian and Chinese cultures, helping Nixon get a clearer picture of the challenges and dangers he would face in seeking peace. In July 1971 Nixon gleefully announced he was planning a trip to Peking (Beijing) the following February to start negotiations with the Chinese. In October of that year, he declared that in May 1972 he would visit Moscow for a summit meeting with the Russians. Both announcements were seen as diplomatic coups for Nixon, coming at a time when his presidency was sinking into despair and rigidity.

In his role on the Advisory Council, Jim encountered several of the men who would play important roles in the Watergate affair. Michener's contact at the White House was John Ehrlichman, whom Jim publicly characterized as "a sturdy, well-spoken, tough young man with above average intelligence and a brilliant capacity to judge what was going on around him . . . that he should have been placed in charge of policies affecting the internal social and economic life of a complex republic was appalling, for he was totally unqualified to judge the social needs of this nation." Michener's dealings with Vice President Spiro Agnew were less frequent. "He lacked the intense control of Nixon but had a superior sense of humor," remarked Michener. As he got to know more of the Nixon team, Jim admitted that they "impressed me as being among the most honest men I ever met in Washington, certainly worthy of comparison with their counterparts in the Kennedy and Johnson Administrations."[20] This generous assessment would gradually change, however.

In addition to his position on the council, which had him driving to meetings in New York and flying to ones in Europe, Jim campaigned in Pennsylvania for Edmund Muskie, who eventually lost to George McGovern for the Democratic nomination for president. Michener contended that the Democrats had surrendered to the ultraliberals represented by McGovern, who had campaigned on an unconditional and immediate withdrawal from Vietnam. He nevertheless backed

McGovern but admitted that he "was not as wildly enthusiastic about him as he was about Kennedy and Humphrey."[21]

As the China trip approached, Nixon requested that more television than print journalists accompany him, primarily because television crews could make his China trip an international spectacle; the print journalists, who for the most part dissected Nixon in the press, would have a lesser role in the auspicious trip. Michener had no plans to go on the press plane accompanying Nixon, but at the last minute, and after some influence peddling by Hobe Lewis, Michener and Bill Buckley got the last two seats on the plane. Lewis wanted Jim to write a feature article on the China trip for *Reader's Digest*, and Michener was eager to reveal this hidden corner of Asia to Americans:

> I had seen China from all angles but had never been allowed inside its borders. I had given up trying. I felt that Communist China would have to be the only nation on earth I had ever wanted to see and failed to enter. . . . That I should have been lucky enough to find a place on the press corps accompanying Nixon into China gave me real pleasure. It is no little thing to make one's way at last into the capital of the world's largest nation after thirty years of trying to get there.[22]

The press plane carried eighty-seven handpicked journalists, cameramen, and technicians representing six magazines, twenty-five newspapers, and three television networks. Arriving in Peking on February 21, 1972, with the Nixon entourage, Jim grimaced at the sparse number of Chinese delegates sent to meet the plane. "When Nixon sees the size of this crowd," cracked Peter Lisagor of the *Chicago Daily News*, "he's going to come out for busing."[23] Later, while strolling through the streets of Peking, Jim saw "a spacious city with boulevards capable of carrying six lanes of traffic, but with few automobiles . . . women walked boldly and elbowed men if the latter got in their way. . . . Peking was immaculate in all respects and made cities like New York and Philadelphia look disgracefully dirty. But it was also a silent city, with no sound of robust laughter or of young boys playing in the streets."[24]

Jim spent a hurried week in China, visiting the Nanyuan's Peoples Commune, an automobile factory, the Great Wall, Hangchow, and Shanghai. Of particular interest to Michener, however, was President Nixon's demeanor while abroad. "I thought the President handled himself superbly throughout the trip," he noted. "He often broke away from protocol and displayed a good deal of easy charm, eating with chopsticks and drinking innumerable toasts. He may have been just what Chinese-American relations needed at this moment in history."[25]

Accompanying Nixon to Russia three months later, Michener found himself in the middle of a tempest. At a press conference set up in the Intourist Hotel in Moscow, Michener listened intently to Soviet leaders discuss the problem of Russian Jewry. There were two million Jews living in Russia who faced some sort of discrimination at the hands of authorities and the police. Michener was hopeful that a meaningful discussion of the problems might take place at the conference but was dismayed by what happened. A reporter from the American Jewish Press Association asked the editor of a Russian literary weekly why the Soviet Union did not publish Yiddish-language newspapers giving Russian Jews news about Jewish communities abroad. Trying to placate the audience, the editor cited two journals that were published in remote regions of the country. He further commented that foreign journalists always overstated the case of a "Jewish problem" in the Soviet Union. Glibly, the editor read from a 1931 novel, *The Golden Calf*, which basically noted that Soviet Jews were a happy lot. Michener thought the whole scene grossly absurd. He rose in protest, muttered something derogatory, and stormed from the meeting. "Nixon would have been justified in sending me home for causing such a scandal," Jim remarked, "but a member of his staff confided: 'You served us well—you made points we wanted to make but couldn't.' "[26] Without further incident, Jim remained in Moscow for the duration of the summit.

With a renewed optimism for peace between the Soviet Union and the United States, Michener returned from Moscow as invigorated as President Nixon seemed to be. For the next month at least, Michener could return to the business of writing, secure in the knowledge that Richard Nixon would have a new mandate to govern the country.

All that changed, however, on June 17, only sixteen days after the Soviet summit, when five men were caught breaking into the Democratic Party headquarters in the Watergate building in Washington, D.C. The press intensified their search for the mastermind behind the break-in, a search that eventually closed in on the White House itself. As the events unfolded, it seemed that the strong bridges that Nixon had built between Washington and Moscow and Peking—indeed between the nation's capital and the American people—were tumbling brick by brick.

PART FOUR

Homecoming
1970–1997

CHAPTER 15

One Man's America

Jim had woken up one day in April 1970 with the entire novel of *Centennial* outlined in his mind, but it was not until August–September 1972 that he was able to give the project his full attention. In August he sent several letters to historians asking for assistance, among them J. Merrill Mattes, an authority on the Platte River. Among other things, he asked of Mattes: "What was the earliest appearance of cholera?" "When was the first mammoth excavated?" "When was the earliest covered wagon caravan along the South Platte?"[1] In September he and Mari moved to Denver, where they set up research and writing headquarters in a high-rise condo in Penn Square, near the Denver Public Library. His apartment overlooked the roofs of historic downtown Denver, and to the west the Rockies thrust their peaks into a cobalt sky. His sojourn in Denver was among his best memories, and he called it one of his favorite places to conduct research and writing.

The decision to write an American novel was reached carefully and slowly. In the late 1960s Jim and Hobart Lewis were appointed by President Nixon to serve on the American Revolution Bicentennial Commission, a group dedicated to formulating a set of ideals that would debut in the bicentennial year of 1976 and, it was hoped, stretch into the next century. Michener's role was to translate the commission's dialogue into literary form and report to Congress on the process. Unfortunately, the commission devolved into partisan rankling and within a year was scuttled. Michener blamed "influential and ill-intentioned politicians" for the loss of the program. "Instead of a feast of the imagination," Michener growled, "we shall have a hastily contrived picnic with plastic hamburgers."[2] The failure of the commission was a bitter pill for Michener. Taking its loss personally, he groped for ways of contributing his own unique voice to the celebration of the nation's two hundredth birthday. "Try as I might, I could find no hope of salvaging any celebration on a national scale. Some of the individual states were conceiving imaginative small programs, but the grand design was dead."[3] When the idea for *Centennial* emerged, he knew he had found the right landscape and characters to give that voice distinct expression.

As Colorado's centennial year of 1976 approached, the state was undergoing important changes in its economic base. The history of Colorado was always marked by boom-and-bust cycles. The traditional staple industries of mining and agriculture were still major players in Colorado. During the Great Depression and its accompanying drought, agriculture was severely affected. The Second World War stimulated farm production to record levels. After the war, as gold, silver, and coal mining slumped and as thousands flocked to the state, the economy was stimulated by more service-related businesses. The mining industry left its mark on the landscape with garish mountains of mine tailings, abandoned shafts, soils filled with radioactive waste, and old rutted roads cut through the forests that often deposited a traveler in the middle of nowhere.

For several weeks Michener haunted the Denver library, famous for its western history collection. The collection was "especially rich in photographs and old ephemera such as real estate handbills, railroad propaganda brochures and contemporary theatrical reviews," noted Jim.[4] When he did not check out a shopping cart–load of books, he was in secondhand stores buying titles of western Americana for his personal library. At one time he had five hundred books surrounding his desk in his living room. His list of people he would interview for the book was equally impressive, ranging in geographical locale from

St. Louis to Oregon. In September Hobe Lewis had offered Jim the research services of two Britons: John Kings and Tessa Dalton, who both lived in the Rocky Mountain region. Kings, a former editor and cattle rancher, explained the beginning of his relationship with Michener: "In September 1972, no longer sitting easy in the saddle in my ranching endeavors, I was covering an international convention of parks directors for *Reader's Digest* magazine when Hobart Lewis telephoned. Would I like to work with James Michener in the preparation of a major novel on the West? He had told Michener of my dual life as a rancher/editor with a knowledge of western history, and had suggested that I might be helpful for those parts of the manuscript dealing with the development of the cattle industry." Thus began a relationship with Kings that was to last to the end of Michener's career. Kings became Jim's chief literary assistant, advising him on all matters concerned with both his personal welfare and professional ambitions. Tessa Dalton, a photographer living in Denver, was assigned to visually catalog the making of the book, in addition to various duties involved with travel and background research. After meeting Kings and Dalton, Jim sent a note to Hobe Lewis: "We have met the two English people and find them delightful prospects for constructive work. Look much better than average. We are all at work."[5] A third member of Jim's research team was Leslie Laird, a former *Reader's Digest* employee who had worked with him on the Kent State book. The three researchers, along with Mari and Jim, began the task of transforming the raw material of the western experience into the novel that became *Centennial.*

Mari Michener, a native Coloradoan, became one of the staunchest supporters of the project. As the daughter of a Las Animas melon farmer, she thought that Jim's book would honor her family as well as the development of agriculture in the Rockies. She therefore returned to Colorado knowing that she would be assisting her husband and uncovering a part of her heritage.

After meeting Kings and Dalton, Michener gave them their first research assignment: to travel by car to Pennsylvania and reconstruct a daily chronicle of a wagon and flatboat journey from Lancaster to St. Louis undertaken by two young people in 1844.[6] This record became the trip taken by Levi and Ellie Zendt in "The Wagon and the Elephant" chapter of the book. Meanwhile, Michener, accompanied by Lauren Wright, a professor of geology at Penn State, headed to the Pawnee Buttes north of Greeley to begin the preliminary assessment of the terrain and the geologic foundations of the area. After visiting the twin buttes, the symbolic landmark in the book, the two visited the ghost town of Keota, set on a windswept rise on the prairie forty miles northeast of Greeley. There Michener met Clyde Stanley, a wiry man in his seventies who had been a homesteader, editor of the town newspaper, land commissioner, and postmaster. "He was a stunning human being," noted Michener. "Wise, gentle, gifted with words, an artist with the printing press, a man who comprehended the great movements of the earth at his doorstep."[7]

In addition to Stanley and Merrill, Otto Unfug of Sterling, Colorado, became Michener's chief adviser on Colorado life before and after the Great Depression. Unfug assembled a group of sixteen men to discuss irrigation issues with Michener. "When you talked with these grizzled veterans you did not talk abstracts," remarked Jim. Unfug also arranged seminars for Michener in homesteading, farming, and cattle raising. One day Unfug loaded Michener into his panel truck and, taking several old county roads, drove deep into the prairie. "He took me to an abandoned line camp," wrote Michener, "one of those informal stations in the midst of nowhere, used by cowboys as overnight stops in the days when ranches ran for a hundred miles in any direction. I can never forget the beauty of that desolate station: a big stone barn whose century-old woodwork interior was as lovely as a Brueghel painting, a small, low-slung stone farmhouse, which nestled properly into its landscape."[8] Later, in an area around Jim's motel, Unfug distinguished between buffalo grass, blue grama, and African grass. "When he was finished—and he took a long time—I understood what grass was, and why it was important to the cattle grower."[9]

All aspects of the western experience fascinated Michener. Like writers before him, he studied the various stages of exploration and settlement, such as the coming of the scouts, mountain men, pioneers, railroad crews, ranchers, farmers, cowboys, and settlers. Just as important as the human experience, however, was the rugged landscape of the West: the prairie, the mountains and mesas, the desert, and the rivers. Michener could walk along a river for hours, watching its meandering path, seeing how it scoured the land, and viewing with unending fascination what philosophers and observers had known for centuries. The river was always the same, always changing. The South Platte, which he called insignificant and "grubby," was hardly an inspiring river, but it was similar to many of the pioneers who settled Colorado: innocuous, durable, tough, and resilient. Jim thought that the Colorado River was more of a waterway, and, of course, it was. Winding through spectacular country, broad in its current and fierce in flow, the mighty Colorado was a showcase of the American Southwest. But for Michener in late 1972, enamored of northeastern Colorado, the South Platte valley would serve quite nicely as the crossroads and ultimately the home for his generations of restless heroes.

The mountains, from Denver in the south to Laramie, Wyoming, in the north, would form a significant backdrop to the human drama along the South Platte. Several peaks rise above eleven thousand feet in elevation. In summer, bare traces of snow on their summits beckon the prairie traveler. Between Denver and Fort Collins lies Rocky Mountain National Park, a feast of alpine scenery. It was the combination of the mountains, the winding of the river, and the plains that inspired Michener to set his story in eastern Colorado. Along with its historical richness, it was an inspiring mixture.

By January 1973 Michener had typed nearly four hundred pages of the *Centennial* manuscript, mostly concerning the geological beginnings of Colorado, the earliest American Indian inhabitants of the region, and the coming of the white trappers. His day began at 5:30 in the morning when he grabbed a towel and took the elevator to the gym in the basement. For a solid hour he used the stationary bicycle and treadmill, topping off his workout with fifty sit-ups. Back in his room by 6:30, he worked until noon, seven days a week, pecking out two thousand words on a good day.[10] Writer's block, a sign of diffidence, rarely troubled Jim. He maintained a brisk pace at the manual typewriter no matter what was going on inside him or around him.

On a raw snowy night in the middle of January, John Kings and Tessa Dalton arrived at Michener's apartment in Denver to report on their findings of the overland journey from Pennsylvania to St. Louis. There were several questions raised by Michener that his two characters, Levi and Ellie Zendt, had to address on their journey: What would have been the condition of the Susquehanna River at the time the two crossed the covered Columbia Bridge to the west bank in February? Would they have taken the old grade road over the Alleghenies or the faster Forbes Road at a time of year when snowstorms could still be a threat? These were just two of the many questions that Michener needed answered, and Kings and Dalton supplied them. Moreover, they returned with population counts, weather records, spelling of place names, costs of tolls, details of wagon building, and hundreds of other facts that became grist for Jim's mill.

On January 19, 1973, Michener, Kings, and Dalton climbed into Michener's Chevrolet station wagon to begin a twenty-five-thousand-mile odyssey through the American West. Between January and May the three would take five separate journeys: the first took them deep into New Mexico, Texas, and Oklahoma; the second from Denver to Chihuahua, Mexico; the third into Wyoming, Idaho, and Montana; the fourth to Nebraska; and the fifth, later in the year, a loop of western Colorado, Arizona, and Utah. Even with a heavy load of research and travel, Michener by March had completed two-thirds of *Centennial*.[11]

Since Michener placed great emphasis on the structure of his novels, *Centennial* posed an interesting dilemma: how to maintain a compelling narrative from the prehistoric times through the 1970s. Michener once claimed that he could write "six or seven good books a year, but it would take me six or seven months with each one to find the right structure."[12] *Tales of the South Pacific* lacked a coherent narrative voice, but that worked to its advantage. "I attempted several types of organization before hitting upon the one I finally used," remarked Michener. "What did work was a loose collection of delicately interrelated stories in which no one character, no one setting assumed priority."[13] His most successful structure before *Centennial* had been the device of the Tell in *The Source*, which helped thread together the various parts of the book. With *Centennial*, after much trial, he devised a contemporary story to help tie together a long historical chronicle across a sprawling geographical canvas with more than seventy characters. He created the character of Lewis Vernor, a history professor, who is recruited by the editors of *US Magazine* to report on the South Platte River shortly before Colorado's centennial celebration. Vernor's narrative is interpolated into the omniscient parts of the chronicle, giving the reader a sense of personality and perspective as the novel progresses through the various eras.

This structure did not come easy. "The more I worked with the intricate interweaving, the more I liked it," said Michener. "But I became aware that in the telling of the twelve long stories that made up the body of the book, I was losing contact with the man I had established in the opening chapter." After working out several solutions, he finally hit upon a device used by Edward Gibbon in his monumental work *Decline and Fall of the Roman Empire.* Writing in faultless prose, Gibbon set down his assertions on the page, presented his evidence as support, and drew his conclusions. "Then," observed Jim, "to reestablish himself with his reader, he added at the foot of each crisp page some of the saltiest, most irreverent and downright witty footnotes ever penned." Michener borrowed Gibbon's literary device to weave together the historical and contemporary strands in *Centennial.* "Therefore, at the conclusion of each of my twelve stories I would add a series of footnotes which would extend the narrative, throw light into the corners of it, and correct misimpressions that might have gathered. It was never my intention to write bawdy or clever notes, in the Gibbon tradition, for I had neither the scholarship nor the wit to do so, but I did desperately want the reader to experience the ebb and flow of historical debate."[14]

Since Michener believed that a novel should be a total experience, he wanted maps to augment the narrative. Jim drew the original maps on anything he had handy: a napkin or a memo pad. These crude drawings, often shaded in colored pencil, of northeastern Colorado and the western United States served as the basis for the later professional maps done by cartographer Jean-Paul Tremblay for the Random House edition. Michener had used maps to great effect in both *The Source* and *Iberia.* "The creation of a universe [for the novel]," Michener remarked, "requires all the art the writer can command; it is a painstaking task which cannot be done quickly, and every component of the finished book must contribute to the illusion."[15]

Michener recorded the process of *Centennial* in meticulous detail. As John Kings noted: "[Jim] entered in a small notebook each segment mailed to Nadia [Orapchuck, Michener's secretary] for final typing, the number of pages, the chapter, and the date sent. Nadia then replied with a series of cards acknowledging the date received, which Jim added to his little notebook."[16] Often the process of circulating portions of the manuscript for editing and proofing was as complex as developing the manuscript itself. "Sometimes," Jim commented, "in the preparation of the manuscript I had segments of it (1) with Erskine, (2) on the way to Erskine, (3) with Nadia being typed, (4) on the way to Nadia to be typed, (5) on the way from Nadia to Erskine, (6) with Kings or Dalton or Laird to be edited, (7) with any of a dozen experts to be read for accuracy. Only the most careful mothering of this flock of papers enabled me to hold them together in some form or other."[17]

Between May and August Michener secluded himself in his Denver apartment writing and rewriting the concluding chapters. During the final throes of the manuscript, Michener's apartment looked like a buffalo wallow, with books tossed askew and papers strewn about his desk and floor; a can of half-eaten pineapple rings stood by the stack of manuscript pages. Mari left him alone to plow through the pages while she went out shopping, meeting friends, and seeing the sights. *Centennial*, however, was not the only thing on Michener's mind that summer. In May Random House published *A Michener Miscellany*, a selection of twenty-five of Jim's best articles for *Reader's Digest* between 1950 and 1970. Michener added his own prefatory notes to the fourteen categories, shedding light on the background and motivations behind the writing of some of the essays. These are some of Michener's best, most insightful essays, relating to cultures of the world and his own personal observations on art collecting and popular music.

The debut of *A Michener Miscellany* was overshadowed that summer by the increasingly bitter Watergate scandal. Wherever Jim went in his travels in the West, the issue repeatedly arose. What should Nixon do? What should the country do with Nixon? These became the two central questions that haunted Michener as he researched and wrote *Centennial*. On the first-year anniversary of the Watergate break-in in June 1973, Michener viewed the situation gravely. On April 30 Nixon's top aides H. R. Haldeman and John Ehrlichman both resigned; his counsel, John Dean, had stepped down earlier. From his apartment in Denver, Jim set aside *Centennial* to write his first public response to the Watergate scandal.

Still an official member of the Nixon administration, Jim felt obligated to support the president and reassure the country that the nation would survive the divisive issue. In a carefully worded and lengthy article for the *New York Times* ("Is America Burning?"), Michener elucidated both sides of the debate. Because his country's future was at stake, he never spent more time weighing the purpose of each word and phrase. "As Watergate began to unfold," he explained in the article, "I had no predetermined villains whom I wanted to see fall. Nor did I have any heroes whom I wished to see triumph. . . . I argued against impeachment and resignation, reasoning that Nixon would have been adequately disciplined by the harsh publicity he was receiving." In effect, Michener expected that Nixon would be humbled enough by Watergate for him to emerge a more effective president. "He will be forced to retreat from his program of executive aggrandizement and return to the sober constraints of the Constitution. . . . Out of this travail," Jim reasoned, "we can get a better Presidency, a better balance in our Government. We can remind future officeholders that they are servants of the people."[18]

The next few months shook Michener's confidence both in President Nixon and the belief that sound judgment would prevail. In mid-July Nixon aide Alexander Butterfield, testifying before the Senate Watergate committee, startled everyone by asserting that Nixon had routinely taped conversations in the Oval Office. The news would provide a way for the committee to substantiate or clear Nixon's role in the cover-up of the scandal. Nixon later rejected the committee's subpoena to turn over the tapes, claiming executive privilege. In October Nixon ordered his attorney general, Elliot Richardson, to fire special prosecutor Archibald Cox, who had refused to accept Nixon's synopsis of certain tapes instead of the tapes themselves. Rather

than comply, Richardson resigned. Cox was then dismissed by Robert
Bork, third in line in the Justice Department. Named the Saturday
Night Massacre, the events further crippled Nixon's efforts to survive
in the White House.

By November Michener was convinced that Nixon was not only
acting in bad faith but was also damaging the nation as well. In a cursory,
venomous opinion piece for the *New York Times*, he bluntly admitted:

> I was wrong. . . . Last June I wrote an essay on Watergate in
> which I spoke of President Nixon with the sympathy and restraint
> owed by any citizens of a democracy to the President. . . .
> When I wrote in June I did so prayerfully, hoping that Mr.
> Nixon would rise to the cruel realities which confronted him.
> I was deceived. Mr. Nixon never intended conciliation. He
> does not know how to bind a nation together, and it's a folly
> to continue hoping that he will learn. He must be neutralized.[19]

What Jim meant by "neutralized" was impeachment or resignation,
nothing more, nothing less. It was one of the first public outcries
for Nixon to be removed from office. Jim soon lost his position on
the Advisory Council for Information. He never, however, regretted his decision to publish his dissatisfaction with Nixon's handling
of Watergate. In the end, he considered it his moral obligation to
the country.

Dubbed by Jim, somewhat presumptuously, as his "birthday gift to
America," *Centennial* took final shape in a Denver high-rise during
late July and early August 1973. Shortly thereafter, the Micheners
returned to Pipersville, so that Jim could begin the intense revision
process with Albert Erskine and Bert Krantz at Random House. That
autumn, while working on the final drafts, Jim returned to western
Colorado, partly to get some western air in his lungs and partly to
do more research on natural history for an article he was writing.
Throughout the winter, he polished *Centennial*. In February he wrote
to Kings and Dalton in Colorado:

I'm working three days a week in New York with Bert Krantz and her eagle-eyed assistant. Five queries a page on a manuscript of 1,300 pages is 6,500 separate questions. They're wonderful . . . they know absolutely nothing about anything west of the Hudson River, so they're especially helpful in checking things I take for granted. . . . We're cutting a lot. The dynamiting of the rattlesnakes: out. Those glorious paragraphs from the local paper on the wreck of the circus train: out. The soldiers hunting bison north of Fort Laramie: out. Two of Lame Beaver's exploits: out. And lots of small paragraphs that added but did not illuminate: out.[20]

It would be difficult for a major novel such as *Centennial* to avoid the epidemic of nihilism that gripped the country during the early 1970s, but the novel is remarkably free of pessimism or despair. It was Jim's first novel of America since *The Fires of Spring*, which was written under vastly different circumstances, when America was emerging from a major world war and feeling a surge of optimism. Written in the darkest days of the Vietnam War, Watergate, and student discontent, *Centennial* remains one of Michener's most enduring works. It is a novel filled with scenes of the frontier, the migrations west, the cattle trails heading northward, those images of western life that Michener first began to consider as early as 1936.

If *Centennial* is a historical novel of the settlement of the West, it is also a cautionary tale of greed, stupidity, and the squandering of the nation's natural resources. Michener is at his best when describing the pioneer experience: a lone white man living in the silent majesty of the Rockies in the 1830s; two exiles fleeing persecution in Pennsylvania for the promise of a new land in the West; a cowboy moving his herd through perilous country; and English dudes carving vast cattle empires in the seas of grass. Other writers, most notably Francis Parkman, Bernard De Voto, A. B. Guthrie, and Wallace Stegner, have described the pioneer experience with beauty, vigor, and accuracy. Michener, however, stands alone in his ability to record how the simplest of details meant life or death out on the prairie. With Wallace Stegner's *Angle of Repose* (Pulitzer Prize 1972) and Larry McMurtry's

Lonesome Dove (Pulitzer Prize 1986), *Centennial*, in the opinion of many readers and critics, is one of the finest epic accounts of the western experience to appear in the last part of the twentieth century.

Centennial was published in September 1974 to widespread critical acclaim. One of the most commendatory reviews was that of Roy Newquist writing in *Palm Springs Life*. The book, wrote Newquist, "is more than a novel. For almost 1,000 pages we are totally absorbed in the story of Colorado and a mythical town called Centennial which sits on the Platte River. . . . It is impossible to name a better novel written by an American. (At the moment, still under its spell, I can't even think of a better novel, period). . . . If you read no other book this season, read *Centennial*. In impact, and total accomplishment, it tops *Hawaii* and *The Source*. As I said it is more than a novel; it is a beautiful and moving experience."[21] Wayne Warga in the *Washington Post* called Michener's novel "a hell of a book. What emerges most clearly is the sense of the American heritage, the formation of this country, and its ideals. We are young, we are new, but we are also durable."[22] Writing in the *New York Magazine*, Eliot Fremont-Smith observed: "Three important things are going for this book . . . one is the momentum of the vast conception; it does carry one along. Another is the sheer bulk of the information that the book imparts— once upon a time a central purpose of the novel. The third is the sense of sharing that Michener constantly evokes. The subject of *Centennial* is our country, our history. If nobody else will throw it a party, Michener will, and everybody's invited in for a piece of cake. You don't throw stones at this kind of a book—though some grinding of same might have helped the old digestion."[23]

In the summer of 1974, when the battle for the presidential tapes reached its height, Hobe Lewis devised a plan that would provide Richard Nixon a graceful exit from his predicament. As Nixon's personal friend, Lewis hated the idea of impeachment or resignation, both of which loomed as likely possibilities in the coming weeks. He asked Michener to rally support for his plan among Democrats, while Lewis approached Republicans. Lewis's plan called for Nixon to make a brief confession on national television by admitting that he had made a mistake by ordering the break-in at Democratic headquarters at the Watergate. If he made such an admission, figured Lewis, key people in the bipartisan leadership might allow him to escape without impeachment or resignation. When Michener and Lewis had secured the signatures of many in Congress, they headed to the White House, where Nixon's secretary, Rosemary Woods, informed them that the president was seeing no one—not even his former treasury secretary and special adviser, John Connally, who had been trying to get into the Oval Office for the last three weeks. Thus Lewis's plan died on Nixon's secretary's desk.

On July 25 the Supreme Court ordered Nixon to turn over the tapes, which he reluctantly agreed to do. Three days later the House Judiciary Committee approved two articles of impeachment against the president. On August 8, his support evaporating, Nixon resigned. Gathering his staff, he read them his somber, enigmatic farewell statement: "Always remember, others may hate you, but those that hate you do not win unless you hate them back—and then you destroy yourself." "His farewell statement," wrote Michener, "was so extraordinary that we have to assume that there had been a total deterioration."[24] Only years later would Jim—or the nation for that matter—understand the depths into which Nixon had taken the government and the country.

Jim celebrated his sixty-eighth birthday on the hill in Pipersville in February 1975. The nation seemed suddenly and delightfully boring: the war in Vietnam was nearly out of the headlines, the presidency of Gerald Ford was remarkably free of scandal, the college campuses had returned to places of learning, and the hill itself was a place of genuine pastoral beauty, even when snow mottled the hills and the bare branches reached lifelessly to the sky.

The success of *Centennial* had left Michener feeling particularly upbeat. He had wanted to return home with a triumphant novel, and *Centennial*'s popularity and critical reception proved to be greater than he expected. He had not written a complex, multigenerational novel since *The Source* in 1965. *Centennial* was as much proof to himself that he was mentally capable of such a feat as it was to his readers and fellow writers. As he approached his thirtieth year at the forefront of American writing, he was quite aware of his strengths as well as his defects. He had discovered the magic of creating a universe in which a reader could spend a few weeks or so. On the other hand, he did not consider himself a great stylist, a good developer of plot, or a great creator of vivid characters. The literati, who always view success with intense scrutiny, thought of Michener as something of an outcast. He appealed to the middle-class reader; his novels were unwieldy and followed a fairly predictable pattern of country and culture hopping. John Leonard of the *New York Times* regretted that Michener in the 1950s developed the large historical novel, preferring instead the more intimate *Tales of the South Pacific* and *The Fires of Spring*. Another critic thought his books were more suitable as a piece of furniture than as a work of art. "Don't drop one on your foot," cracked another pundit.[25] Most critics agreed that Michener lacked a sense of tragedy. Random House, of course, thought him one of the most bankable authors in the world. In America, he was an icon, which no doubt made him feel that he was destined for immortality. Well into his career, Michener continued to distrust the value of criticism to his work: "Few people listen to critics more than I. If Vincent Canby says a movie is good, I go see it. If Jonathan Yardley or Anatole Broyard tells me a book is first rate, I go buy it. If John Canaday or Jack Kroll assures me that a picture is worth looking at, I look. But I never bother with what critics say about my own work; indeed, I refuse to read them. A critic is most helpful in advising you how to spend your money; he is useless in telling you how to spend your life."[26]

For more than a year he had been researching and writing a nonfiction book about America's national obsession with sports, which, like many of his topics, had been marinating for several decades. Jim had always maintained that engaging in sports at an early age had saved him from becoming a juvenile delinquent. While playing basketball in high school and at Swarthmore, he became a collector of sports trivia and statistics. "I could recite the batting order and batting averages of every team in two leagues," he once commented.[27] Early interest and his later involvement as a fan of Philadelphia sports teams—the

Eagles, Phillies, Flyers, and 76ers—gave him the impetus to write a comprehensive book about the American sports scene.

As early as 1973 he sat down and discussed the project in Doylestown with Joe Avenick, a Philadelphia sportswriter, and Ed Piszek, a business entrepreneur and millionaire who, as president of the company, made Mrs. Paul's Kitchens a leader in the frozen-food industry. Piszek, known as "Mr. Fishcake" because his company sold them, helped finance Jim's ninety-page patriotic tract *The Quality of Life* in the early 1970s and was eager to assist him in another project. Piszek suggested the idea of a sports book that Avenick could help Michener research and write. Since Michener's heart was in sports but he had limited knowledge of the jargon and inside operations, Avenick's services could be especially critical.

During the writing phase in the summer of 1975, Michener accompanied Piszek, Avenick, and John Cardinal Krol of Philadelphia to the Holy Land. Later, Avenick collaborated in the writing of an article with Jim for the *Saturday Evening Post* titled "Pilgrimage for Peace," which appeared under Michener's byline, about Krol's travels to the Middle East. As it turned out, Avenick would play a more crucial and perhaps a more controversial role in the writing of *Sports in America*.

Avenick was hired by Piszek to help Michener research the book on sports. As Avenick explained in an interview, Michener would outline the various points he wanted to cover in the book. Avenick would then research those points and write the draft that Michener would use to write the finished manuscript.[28] The degree to which Jim used Avenick, without giving him any credit on the book's cover, became a point of contention.

In his autobiography, Michener clearly explains how he employed researchers on projects:

> How big of a research staff do I employ on a full time basis? One: me. On two occasions, the book on sports and *Centennial*, I had the part-time help of two different bright young men, but they were assigned to me by others who owed me courtesies that could not be discharged by cash payments, and I must

stress that they were finders and judges of information, not writers of prose. When such helpers bring their research material to my attention, I still do all the reading, evaluating and writing.[29]

According to Avenick, his services went far beyond a mere "finder of data." "I wrote the rough draft of Chapters 2 through 12," claimed Avenick, "using the notebooks and outline that he had given me. I then did oodles of research, re-writing, copyediting, proofreading and the index. Along the way, Michener and I traveled throughout the U.S. to sporting events. He also sent me alone to some events."[30] In his "Author's Note" at the beginning of *Sports in America*, Jim acknowledged Avenick's role this way: "The writing of this book was aided considerably by the research help provided by Joseph Avenick. A former sportswriter for various newspapers, he has an affection for games, a familiarity with the players, a knowledge of their records, and acquaintance with the literature about them. . . . Working with him was both instructive and enjoyable."

To what extent did Michener rely on his researchers/writers? In most cases, his methods were aboveboard. But at least in two cases— *Sports in America* and four years later in *The Covenant*—it may be apparent that Michener was guilty of excessive collaboration without proper acknowledgment. As for *Sports in America*, Avenick put in a great deal of work with little recognition. There were good reasons, of course, for Avenick to remain in the shadows for this book. The first was Michener's self-imposed deadline, which meant that he had to compress years into months and months into days to reach a satisfactory end to the book. He needed Avenick's legwork and writing skills to reach that goal. The second was his reputation, which by 1975 had become considerable. He wished to share no glory with *Sports in America*. It would bear only Michener's name on the cover, even though Avenick played a central role in its development. Throughout the research and writing phase, Michener maintained total control. After Avenick turned over his drafts to him, Jim went to work revising them. However, since good nonfiction prose is difficult to revise, Jim let most of it stand with few alterations.

Later, in a letter to Avenick, Jim even mentioned Joe's vital role in *Sports in America*: "Your ability to write the first draft of nearly every chapter and your keen eye regarding sporting characters and sports facts/figures has [*sic*] saved me a tremendous amount of angst. . . . I also anticipate continuing our successful collaboration when we begin the Maryland novel this fall. I suspect you'll be visiting me quite often in St. Michaels."[31]

Avenick's role clearly exceeded that of a researcher, but Jim never admitted it. Perhaps as a way to appease Avenick, Michener asked him for assistance on his next major novel.

In spring 1976, just prior to the publication of *Sports in America*, when he was traveling constantly, Jim met Joe Avenick for dinner at the Green Turtle Inn on Islamorada in the Florida Keys, near Avenick's home. Avenick introduced Jim to an attractive divorcée in her mid-thirties who went by the name of Melissa, sometimes called "Missy." She lived in town and had two horses in training at the racetrack in Miami. Jim and Melissa quickly became friends and companions.

For the next eight years or so, Michener and Melissa had a clandestine relationship. He frequently dated her when he traveled to Florida. At times she accompanied him on trips around America. Twice they flew to Europe together, once to the Isle of Capri.

Although she had little idea of Jim's celebrity status when they first met, she quickly became enamored of his power in the literary world. Melissa was a safe person in which to confide: unattached, vivacious, outside the world of publishing, financially comfortable. At times she was capable of salty humor and an off-color joke. She never pressured Jim to leave Mari for her. Several months after he met Melissa, he began a novella titled "Matecumbe"—a love story with a character based on Melissa set in the Florida Keys. Despite Michener's attempts to have it published, Random House twice turned him down. Erskine went so far as to label the book "iconoclastic self-abuse, better suited for a supermarket tabloid."[32] To this day, "Matecumbe" remains among a number of Michener's works, including one on Austria (given to Joe Avenick by Michener), Jim's Russian novel (now in the University of Northern Colorado archives), and a manuscript on fortune-telling (also at the University of Northern Colorado), that never reached print. Neither the manuscript titled "Matecumbe" nor the one on Austria has been fully authenticated. As for Melissa, she seems to have disappeared from Jim's life in the early 1980s. However, she most likely inspired the character of Melissa "Missy" Peckham, the feisty, industrious heroine of Michener's 1988 novel, *Alaska.*

Because Jim traveled so much and engaged in various writing projects, Mari never discovered her husband's relationship. On July 1, three days before the nation's two hundredth birthday celebration, Jim and Mari packed up and headed to their cottage in the fishing hamlet of St. Michaels, Maryland, located on Chesapeake Bay several miles and virtually a few hundred years away from Washington, D.C., and Baltimore, across the water. (According to Jim, they moved in at 10:00 in the morning, and he was at the typewriter by 11:00 "with a full head of steam.")[33] Mostly composed of watermen who sailed daily on the bay in search of crabs, oysters, and clams and retired professionals from the eastern seaboard who came there to escape, the village exuded maritime charm. Overhead in autumn, several thousands of Canada geese winged south from James Bay, often blackening the sky with their numbers.

The previous summer the Micheners had rented a white, two-bedroom, furnished bungalow four miles from town. A year later they would buy the place. Loblolly pines flanked the stone-colored drive. The front of the house faced Broad Creek, which ran into the Choptank River and the Chesapeake. After moving in, Michener painted his name on the mailbox fronting the road, signaling that he had settled in the region for a prolonged stay.

Chesapeake and Michener seemed like a perfect fit. With hundreds of miles of serrated coastline and numerous coves, inlets, and islands, Chesapeake was a region rich in natural and historical possibilities. Rogues and rascals colored its past, much like the characters who clinked their spurs on the streets of *Centennial.* In many ways, *Chesapeake* was the antithesis of his Colorado novel. Whereas eastern Colorado was landlocked, semiarid, and dusty, Maryland's Eastern Shore was much like a Constable painting: silvery, watery, and delicious. "I decided to write the book because of the bay and its people," Michener observed. "The area has always captivated me. It's a great body of water, a great inland sea. I first sailed the bay in about 1927 when a college friend at Swarthmore had a boat at Rock Hall. I kept coming back to it, sailing with other people who had boats here, over the years. But all I ever knew was the water, the sailing. I knew a great deal about the bay itself, but nothing about the land of the interior. It was almost as if it were populated by aliens."[34] As was customary with a Michener project, he read voraciously on the area. "I work on the theory of total immersion," Michener quipped. "I'm a Baptist in that respect. A man is saved only when he goes all the way under. This sprinkling water on the head ain't much my style."[35] In addition to books on natural and social history, he preferred two books about the Chesapeake area: John Barth's *The Sot-Weed Factor* and William W. Warner's Pulitzer Prize–winning *Beautiful Swimmers: Watermen, Crabs, and the Chesapeake Bay.* These books, he felt, captured the spirit of Chesapeake, and, of course, he was anticipating that his novel would also. While in Maryland, Michener met Barth, an Eastern Shore native, several times, mainly at Johns Hopkins University in Baltimore, where Barth taught writing courses.

Jim quickly converted the spare bedroom into an office by moving in his boxes of books and a heavy oak desk. He leaned paintings against the wall, where they stayed for months. A portable record player stood beside the desk, and a Pepsi-Cola carton served as a prop for any book he wished to examine. Wires snaked across the oak floor. Outside, two herons, which the Micheners named Victor and Victoria, had taken up residence in the semistagnant pool behind the house. In the late afternoon, a neighbor's Irish setter named Brandy often swaggered by to join Michener on his walks through the nearby woods. For the last few years, Michener had walked in pain, the result of the deteriorating bone in his hip. A sturdy walking stick assisted him on these jaunts, but the nagging discomfort of bone rubbing on bone became part of his life.

Mari's role had changed little in the twenty years of their marriage. She made Jim's appointments, answered the telephone, retrieved books from the library, cleaned the house, and occasionally cooked. She saw to it that Jim got his rest, watched his diet, and stayed on course with his writing. Jim fretted that he was a nuisance working at home. "It's most difficult for a wife to have a husband who works at home," he wrote privately. "Why doesn't he get in the car and drive down to the station and go into New York like other decent men? What in the hell is he doing around the house when I want to clean, and who does he think he is asking me to get lunch for him? I'm reasonably certain that Mrs. Beethoven would have been a lot happier if Ludwig had a good nine to five job teaching scales at the local junior high. . . . Mari has been unusual in her capacity to adjust to having her man at home throughout the day."[36]

In July 1976 he began the plot outline for *Chesapeake*. To avoid any arguments over dates and events in the region's history, Jim made the locales and characters entirely fictional. "I didn't use real settings or any real people," he explained. "Of course the bay itself is real and the Choptank River, and their geographical relationship to the Western Shore rivers like the Rappahannock and so on. I've tried to be very careful about that." He avoided using the names of actual towns like Trappe or Easton because it would put them into a historical setting, "where everything you say is erroneous, or at least up for review."[37] He therefore invented four imaginary sites and placed them on a map where there existed only marshland or vacant coastline.

Michener wanted to avoid a genteel novel of the Eastern Shore. Shaping his characters from tough, hard-bitten watermen and their women, oyster dredgers, crabbers, and the like, he created underdogs fighting for their own values against the powerful landowners inland. He also focused on slavery in the Eastern Shore and modern-day race relations. According to Michener, the slavery problem evolved into our contemporary difficulties with race relations, and both should be at the forefront of our national conscience—slavery for our historical perspective and race relations as something we should always strive to improve. "It would be very deficient if I did not cover these issues," he remarked.[38]

Jim invited Joe Avenick down from New Jersey to assist him with the editing phase. Michener and Avenick labored over the fictional family and place names in the novel. The two would toss back and forth a name. Michener would scramble the letters and pronounce it a different way. He might even spell it backward, weighing the euphony of the word. Through playful banter, Michener and Avenick corrupted the real town name of Pocomoke City in southern Maryland into the fictional "Patamoke." "Most trips ended," remarked Avenick, "with my taking home some pages, reading them at home, and coming back to talk about suggested edits with Michener. I had nothing to do with structure and plot, just copyediting, i.e., making sure the same word was spelled the same throughout; verifying facts, the integrity of sequence; and period accuracies."[39]

Through the fall and early winter of 1976, Michener wrote the early draft of *Chesapeake*, aided by a host of researchers who fed him a constant stream of technical information. As was customary, he acknowledged these helpers at the beginning of the finished book. While he toiled in the mornings, the afternoons were reserved for research and enjoying the surroundings. To accomplish the former, he spent numerous hours at the boat-building yard of Jim Richardson, who briefed Jim on the techniques of transforming oak logs into hand-hewn vessels. Or he helped dredge oysters through the long winter afternoons. "After I spent two days aboard a dredge boat," he confessed, "I came home and told Mari I didn't care what she was paying for oysters, it wasn't enough. That's hard work!"[40]

Michener would have preferred to work straight through on a manuscript, but often there were inevitable distractions and interruptions. In January 1977 he was invited to the White House to receive the Presidential Medal of Freedom, the nation's highest civilian award. A number of his Doylestown friends, including the Silvermans, attended the ceremony in the East Room. Along with twenty-one other prominent Americans, including General Omar Bradley and artist Georgia O'Keeffe, Michener received his award from President Ford. Michener's Medal of Freedom citation reads in part: "Author, teacher, and popular historian, James Michener has entranced a generation with his compelling essays and novels . . . the prolific writings of this master storyteller have expanded the knowledge and enriched the lives of millions."

Meanwhile, Ed Piszek had emerged as a significant patron of Michener's art. "For a decade," Piszek recalled in his memoir, "I had admired Jim's work from afar. Though I was no writer, our ambitions and interests seemed not so every different."[41] Piszek began funding some of Jim's trips abroad, particularly when they involved promoting Polish American culture. Michener, who was financially secure, nevertheless willingly accepted Piszek's friendship and patronage. In January Piszek and his staff at Mrs. Paul's Kitchen began collaboration with *Reader's Digest* to bring Michener and his world to public television. *James Michener's World,* a series of (a fifth was added later on Poland) four programs highlighting Israel, Hawaii, Spain, and the South Pacific ran on PBS from summer 1977 through summer 1978. The series, which led viewers on a travelogue of countries found in Michener's works, featured Michener as host and narrator. His role meant extensive travel around the world; often he flew late at night back to Maryland to resume writing *Chesapeake.*

Jim felt honored to follow in the footsteps of scholars and educators who hosted popular programs on PBS, men like Kenneth Clark, whose *Civilisation* series was a worldwide success. *James Michener's World* achieved a stunning ratings success for PBS. Although critics praised Michener's writing credentials and erudition, some criticized his steely reserve on camera. Writing in the *San Francisco Chronicle,* Terence O'Flaherty observed: "Michener is a man of cold curiosity, voluminous knowledge and retentive memory, but he lacks the sensitivity that comes with a sense of humor and without it he is a pompous bore."[42] The *Hollywood Reporter* was equally negative: "The biggest disappointment of all is Michener himself who turns out to be a diffident screen presence with an earnestly dull narrative style."[43]

Nearly exhausted from a regimen of travel, Michener returned home in the spring of 1977 and by early summer had finished *Chesapeake.* At this point in the development of the manuscript, he called in one of his chief researchers, Dickson Preston, an authority on the history of the Eastern Shore and a biographer of Frederick Douglass, to read the draft and edit the most minor of mistakes. By now, Michener was aware that his age might be a factor in making simple errors in the text. So Preston did "a page by page check for accuracy. At his request I was tough to the extent of feeling that I was a nagger or a nit-picker."[44] When Preston was finished, Michener turned over the manuscript to Erskine, Krantz, and a copyeditor, the three of whom spent three months further combing it.

In summer 1978 *Chesapeake* made publishing history when advance orders, totaling 250,000 copies, helped make it the number one best seller even before publication. Like *Hawaii* and *Centennial, Chesapeake* is a novel of settlement and the difficulties that ensue when people abuse their authority and squander the environment. Spanning nearly five centuries, the novel weaves a tale of the lives and misfortunes of five families—the Steeds, Turlocks, Paxmores, Caters, and Cavenys. It also includes generous slices of history: pirates, evil slavers, sea battles, oyster conflicts, Cromwell's castigation of Catholics and Puritans' oppression of Quakers, and meetings with Ben Franklin, John C. Calhoun, Henry Clay, Daniel Webster, George Washington, and Adolf Hitler. In addition, Michener includes the Watergate scandal and the lives of Canada geese on the Eastern Shore. In true Michener style, little, if anything, was overlooked. Once again, he returns to themes of religious tolerance and ethnic understanding as the necessary underpinnings of a civilization.

Critics from the major newspapers, wary of record presales of *Chesapeake,* continued their barrage of Michener's art. Boyd Gibbons in the *Washington Post* proclaimed: "The novel is, at times, impressive, for Michener is a tireless researcher; he always has the story—if not the reader—by the throat, and some of his passages of action and violence are vividly written. On the whole, however, I found *Chesapeake* exasperating to read. When the moment calls for humor, subtlety, or even silence, Michener too often either leaps onstage to lecture on the obvious, or he reaches for *Pomp and Circumstance* and proceeds to play it on an atomic organ. . . . *Chesapeake* is an interesting and ambitious quilt of history, and with some nice touches here and there, and the telling never lags. But overall there is a shallowness about this book and the people in it. An experienced writer has become careless with the craft of good writing, and it shows."[45] Jonathan Yardley in the *New York Times* and Gary Wills in the *New York Review of Books* offered their own insights but generally echoed these sentiments. More receptive comments came from reviewers at smaller newspapers, many of whom had followed Michener's long career. Writing in the *New Hope (Pennsylvania) Gazette*, Charles Shaw observed: "This is the best book Michener has written. . . . It reads better than his other long books; in fact it reads beautifully, flowing more like *The Fires of Spring* and *Sayonara*. It is never the least bit wooden as, I regret to say, parts of his other opuses are."[46] For many readers, perhaps because they are familiar with its setting and knowledgeable of its history, *Chesapeake* is Michener's finest work, the closest he came to penning a great novel about a culturally rich section of America.

After finishing *Chesapeake*, the Micheners decided to remain in St. Michaels rather than return immediately to Pipersville. They would end up staying in the cottage near the bay for the next four years. The village united in protecting their privacy while according them the status of a royal couple.

CHAPTER 16

The Covenant

On a cool soggy day in New York in mid-March 1978, Tony Oursler, an editor at *Reader's Digest*, telephoned Michener at the Random House offices on East Fiftieth Street, where Michener and Albert Erskine were hashing out the final corrections for *Chesapeake*. Oursler wanted to talk to Jim about a project that had crossed his desk. Pulling on his raincoat, Jim walked up to the University Club. Over a glass of beer, Oursler mentioned that a young South African writer, Errol Lincoln Uys (pronounced "Ace"), who worked as an international editor for the *Reader's Digest* in New York, had raised the possibility of writing a novel of South Africa, an idea that Oursler thought was brilliant and wanted Jim's counsel. South African apartheid was an incendiary issue in America, and its development, reasoned Oursler, would make a fascinating book. Working at the Pleasantville, New York, headquarters of *Reader's Digest*, Uys was a former editor in chief of the magazine's South Africa edition who had entered the United States in July 1977 on a visa sponsored by the *Digest*.

For several minutes Oursler and Michener talked over the project. Jim liked it immediately. He had first thought of a novel of South Africa as early as 1971, when he had traveled to several surrounding countries, including Angola, Rhodesia (Zimbabwe), Mozambique, and

Swaziland. "The land was a revelation," he remarked, "one of the most beautiful I have seen. The people were outgoing, eager to talk about their problems and challenging to be with. And the sense of history about to happen was overwhelming."[1] He returned home determined to write a novel of South Africa. Basic themes he wished to include were the Bushmen moving south across the desert, the coming of the Huguenots, the Great Trek of the Dutch, and the Mfecane, the amazing uprising of the Zulu in the 1820s. He also wished to include modern South Africa and the issue of apartheid. "But when I came to draft the novel," Jim explained, "it dealt with all these matters from the outside, as seen by a visitor. The novel had to be written from the inside, and I did not at the time know enough to write in that fashion. So I dropped the subject and wrote instead *Centennial* and then *Chesapeake.*"[2]

Oursler and Jim agreed that the current ambitious novel needed someone of Michener's stature to bring it to successful completion, something Oursler had discussed with Uys. Uys proposed that he and Michener might work together on the project, benefiting from each other's ideas. In considering this partnership, Jim had to weigh two things: first, was this a writer-editor-researcher who could pull the enormous load of the project and yet add creative ideas, and second, could they negotiate their differences professionally and peaceably?

In the meantime, Uys got to work polishing the forty-page proposal for the South African novel, which he sent to Michener in April. Reading it in St. Michaels, Jim declared: "I had the pleasure of reading Uys's notes on a proposed book about South Africa. I was impressed with his organizing ability, and his keen insight into the problem of arranging a mass of material so as to be useable, especially in fictional form. . . . We have both done a great deal of thinking on this matter, along our separate lines, and we have come up with striking parallelisms, as I suppose any two reasonably intelligent persons would, faced with identical data." Jim quickly telephoned Oursler, announcing that he and Uys should begin work "right away."[3]

For Uys, a young writer who had been in America less than a year, working with one of the country's leading writers was both intimidating and exciting. At thirty-four years of age, he looked forward to a career as a successful novelist. He envisioned a book that would capture South Africa's rich and violent history and one that would fit nicely with Michener's concept. Michener commented: "I am mightily impressed with Uys's keen instinct for weaving strands together, and I am sure I could learn something from him. . . . I would like nothing better than to sit quietly with him and kick these ideas about for some days to see which are fruitful for my approach."[4]

From the outset, Uys was aware of his precarious role in the South Africa project. "I was an employee of *Reader's Digest*," he explained, "which sponsored my move to the United States. My immigration status and that of my family was [*sic*] entirely dependent on my good standing with the *Digest*. . . . The arrangement made between Michener and the *Digest* was that he would engage my services as editor/researcher and that my salary would be a write off against future payments by the magazine for rights to *The Covenant*. That my involvement was to go far beyond this became apparent from the start."[5]

Uys did not raise the subject of collaboration with Michener. They never discussed whether Uys would be a coauthor or have his name appear as "with" on the cover. "I was in no position to make assertions regarding my role in a book authored by one of the magazine's star contributors," Uys explained.[6]

Uys traveled to St. Michaels in May to begin work with Michener. Working closely together over the next two weeks, they "thrashed out the framework for the novel, its plotting and family lines, and its major characters."[7] Uys had begun using the future name of the novel, "The Covenant," which refers to the Day of the Covenant, a religious holiday in South Africa commemorating the vow to God the Voortrekkers took on the eve of the battle of Blood River in 1838. After a decisive victory, the white settlers interpreted their triumph as a sign from God that they were to rule this land and subjugate other peoples who threatened their covenant with the Almighty. South Africa was their Canaan, their promised land, and they would defend this belief well into the twentieth century. Michener thought the title entirely appropriate:

> Errol's suggestion that the novel be titled *The Covenant* is a sturdy one. . . . But I would not like, at this time, to fix upon

a title, for I have never done so until the manuscript was finished, and even then I have usually left the final decision in the hands of Random House. I am not good at titles and feel that naming a book too soon during the gestation period puts a curse on it. But I see much merit in *The Covenant*; it's better than anything I had in mind, and I will keep it strongly on file."[8]

After witnessing two decades of racial unrest and contemplating heavily on the subject, Michener felt that he had a platform to address the intractable white-controlled government of South Africa. American blacks had made enormous gains in the past few years, and he predicted such success for other countries on the verge of integration. He pointed to Hawaii as one of the best experiments in racial harmony. However, if he saw a willingness in Honolulu to achieve integration, he did not share the same vision for Cape Town or Johannesburg. Nor did he feel that Japan or India had made enough progress on this issue. In addition to writing a novel on the evils of racial separation, Jim assumed his role, like so much in his life, as if it were his ethical duty.

Michener studied South African history, particularly the issue of apartheid, with careful scrutiny. Although South Africa had a long history of racial discrimination and white superiority, apartheid was not officially adopted by the South African government until 1948, when the white Afrikaner Nationalist Party rose to power. This system of legal discrimination allowed the five million whites to revoke the rights of more than twenty-five million nonwhites. According to the mandate of the Afrikaner Nationalist Party, the goals of apartheid were to affirm racial separation and maintain white authority. "The preservation of the pure race tradition of the Boerevolk," proclaimed the party, "must be protected at all costs in all possible ways as a holy pledge entrusted to us by our ancestors as part of God's plan with our People. Any movement, school, or individual who sins against this must be dealt with as a racial criminal."[9] The ensuing laws classified people according to three racial groups: white; Bantu, or black Africans; and coloured, or people of mixed heritage. Later, a fourth group composed of Indians and Pakistanis was added. Laws dictated the regions where people in a group could live, what jobs they could hold, and the schools they could attend. Blacks could not own land, engage in political activity, or exercise any of the freedoms associated with a twentieth-century democracy. Blacks were forbidden from entering white-zoned areas, unless they were domestic workers whose jobs took them into those restricted sections. The Pass Laws Act of 1952 required that blacks carry a passbook, known as a dompas, which contained the person's fingerprints, photograph, personal information, place of employment, and permission from the government to work in a certain zone. The person's employer also wrote a performance report in the dompas. If a worker offended his or her employer, the employer could decline to endorse the passbook, which could prevent the employee from returning to work.

International condemnation of apartheid coupled with resistance by South African residents—black, coloured, and white—led to United Nations sanctions against the government of South Africa in 1977. Slowly, the government adopted a series of reforms, which included allowing the formation of black labor unions and encouraging some political activity by blacks. When Michener and Uys began their work in early 1978, the situation was tense and volatile but showed signs of improvement.

After completing two months of intense work on *The Covenant*, Michener left for a research trip to South Africa, arriving in Johannesburg on July 11, 1978. Uys arranged for Philip Bateman, a former *Reader's Digest* editor living in Cape Town, to serve as Michener's guide in South Africa. According to Jim, however, Bateman ended up being his escort, interpreter, ombudsman, driver, and overall guru during the trip. On the drive from the airport, Michener turned to Bateman: "One thing we need to establish is this isn't a light trip. We need to keep the press away and it's not lots of parties and drinking. It's a working research journey."[10] Jim further remarked that he wanted to keep the trip as secret and low-key as possible.

Before embarking on the circuitous six-thousand-mile journey through South Africa, Bateman sized up his famous visitor from America: "He had a razor sharp mind. Many people found him slow and sonorous, which he indeed could be. Yet when he identified someone as bright he would produce questions in rapid fire succession, exchanging information at an enormous pace. I asked him why he was such a chameleon. 'I assess them first and see how much they can handle.'"[11]

To accommodate Michener's intense curiosity, Bateman had set up a schedule of appointments that was a veritable "Who's Who of South Africa," ranging from the leading anthropologists and scientists to the prime minister, a diamond tycoon, and a "famous liberal cleric who was under house arrest."[12] Studded with the country's leading scholars, academicians, historians, and artisans, it was an itinerary worthy of a foreign potentate.

While Jim toured South Africa, Uys busied himself strengthening the storyline and reworking the character relationships. He exchanged letters with Jim on these issues. A typical one from Uys ran: "Our missionary could well be Vera Saltwood's brother . . . an insufferable young man who'd be at his peak when slavery ends. He could be cranked into the 1813–1833 period without difficulty and be a valuable link to the Xhosa."[13] While on the road, Michener responded:

> I liked your suggestion about the brother-escort, but now feel it has to be a Saltwood. The more I work with this material the more convinced I become that is the way to go. We shall have so many characters as it is, that the closer we weave the net the better: keeping the name Saltwood before the reader will be an asset, and the more varied the performers under the name the better . . . please continue to give this your most careful thought, as mine produces little except a conviction that we need the character and can use him to tremendous effect if we can come up with the proper structure.[14]

After a week of touring museums, visiting memorials, and interviewing prominent citizens in Cape Town, including an authority on Bushmen, Michener and Bateman began their overland motor journey by heading for Swellandam and Port Elizabeth. Several days down the road, Jim noted: "I'm traveling with a man who absolutely refuses to ask anyone where anything is; as a result I'm seeing one hell of a lot of South Africa."[15] By August 21 Michener was back in St. Michaels and, characteristically, back at the typewriter. He arrived in Maryland prepared to write what was arguably the most difficult novel of his career.

As he predicted, the first three chapters came off the typewriter quickly and were on their way to Nadia to be typed by the middle of September. "I will spend all of October on television," he told her. "Then Uys and I will resume in November and keep working until we finish, God willing."[16] Michener planned the writing process in three phases: the original manuscript, or the first draft, with few outside reviews; the "real manuscript," with Michener's and Uys's revisions, ready to be typed by Nadia; and the final manuscript, which was ready for Erskine and Krantz at Random House to make their additions and corrections. The process would ultimately take more than a year and a half to complete.

His six-week trek through South Africa had provided Michener with additional information he needed to begin the book, but this enterprising of a novel needed more than a quick education in a foreign culture. It needed the expertise of someone who was raised in its schools, was steeped in its history, was familiar with its struggles, and had experienced the misery of apartheid firsthand. Errol Uys brought a nuanced and informed perspective to *The Covenant*. He was adopted by parents who divorced when he was in his teens. While he freelanced for newspapers, he drifted from one odd job to another, once selling women's underwear and studying law. Down-and-out at one time, he came home to find his roach-infested room had been burglarized. "The thief had a sense of humor," admitted Uys. "Finding several pairs of cufflinks, he stole one from each pair." He bummed around South Africa, absorbing its heritage and specialized speech patterns. After landing a reporting job at the *Johannesburg Star*, he began writing feature stories about the drought in South Africa, the destruction of precious forests, and the shantytowns of Soweto. "Not long after my trek around South Africa," Uys wrote, "I took a job as editor of the *Post*'s Cape Town edition. I ran a newspaper in the heart of District Six, the Harlem of Cape Town, a vibrant, jazzy, violent quarter, where kings and jesters like Sydney Magoni would walk into my office and strip—to prove he was the most-stabbed man (fifty times) in the district."[17] In the early 1970s he came to work as editor in chief for the South Africa bureau of *Reader's Digest*, a position he would hold until his immigration to America in 1976.

On September 11 Uys met Jim at St. Michaels, where Jim related the details of his South African adventure. Errol brought with him more storyline suggestions and changes for Michener to consider. Since *The Covenant* involved the lives of three families and their descendants—the Van Doorns, who were Dutch; the Saltwoods, who were English; and the Nxumalos, who were black—both Uys and Michener sought balance and equal treatment of the families. The two agreed that the Van Doorns and the Saltwoods could be successfully developed. The experience of blacks in South Africa, however, needed more research to attain parity with the other families.

For unknown reasons, Bateman had not introduced Michener to any black leaders while in South Africa. At their September meeting, Uys suggested that he would spearhead some introductions for Michener and also begin developing the characters in greater depth and detail. Late in September he wrote Michener: "I met the problem of contacting South African blacks head-on; and came up with an immediate breakthrough. . . . I've confirmed two participants—David Sibeko, the 'political' [leader] with a good Transvaal background and grandfather who rode with the Boers, and Bernard Magubane, Associate Professor of History at the University of Connecticut, a specialist in a 'black' view of SA history."[18] Single-handedly, Uys continued to arrange interviews with important leaders connected to South Africa's struggle for equality.

While Uys worked and researched in New York, Michener continued writing the first draft. He asked Uys to work independently and not bother him with revisions until the first draft was complete. Uys complied but periodically sent him suggestions. In December Uys wrote that he had made significant progress on chapters dealing with the Voortrekkers and the sections on apartheid.[19] As Uys further probed the divisive issue of apartheid, he confessed to Jim: "I know how distressed you felt having committed yourself to the apartheid chapter. Believe me, my own despair grows apace. At the bottom of it, I suppose, there is some guilt at not having done that much more, over there, toward helping break down the 'obscenity' of the system. That word keeps cropping up."[20] Eight months into the research of *The Covenant*, combined with intensive discussions with Michener, Uys believed that he, in fact, had entered into collaboration with Jim on the book. Although Michener never mentioned how he was treating Uys's involvement, it was apparent to Uys that he was playing a significant role in the writing of the novel. Moreover, he thought Michener would acknowledge his dedication by including him as a coauthor, as "with Errol Uys" on the cover, or offer him a share of the royalties. As the writing progressed into the new year, the bond between the famous novelist and his young protégé increased and intensified. "We had some violent arguments on some points," noted Michener, "on some of which I knew more than he did; but usually he had a keen sense of what should be done and was invaluable."[21]

When Michener felt that his draft was ready for review by experts, he began circulating sections and chapters to designated authorities. Most of the experts resided in South Africa, but some lived in various parts of Europe and America. On each chapter or section in question, Michener typed a prefatory note: "This m.s. is being submitted to you in hopes that you will give it your most careful attention. Absolutely everything is up for review: the data from your field of expertise; the language; the customs; the inferences; and above all the major facts which might be in error. I would appreciate your guidance on even the most minute points, as I always strive to avoid ridiculous error."[22]

Throughout the first six months of 1979, chapter reviews and comments filtered back to Michener, who read and studied each response carefully. He called the reports "invaluable, for they put me in touch with the wisest people in the world. And I sometimes think they enjoy catching me in error."[23] A typical one came from Philip Tobias: "Thinking over the chapter as a whole in the wee hours of the morning, perhaps I should indicate what may be a fundamental problem. The chapter is based on the assumption that robust australopithecines (Brutish) and Gracile australopithecines (Australopithecus africanus) lived side by side, that is, were contemporary over a lengthy period. In fact, there is little evidence for such contemporaneity."[24]

When Uys read parts of the manuscript, he had his own criticism of Michener's handling of the South African Boer type: "Not one of the characters even suggest[s] a picture of the 'frontier Boer,' i.e., the wilder, independent, hard as nails individual. What we have is the picture that evokes an American *Centennial*-type character. . . . Sure we might argue the American reader only needs a simplistic view. But it's wrong, I think, to offer him this [version] simply. It just was not so."[25]

Uys returned to St. Michaels to complete the final revision phase between September 8 and December 21, 1979. Often Uys handed Michener whole prose passages running several pages for Jim to scan and use in the narrative. Jim would alter them slightly, reword sentences, or copy them verbatim into the text. Such behavior at least confirmed in the back of Uys's mind that Michener would offer him a coauthorship or part of the royalties. Neither was forthcoming. Working fifteen-hour days, plodding line by line, the two went through the manuscript. By the middle of December, their work almost complete, Uys worried that Michener might not fully acknowledge his contributions. This became apparent when Michener showed Uys his planned "Author's Note" that would be placed at the beginning of the book, indicating, in part, that Uys had "read the manuscript seven times." The note gave the impression that Uys's contributions only occurred during the final drafting of the manuscript as a copyeditor.

Uys's fury slowly simmered. He was raised in a tradition where one's work had to be dutifully honored, and he felt the need to confront Michener about this obvious plagiarism. Toward the end of their time together, Uys asked Michener about their collaboration. Jim offered Uys help getting his next book published; at one point he offered him a trip to Europe for his time and contributions. Uys brushed off these feeble gestures. He probably would have had much better bargaining power had he been a more established writer and not been tied to *Reader's Digest*. In the end, Michener offered Uys very little that had to do with *The Covenant*, which left Uys disheartened and resentful. As a parting gesture of goodwill, Michener gave Uys a Christmas goose. "It was a wry Dickensian twist," remarked Uys. "The bird, loaded with shot from end to end, was inedible."[26]

Ultimately, Jim asked *Reader's Digest* to pay Uys a $5,000 bonus for his contributions, a meager sum considering that rights to the Literary Guild edition fetched $1.5 million several months later and the eventual hardcover and paperback sales exceeded $2 million. With Joe Avenick in *Sports in America*, and perhaps more conspicuously with Errol Uys in *The Covenant*, Michener committed two scarlet literary crimes and used his celebrated status in publishing to get away with them.

In an interview with *Playboy* magazine, conducted less than a year after the publication of *The Covenant*, Michener reiterated the stance he took in his autobiography regarding the use of researchers: "I do all the research myself. Now, there are several exceptions to that: *Kent State . . . Centennial . . .* and for *The Covenant*, I sought help, but the whole body had been laid out. In all the other books, nobody. And even in those cases, I did all the research myself."[27]

When word got back to Michener that Uys was claiming that he had written significant parts of the novel, Michener sent the South African writer a letter, stating in part that Uys had two choices: either he could keep quiet about his role in *The Covenant* and achieve later success with another novel, or he could keep up his present course and fall into worse "miasmas." "I'll invite you," the letter continued, "to choose the one that attracts you most."[28]

It should be noted that *The Covenant* was written not in South Africa but far removed from it in St. Michaels, Maryland. Most all of Michener's large novels—*Hawaii, The Source, Centennial, Chesapeake, Texas,* and *Alaska*—were written in residence in those regions covered in the books. That *The Covenant* emerged as a remarkable piece of authentic history and a valuable anthropological record as well as a sound novel is a testament not only to Michener's talents as a story-teller but also to Errol Uys's exceptional knowledge of South African culture.

Random House planned a November–December 1980 publication to capitalize on the holiday buying season. In August and September *Reader's Digest* issued condensed versions under the titles "Keepers of the Covenant" and "The Star of Freedom," respectively. Michener anticipated some criticism in the South African press, but in no way was he prepared for the novel's virulent reception in that country. South African writer W. A. De Clerk declared that *The Covenant*, as previewed in *Reader's Digest*, was "pretentious literary trash," which he hoped "the government would not ban because it would only give the book underserved notoriety."[29] Another South African writer, Andre Brink, pounced on a certain section of the story developed by both Michener and Uys. In the novel, a white South African family is reclassified because officials discover a three-hundred-year-old mixed marriage in their family tree. Brink said flatly: "To suggest that a family could be reclassified on the basis of something that happened in the 17th century is ludicrous and ridiculous."[30] Brink isolated an incident in the novel in which Michener has his character Detleef van Doorn, the race board chairman, describe one of the tests used to determine race. "We twist the hair over ears tightly round the pencil . . . if the subject is white the hair unravels quickly when the pencil is withdrawn. With blacks, as you know, the hair remains crinkled." A little girl named Petra, a member of the family being investigated, is asked to slip down her dress so that the board can examine a small triangle at the base of her spine. "If that's dark, you can bet she has Bantu blood," the board is told. The mixed marriage in 1694 is revealed, and the family, now reclassified as coloured, is forced to move to a coloured settlement near Cape Town. In another scene, a black man being interrogated by the Security Branch is beaten and has an electrical cattle prod attached to his genitals.

Michener rarely if ever responded to criticism, but he maintained that all the incidents in the novel were based on fact. "Rest assured," noted Errol Uys, "there were instances where investigators delved into family lineages as far back as they could go."[31] In an article in the *Washington Star*, Judith Chettle, wife of John Chettle, director of the South Africa Foundation, a Washington, D.C.–based group supportive of the South African government, remarked: "Michener describes with sensitivity and insight the expulsion of a little girl . . . from her white school because it is established after complaints and a humiliating physical examination that she should be classified as colored. The incident is based clearly on an actual case, and no other event in the book illustrates more tellingly the enormous sacrifices that the maintenance of the covenant has demanded of the innocent."[32]

Later in the year Brink, writing in the *Washington Post*, expanded his criticism by trying to make the case that Michener's book was hardly the "epic" of South Africa that it pretended to be.

It may seem courageous for a man to take it upon himself to "explain" South Africa to the world. However, if that explanation relies on the most facile of clichés . . . one feels apprehensive about both the motive and the achievement. . . . In previous works Michener may have impressed through an ability to sweep through vast tracts of history, but here he only plods and dodders. Wading through this boring "epic" one feels like one of the large birds of Africa taking run, great unwieldy wings flapping, in order to gain the momentum required to become airborne: only this one never takes off, never soars. . . . Stylistically, *The Covenant* is a depressing experience—not because it is badly written but because it is mildly competent—the work of a tired pedestrian plodder, far removed from the crispness and brightness which, so many years ago, characterized the author of *Tales of the South Pacific*.[33]

As to why so many South African readers condemned Michener's novel, Uys offered an observation: "Mr. Brink, as with other Afrikaner writers, seemed to be in a rage that an American author would pull off their 'epic.' Maybe it was because James Michener got to the heart of their shame."[34]

Disagreeing with Andre Brink on the merits of the novel was Alan Paton, author of *Cry, the Beloved Country*, who was perhaps the most respected writer in South Africa at the time. Although he did not go so far to label *The Covenant* South Africa's epic account, he did single out Michener's ability to reveal the truth and hypocrisy of Afrikaner culture. "White South Africa is a society corrupted by racism," Paton noted. "Michener sometimes exaggerates and over dramatizes, but he is exaggerating the truth. . . . I cannot call this anything but an extraordinary book."[35]

Within a month of the publication of "Keepers of the Covenant" in *Reader's Digest*, the South African government announced the banning of Michener's 881-page novel. The ban affected the book only and did not include magazine excerpts or condensations. According to the guidelines set forth by the Directorate of Publications, a book could be banned if it was "harmful to the relations between any sections of the inhabitants of the Republic" and was "prejudicial to the State, the general welfare or the peace and good order." Michener reacted officially by admitting that he was "saddened" by the move but added that it was "of almost no significance."[36] Inside, however, he was furious: he was being punished for telling the truth, and the move affected his royalties in the country.

After some appeals, the government reversed its decision and lifted the ban of *The Covenant*. Although it gave no reason for doing so, it was widely speculated in South Africa and America that the board had rushed to judgment on Michener's book, not realizing the extent of the propaganda damage done by banning the novel. As the board had a chance to examine the book in detail, it realized that the novel was not as threatening as first thought. Consequently, with as little fanfare as possible, it quietly lifted the ban. News of the banning and "unbanning" of the book only boosted prepublication sales in America and Europe. In November *Ladies' Home Journal* ran an excerpt from the book. In January *People Weekly* began the first of three serials of the novel. Once again, sales soared before publication.

For many Americans who viewed South Africa through the single lens of apartheid, the publication of *The Covenant* provided them with a wider exploration of a richly textured and often violent heritage. "*The Covenant*," wrote Alison Comey in the *Baltimore Sun*, "is an exhaustive demystification of America's particular scapegoat, South Africa; without knowledge of its complexities, no armchair diplomat can presume to judge that country's turmoil."[37] Reviewers in the major dailies continued the Michener line. John Leonard in the *New York Times* called Michener "as sincere as shoes." Matt Rouse in the *Cincin-*

nati Enquirer labeled *The Covenant* Michener's most "over-written, molasses-paced, forbiddingly dense novel yet. . . . Regardless of the fact that even as he instructs us with valuable history lessons, he threatens to annihilate our sensitivities to language and to the art of storytelling."[38]

Looking past the usual terms associated with Michener's novels—verbosity, shallow characterization, and pedestrian style—William McWhirter in *Time* wrote insightfully:

In his 30th book, Michener manages to cover 15,000 years of African history, from the ritual-haunted tribes of Bushmen to present-day Afrikaners obstinately jeering at appeals for "human rights." . . . If Michener cannot uncover the African soul, he understands the African soil—the blood that has spilled on it, the exploiters who have trampled it, the survivors who must scratch it for a living. *Covenant* derives from an Old French word meaning "to be suitable." To dramatize a complex and tragic history, whether of Asia, America, Europe, or Africa, is beyond the power of all but a few popularists. Of those few, James Michener remains the most suitable bridge between the protagonists of history and the outsider.[39]

Writing in the *Columbus (Ohio) Dispatch*, Jeanne Bonham remarked: "It is impossible to come away from the sobering experience of reading this novel and not understand Africa, at least from Michener's point of view, and the development and reasons for apartheid, the system whereby the races are kept completely separated. *The Covenant* is another solid achievement for James Michener."[40]

Michener reckoned that he spent $122,000 in out-of-pocket expenses on writing *The Covenant*, "which explains why a beginning writer could never have attempted such a feat."[41] It was a massive project and one of the most physically and mentally demanding. It was also one of his most satisfying. By capturing an important moral struggle that held the world's attention, he attained a mastery of content and narrative that he never quite achieved again. Other novels would follow, but they would lack the heart and soul that Michener put into South Africa's quest for human equality and freedom.

The rejection of *The Covenant* by the South African government troubled Michener but ultimately hardened his resolve. He predicted in ten years time his novel would be regarded as "an important ecumenical statement very favorable to the nation as a whole."[42] Despite the government's criticism of the book, and in many cases because of it, *The Covenant* enjoyed wide popularity in Africa as well as in South Africa. In February 1990, nearly ten years after its publication, Nelson Mandela, the voice of oppressed blacks for several decades, walked out of prison a free man. Working with President F. W. de Klerk, Mandela helped to abolish apartheid. In 1994, in South Africa's first democratic election, Mandela became president and ushered in a shift from a white- to a black-controlled government. Such abrupt changes, Michener thought, were extraordinary. "I did not expect to see South Africa turn into a one-man, one-vote free democracy in my lifetime," he declared. "De Klerk and Mandela have been able to bury old animosities and begin new lives for their nation. The country's transition was a highlight of the decade."[43]

CHAPTER 17

The Great Ennobler

Young Jim Michener grew up in Doylestown knowing that the road to the east dead-ended in a farmer's field, while the road to the west continued over the rolling hills toward the Pacific Ocean. Escape and exploration were at the heart of his youth. Although the methods of exploration varied—from cars, trains, and ships in his youth to commercial and jet fighter planes in his maturity—the need for escape never left him. His love of aviation was tested in three separate crashes, but ultimately he came to love this mode of travel the best.[1] He never forgot the irony of crashing in the Pacific Ocean the same week that the Russians launched *Sputnik*, the first satellite in space. During island-hopping inspection tours in the South Pacific during the Second World War, accompanying fighter pilots in the Korean War, and flying with SAC squadrons around the world, Michener was at home in the air. He came to respect pilots and the crews who flew lonely missions all over the globe. Later, he would place astronauts in that elite group.

It was only natural that he embraced the excitement of America's space program that burgeoned in the late 1960s and early 1970s. Like most Americans, Michener was thrilled by the Gemini and Apollo programs, the landing on the moon, and the prospect of further missions that sent humans into space. In summer 1976, while working on *Chesapeake*, he was invited by the National Aeronautics and Space Administration's (NASA's) Langley Research Center in Hampton, Virginia, to join a panel of celebrities to speak on the topic "why man explores." Joining him in the group were science fiction writer Ray Bradbury, oceanographer Jacques Cousteau, *Saturday Review* editor Norman Cousins, and Massachusetts Institute of Technology (MIT) professor and scholar-philosopher Philip Morrison. From that inspirational symposium came a government offer to help articulate the aims and ideals of NASA's program for the middle-class reader. In 1979 Michener was appointed to NASA's Advisory Board, a position that required a top-secret clearance. That same year *Voyager I* and *Pioneer II* flew past Jupiter and Saturn, respectively.

Although other books loomed in Michener's mind—Texas and Poland were in primary spots—he chose instead to focus on the space program, beginning the initial draft of *Space* in late 1980 and early 1981. Shuttling between St. Michaels, Houston, and Cape Canaveral, Jim insinuated himself into the space program and roamed where most average citizens were forbidden to go. He chatted with astronauts and engineers. He stuffed himself into capsules, trying to simulate the conditions of orbiting astronauts. He spent an entire day in mission control monitoring operations in space.

Back in St. Michaels, he wrote *Space* with relative ease. The short time span of the novel, between 1944 and the early 1980s, allowed him to work quickly through the narrative. Playing the wily fox, he suspected that his readers—and certainly the critics—would be surprised about his chosen venue. No doubt some had even tried to speculate about which region or country he would choose next. Of course, they were thinking "over," and he was contemplating "up."

Space went on to receive highly favorable reviews, some of which came from respected writers who regularly authored articles for science journals. Most reviewers were impressed that Michener's erudition and knowledge extended well beyond the historical novels they were accustomed to reading. Henry Macdonald in the *Washington Times* remarked: "*Space* succeeds well, treating its subject with intelligence and integrity. Not only does Michener demonstrate in this book a mastery of the science and history of man's 'conquest of space' but, more importantly, he conveys in his account an uncommon sensitivity to its philosophical and religious implications."[2] Ben Bova, writing in the *Washington Post*, observed that "Michener is, if nothing else, a solid reporter. He studies his subject matter thoroughly and writes about it in unadorned prose. Better than most writers, he gives his readers an understanding of the men and women involved in the mighty saga of space."[3] Reviewing the book for the *New York Times*, John Noble Wilford remarked that "the author has, as usual, done his research well. He has also managed to develop his sprawling narrative around all of the major political, social, and technological themes that resonated during the years of the first exploration of space. [This is] a sympathetic and historically sound treatment of an important human endeavor that some day could be the stuff of myth or at least of grand chronicles in the tradition of Hakluyt."[4] Karl Keller in the *Los Angeles Times* declared, "Michener, for all his flaws, is the Great Ennobler."[5]

In May 1981 a seventy-four-year-old James Michener reacted with alarm to the news that an assassin's bullet had nearly taken the life of his friend Pope John Paul II in Rome. As it turned out, the alleged assassin was a Turkish dissident and not a gunman hired by a foreign government, as Michener first suspected. Jim had known the former cardinal of Krakow, Karol Wojtyla, for almost ten years. Jim first met him in 1974 on a trip to Poland with Ed Piszek. In 1977 Piszek's movie company, Emlen House, filmed Michener on location throughout Poland for the PBS documentary *Poland: The Will to Be*. In between takes, Michener chatted with Wojtyla, and the two quickly developed a congenial friendship. "When our television interview was over," Michener remarked, "Cardinal Wojtyla took me by the arm and asked if I thought he had done well. I told him he was fabulous and I meant it. He next asked if I thought he could get a job in Hollywood. I replied that there was no doubt about it." In the next few months, Michener visited the cardinal at the Vatican in Rome, where they dined on stuffed cabbage and Polish white wine. "We enjoyed each other's company immensely," noted Jim. "The cardinal is a brilliant wit."[6]

The following year, Michener and Piszek were back in Warsaw for the European screening of the documentary on Poland. While there, the two learned that the Vatican had elected Karol Wojtyla as the next pope. After a jubilant celebration, Piszek and Michener returned by cab to their hotel. Michener was clearly troubled by the news that a Polish cardinal was now pontiff and what that meant for the people of Soviet-dominated Poland. What would happen to the tenuous relations between the two countries, one seeking to control, the other, predominantly Catholic, pursuing greater independence? Would Soviet tanks eventually rumble into Warsaw as they had into Budapest in the 1956 revolution? "In Hungary," he told Piszek, "I saw the same thing happen. Well, not quite the same. But Hungary was ready to break free. It seemed unstoppable. You know what this means, don't you?"

"I think so," said Piszek.

"They'll kill him. Or, they'll have to let it go."

Of course, by "they" Jim meant the Russians or, more particularly, the KGB. "Or let what go?" asked Piskek.

"Poland. The whole country. They'll have to let it go."[7]

As tensions escalated throughout the 1970s in Poland, Michener had planned a novel of the country, a book that would capture the history and culture of this crossroads of turmoil in Eastern Europe. Wedged between the great—and often warring—powers of Russia and Germany, Poland was under the persistent threat of invasion. After wars and peace treaties, its borders expanded and contracted over the centuries. As he had in Israel, Afghanistan, and South Africa, Michener wanted to write about these dramatic events in a novel. By 1981, however, it appeared that the book would go the way of other Michener projects and be shelved forever. Other projects lured him more, including one on Texas and another on Alaska. And so, while Lech Walesa stirred up Polish workers in the Gdansk shipyards and while a Soviet threat remained to smash any move resulting in Polish independence, Michener, still in St. Michaels, set his sights on Texas.

In July 1981, however, Piszek and Michener lounged on Jim's backyard patio. Behind them, the waters of Broad Creek glistened in the sun. Ed knew that he was running out of time to encourage Jim to consider writing the novel of Poland. After Jim told him that he was planning a novel of Texas, Piszek mustered his courage and told him that there would never be a better time to write the Polish novel. "Under ordinary circumstances," said Piszek, "I'd never tell you what to write about, but I have to say this. We've traveled Poland together over and over. You know the country inside out, as well as any man. Jim, if you don't tell the story, who will?"[8]

Jim told him he would seriously consider it but to give him time. Piszek returned to Pennsylvania. The following day, Jim telephoned Piszek and told him he would write the Polish novel, rattling off a host of names of people he needed to help him with the research.[9] Days later, Piszek wrote Michener: "Please guide me to the proper cooperation on this project. Man, I don't want to foul this one up. I can face victory and somehow I'll face defeat, but a self-inflicted error would be impossible for me to face. Please be kind and steer me through the cooperation you seek. Don't let my zeal trip me up."[10]

On July 17, 1981, as his notebooks document, Jim committed himself to the novel of Poland, which remained untitled until shortly before publication in 1983. "On this day I sat in my office and coldly pondered what problems I would face if I decided to proceed with the novel I had in mind. I typed out a short outline identifying the seven main episodes covering the period from 1242 through 1944 and two short opening chapters for the opening and closing." On August 30 he flew to Poland "for an extensive exploratory trip to the sites I would want to emphasize. . . . I met leaders of the government, the two heads of the Catholic church, labor leaders, and scores of private citizens."[11]

In early September, after meeting with Lech Walesa, the Solidarity labor movement leader, Michener knew trouble was brewing in Poland. Walesa, a former electrician turned labor firebrand, was at the center of the turmoil. Formed in September 1980, Solidarity, a national federation of trade unions, became Poland's first independently recognized union since the end of the Second World War. Adding further weight to the movement and perhaps creating more friction with the Soviets was Pope John Paul's official sanction of the union. Solidarity and Lech Walesa aggravated the Soviet-run government, which tried to restrict the union's activities. Several showdowns and strikes occurred in the following months. In January 1981 Walesa was received by the pope in Rome, further irritating the government authorities. In September, shortly after Michener's visit to the Gdansk shipyards, Solidarity held its first annual congress. Walesa was elected its chairman and chief spokesperson, frequently using this platform to approach trade unions around the word for support and encouragement. With an outspoken union leader in the Baltic ports, an unyielding government in Warsaw, and a patriotic Polish pope in the Vatican, Michener sensed that an international drama was taking shape. Little did he know that the events in Poland and Europe would foreshadow the breakup of the Soviet bloc and within the decade lead to the ultimate collapse of the Soviet Union.

In late September Michener returned to St. Michael's to resume writing the novel. For the next seventeen months, while turmoil continued in central Europe, Michener committed the Polish struggle to paper. The project developed into one of his most joyful and satisfying, largely because it served to replace his elusive Russian novel, and like *The Covenant,* it connected decisive current events with historical ones.

Keeping his pledge to center his next project in Texas, Jim and Mari moved the first part of October 1982 to Austin, where he could use the extensive research facilities at the University of Texas. They retained the home in St. Michaels and the one in Pipersville, as well as the condo in Juno Beach and one in Honolulu, which his former secretary, Evelyn Shoemaker, lived in rent free. *Poland* was in Erskine's and Krantz's hands, being worked over for style, content, and consistency. Once settled in a rental home near the campus, Jim worked on questions on the Polish manuscript with John Kings, his assistant on *Centennial,* and his new research assistant, Lisa Kaufman, a graduate student at the university.

To say that Texas unfurled the red carpet for Michener is something of an understatement. Early in 1981 Governor Bill Clements, aware of what *Centennial* did for Colorado, urged Jim to write a similar book of the Lone Star State, offering him as bait the research bonanza of the University of Texas. Michener grabbed. After word got out that he was moving to Austin, people sent him their Texas family histories, hoping their ancestors might appear in a Michener work. The University of Texas supplied him an office and secretarial help. Reporters from Texas newspapers and magazines descended on him, hoping for some tidbits of his forthcoming book. For Michener, who welcomed the adoration, it was quite overwhelming.

He began the historical research on *Texas* as he finalized *Poland.* By April 1983 the latter project was entering its final phase before publication. Random House had hired two Polish scholars, Klara Glowczewska in New York and Marian Turski in Rome, to vet the final manuscript and offer their suggestions, which they did, further tying up Michener with revisions into mid-April.

Owen Laster and Albert Erskine discussed the title. Both thought "Polonaise" would be a suitable name, but later it was revealed that British author Piers Paul Read was publishing a novel with the same title. Legally, Random House was free to name the book what it wished. Consequently, both Laster and Erskine pressed for "Polonaise." Michener, however, recognized that naming the book would constitute an ethical breach of trust between writers, so he asked them to reconsider. After much debate between William Morris and Random House, the title *Poland* was selected. While the debate was going on, Michener spent three days rewriting passages that might be affected if the title was "Polonaise." "So all the rush work goes down the drain," lamented Michener after the decision, "but now I've grown to like two or three of the changes I drafted in order to utilize the new title . . . the improvements I've made work just as well with either title."[12]

Poland, Michener's sweeping work of that country's anguished history, appeared in early September 1983, making it his fourth major novel in six years. Writing in the *Detroit News,* reviewer Lisa Schwarzbaum observed: "This is a classic Michener production, an expertly synthesized novel weaving fact and fiction into the kind of detail-packed, sympathetic rattling good read one has come to expect from the master of the massive. By tracing the fates over the centuries of three fictional families—the Counts Lubonski, the petty nobles Bukowksi, and the peasants Buk—you have the story of Poland from the time of Genghis Khan and the Tartars in 1204 through the time of Lech Walesa and Solidarity in 1981."[13] Other reviewers cited Michener's harrowing version of the Holocaust, while others marveled at Poland's ability to endure "cycles of devastation and renewal."[14]

Donning his new Stetson and grabbing his venerable walking stick, Michener spent his afternoons sauntering the hills around his rented home on Mount Bonnell Road in Austin. These were generally happy and uneventful solo journeys. However, in the Micheners' car, usually driven by Mari, things were different. Impatient Texas drivers, seeing their Pennsylvania license plates, bawled: "Go home, ya damn Yankees," as they barreled past. But Michener, just another "durned northerner" for all anybody knew, had no plans to return home. Instead, he dug his heels into Texas and prepared to write his epic of the Lone Star State. He grew to love Texas: the chili cook-offs, the Friday night high school football games, the cattle auctions, and the afternoon chats with geographers, historians, and geologists.

In the autumn of 1982 Michener was asked to serve on the Board for International Broadcasting in Washington, D.C., which managed two powerful anti-Communist news stations, Radio Free Europe and Radio Liberty, both originating from Munich, Germany. The appointment stemmed from his firsthand experience in Poland, Hungary, and Russia. The chairman of the board was his old friend and confidant Frank Shakespeare, who had first recruited Michener in the early 1970s to serve on the Advisory Council for Information. Of the government agencies in which he served—the USIA, the NASA Advisory Board, the Postal Stamp Committee, and the Board for International Broadcasting—Michener considered the last his most important role, for it brought him "into daily conflict with Communism in all its various manifestations."[15]

Composed of nine members, the board featured Shakespeare, a Republican; four other Republicans; and four Democrats. Among the Republicans were billionaire Malcolm Forbes, Jr., and Arch Madsen, who administered the radio empire of the Mormon Church. Among the Democrats were labor leader Lane Kirkland and the Catholic theologian Michael Novak. Despite their different political stripes, the group, according to Michener, got along well. Shakespeare administered the board with the same courtesy, efficiency, and no-nonsense American pragmatism as he had the Advisory Council for Information under President Nixon.

Radio Free Europe, broadcasting into the captive nations behind the Iron Curtain, and Radio Liberty, broadcasting into the republics governed by the Soviet Union, were both venerable institutions heading into the 1980s. As Michener saw it, the board's greatest challenge was to provide accurate news and information while avoiding starting a revolution in the various countries. Michener recalled painfully that in Hungary in 1956 American broadcasts "ignited false hopes among the freedom fighters. I was one of several who kept reminding Frank that our stations must never again raise hopes behind the Iron Curtain that we would be unable to support, and he was careful to broadcast truth, not to incite rebellion."[16] Under Shakespeare, the board stressed accuracy and objectivity, but often individual broadcasters made on-the-air blunders that were reported back to Washington. Some notable miscues reported to the American government were when the broadcasts "(1) referred to the Soviet Foreign Minister as a bandit; (2) compared former Soviet officials to Nazi war criminals; (3) called a British author a Communist agent; (4) used an anatomical obscenity to describe a Polish government official; and (5) described a prominent American actress as having a pro-Marxist outlook and 'warm sympathies' for the Soviet Union."[17]

When cries were heard that Radio Free Europe and Radio Liberty were becoming obsolete and their funding should be cut to help trim the federal budget deficit, Michener quickly responded in an op-ed article for the *New York Times*:

For decades the Soviet Union has conducted attacks against these broadcasts. They have been denounced "as an instrument of the CIA," "subversive radio stations" and as "a relic of the cold war." . . . Radio Free Europe and Radio Liberty are no more relics of the cold war than is the Atlantic alliance. Both are important mainstream instruments of American foreign policy. . . . Consequently, we must have a clear national commitment to support this vital organization, which is little appreciated in the West but highly valued by millions in the East.[18]

Jim's office at the Barker Texas History Center on campus was his first outside his primary residence since his days at Macmillan in the 1940s. It was spacious enough to accommodate several desks, type-writers, books, souvenirs of his Texas travels, and several assistants coming and going throughout the day. Three Texas state maps were also plastered on the walls, each one covered in colored stars indi-cating places where Michener and Kings had spent the night. "There are so many stars they [the maps] look like they have the measles," quipped Michener. "We've been literally everywhere."[19] In early 1983 the university made him a visiting professor, a position for which he took no money. His office staff consisted of Kings and Kaufman and two graduate students: Jesús "Frank" de la Teja, born in Cuba and fluent in both Spanish and English, and Robert Wooster, born in Beaumont, Texas, son of a Texas history professor. Wooster's role was to research Anglo history in Texas, while de la Teja focused on the Spanish cultural influence in the state.

After the group convened several times, Jim reminded them of two special conditions they should be mindful of during the work on the manuscript, both of which reflect the issues raised by his previous collaborative work with Joe Avenick and Errol Uys. "Please *never* bring to my attention any fictional material because I have no right to use the creative ideas of another writer," he told the group. "Secondly, when I say that if Frank, for example, finds that my treatment of 'x' and 'j' is faulty, I would appreciate a statement from him in writing as to what is *not* faulty. By that I mean a reworking of a paragraph, no more. You are not asked or permitted to do any writing on the manuscript."[20] Clearly, Michener had decided that any creative work on the manuscript would be entirely his own.

Undaunted by the vastness of Texas—in fact, attracted by it—he commented on the task before him: "The magnitude of Texas is for-bidding, but I've never walked away from a subject just because of its size. I am more than able to handle this undertaking physically and mentally. I have a better imagination today than when I was twenty. I always worked harder than I had to, and that continues to be the case."[21] With all the attention paid him by Texans, Michener was quite clear that no one—not the governor or the president of the university or the various influential people he met—was going to prejudice his view of the state. "At no stage," remarked Kings, "would he be beholden for its contents to the state or to the university. That was the way it was from the beginning and remained so during the entire preparation of the manuscript."[22]

By the summer of 1983, after residing eight months in Austin, Kings and Michener had crisscrossed the state and logged seven thousand miles. By the following summer they would double their mileage. If they traveled by car, Kings drove; if they had great distance to travel, they chartered a light plane or helicopter. "Everywhere we went," observed Kings,

> we found overwhelming hospitality, usually having to interlace our own research with social functions, meetings and confer ences planned well in advance of our arrival. Press interviews innumerable, TV spots, book signings all became part of the accepted pattern of these trips. We attended fairs, jamborees, reunions, conventions, prayer meetings, hoe-downs, armadillo races, German days, Scottish days, football training camps, Ranger reunions, surveyors' reunions and everybody else's reunions. . . , The research has been richness itself.[23]

Both Michener and Kings knew that it would be a gamble for Michener's project to make a significant contribution to the culture of Texas. "Texas is like a kaleidoscope; shake up the elements of its history and you see some new pattern emerge. Shake it again, hold it to the light, and yet another resolution suggests itself. As easy as Texas history may be at one level of comprehension, so it is ten times more difficult in an abstract sense to equate a much more subtle content," Kings further observed.[24]

To stake his claim in Texas literature, Michener chose a structure similar to *Centennial* and *The Source*: more than four centuries of history were framed by a modern story in which the central characters are pulled into the historical events by their ancestral ties. For instance, the opening features a governor's task force that convenes to find ways of instilling uniqueness in the state's children. The task force brings together the narrator, Travis Barlow, and several other diverse members who have deep roots in Texas and therefore have many intimate thoughts and feelings to share with each other about the state's history and contemporary problems.

Michener always worried about the beginnings of his novels. Most of the leads for articles in *Reader's Digest* were written by a staff writer. He confessed to his editor Hobe Lewis that he was "pitiful" at writing openings, whereupon Lewis would remind him that they employed only the best cutters and lead writers and that Michener should keep writing in the style that he found the most comfortable.[25] Jim labored to give them luster and personality, attempting to avoid a lead that sounded as though he were introducing a history text. The frame structure, usually varied in each book, became his favorite way of opening a novel.

The first chapter of *Texas* went through only minor changes. Michener typed out the first sentence in January 1983: "I was surprised when shortly after New Year's Day of 1983, the Governor of Texas summoned me to his office, because I hadn't been aware that he knew I was in town."[26] Lasting ten pages, the frame opening introduces the narrator and his fellow members of the task force: Ransom Rusk, a billionaire and descendant of an American Indian agent; Lorenzo Quimper, a Texas "mover and shaker"; Lorena Cobb, the descendant of plantation owners who settled Texas in the 1840s; and Professor Efrain Garza, who startles the group by admitting that his ancestors explored the Texas countryside in 1539. From this admission, the story begins in 1535 and proceeds through the lives of Garza's ancestors.

Like *The Source* and *Centennial,* the task force reappears at the close of several of the historical chapters. Of the three novels, however, the opening for *Texas* is the weakest, primarily because Michener relies too heavily on being glib and disingenuous. His narrator, Travis Barlow, offends Texans by claiming that "when good Texans die they go to Colorado." Next, after claiming that Portuguese drivers were wild, Barlow asserts "they were only in training for driving in Texas." The final affront is an unfortunate reference to Charles Whitman, the man who massacred sixteen people from the tower at the university in 1966. Barlow recalls this tragic incident and then in the next sentence "salutes" the tower as he passes by.[27]

His four assistants on the project—Kings, Kaufman, de la Teja, and Wooster—each received a copy of every chapter, which they reviewed and commented on before returning it to Michener for his next revision. Kaufman and Kings suggested that he remove the Texas jokes and the Whitman reference in the first draft, a recommendation that Jim did not take. For reasons only known to Jim, he left them in the final text.

Despite the many squabbles over usage and content, Jim finished the first draft containing fourteen chapters of *Texas* by October 1, 1983. He wrote Laster and Erskine that although the good news was that the draft was finished, the bad news was that it would take until the following August for him to deliver the final manuscript. At a massive size of 2,084 pages and estimated by Jim at 583,603 words, the manuscript was the largest Jim had ever written. Even after revision and severe cutting, *Texas* would top 1,900 manuscript pages. "The other slice of bread in the good news sandwich," Jim added, "is that I would judge as of today the persons working with me here in Texas would be able, should something happen to me, to complete the editing by themselves. . . . Of course it would be considerably better if I were to complete the entire revision, because much needs to be done, but the manuscript as it stands is a good narrative, too heavy on history in parts and requiring some shifts in emphasis and much strengthening, but totally viable." Jim stressed that such information was to be kept confidential. If anyone asked, Laster and Erskine could say with accuracy, "Jim was about halfway there."[28]

Michener further remarked in his letter that he had removed an entire chapter of nearly 150 pages detailing the lives of Sam Houston and General Santa Anna, which he called "Two Eagles." He hated doing this, because he felt these two men represented the conflicting currents of Texas history. But he also knew that such a digression would impede the flow of the narrative. Six years later, in 1990, the State House Press in Austin published the chapter as a separate volume under the title *The Eagle and the Raven.*

For the first eight months of 1984 Michener worked on the second, third, and final drafts of *Texas.* The research team in Austin added a fifth member, Anders Saustrup, who was hired to "scour the records of Texas history to verify dates, places, people, facts, hearsay, to the extent that only a dedicated mole could pursue. With an inquiring European and Yale-trained mind," according to John Kings, "backed by twenty-two years in the state of Texas, Anders became the last barrier through which the manuscript had to be sieved, chapter by chapter, before we were content to let it pass on to Random House." After Anders performed his editing duties, the other four did a final "vacuuming" of the manuscript, which involved annotating a clean copy in four different-colored pens. "Jim would then accept or reject these final suggestions," explained Kings. "They would be cranked into the final disk and the chapter at last printed out for forwarding to Erskine at Random House."[29] Jim mailed a manuscript for Erskine's comments in the middle of August. Erskine responded with the first round (seven pages) of suggested cuts and edits on August 26.

As usual, Erskine was helpful, critical, and complimentary. The *Texas* project marked the thirtieth year of their special relationship. In many ways it recalled other editor-author relationships, particularly those of Max Perkins and Ernest Hemingway and Saxe Commins and William Faulkner. Erskine, however, had perhaps the most demanding role among editors. Unwilling or simply unable to say something succinctly, Michener wrote ten pages to someone else's one. Erskine's task was to shape, focus, and trim Michener's excessive verbiage. Helping to edit nearly twenty of Michener's books, some of massive scale, Erskine succeeded brilliantly. Beginning with *Sayonara* in 1954, Erskine picked up where Saxe Commins left off and gave the wordy Michener a distinct voice that carried the author to international fame. Erskine, who also edited Robert Penn Warren, William Faulkner, and John O'Hara, maintained that his first rule of editing was "If you try to fix a paragraph three times and it still creaks, kill it."[30] Quite simply, without Erskine, Michener would have faded because his excesses would not have been tolerated for very long.

Using the mail, Michener and Erskine worked on the changes to *Texas* through September and October. Erskine wanted a much leaner book, so Michener often had to make drastic cuts in chapters. Often these cuts were painful, like amputating a finger, but Michener yielded to Erskine. Meanwhile, Michener gave his alma mater, Swarthmore, a gift of $1,998,000—what he considered interest on his original $2,000 scholarship in 1925. "Michener's achievements," remarked an anonymous editorial in the college newspaper, "certainly serve as ample testimony to the value of his Swarthmore education. Those now in school can look to Michener's accomplishments for inspiration when the grind of studying seems overwhelming. In the end, as Michener noted, the training can be invaluable."[31] Swarthmore was just the beginning of Michener's philanthropy. In the next few years he would pledge significant amounts to the University of Texas, the University of Houston, Eckerd College, the University of Iowa, Sheldon Jackson College, and the University of Northern Colorado. On October 12 the University of Texas announced that it would form a permanent affiliation with Michener by making him a professor emeritus. The university regents granted Jim an emeritus appointment because he was more than seventy years old. As earlier, the appointment did not provide a salary but would continue to support his research. "For the past two years," Michener told the press, "I have enjoyed a fine relationship with the University of Texas and now accept most warmly the opportunity to continue and to expand the association. The University and the State of Texas provide a stimulating atmosphere in which to work, and I look forward eagerly to the challenging days ahead."[32]

As publication of *Texas* neared in the spring and summer of 1985, Random House initiated a massive publicity campaign for the Michener title. Word-of-mouth promotion had already made the anticipated publication a statewide event. If recent sales of Michener's novels were any indication, *Texas* was going to exceed all expectations. According to Random House figures, hardcover sales of previous Michener titles were *Centennial*, 469,786; *Chesapeake*, 890,237; and

Space, 613,841. The publisher scheduled a first printing of 750,000 copies, hoping that *Texas* would outsell any of those books. At that time it was the largest printing for a hardcover American novel. Within a few weeks of publication, Random House ordered a fifth printing, which brought the total copies to 1.1 million. In comparison, other Random House authors, such as Gore Vidal and Norman Mailer, had first-run printings of less than 200,000 for their recent works. In an agreement with Random House, the University of Texas Press printed its own two-volume collector's edition, profusely illustrated, bound in buffalo hide, embossed with a lone star, and priced at $125 each. Profits from this edition supported the university's writing program. Dubbed by the press "the most prized creation of the Texas sesquicentennial," promoted both regionally and nationally, *Texas* was Michener's most ballyhooed novel.

As with *Centennial* and *Chesapeake,* Michener tried to establish himself in a region with an already significant literary tradition. From J. Frank Dobie and T. R. Fehrenbach to contemporary writers Elmer Kelton and Larry McMurtry, Texas writing was a rich blend of the traditional and the modern. Jim insisted that he was not in competition with these writers, although some critics tried to single him out as a Yankee interloper in Texas literature. Texas writers, in particular, picked Michener's novel apart. Writing in the *Chicago Tribune,* Larry L. King, author of *The Best Little Whorehouse in Texas,* aimed his comments directly at Michener's conceit: "One reason I felt I was eating a washtub of tapioca while pawing through *Texas* is that it contains very little vinegar or spice. The good Lord knows my native state with its long practices of discrimination against minorities and women, labor, the poor and the disadvantaged . . . easily lends itself to being satirized or chastised. Author Michener turns a blind eye or a bland eye pen in these matters. He does not, therefore, write of the Texas where I grew up and the Texas I have observed for nearly fifty-seven years. This book might more accurately have been called 'Frontier Days,' or 'Romantic Texas,' or 'Hooray for Old Times.'"[33] Another Texas writer, Peter Lasalle, observed in the *Los Angeles Times*: "Michener's novels don't really have plots but rather strategies that convey mounds of information . . . the prose is sadly lackluster and cliché-ridden. The dialogue is often solid oak. . . . On the other hand there is enough sense of the complexity of issues to frequently make this engaging reading. . . . It doesn't take a shrewd oilman with a studio name like Ransom Rusk to tell you that recent Michener fare isn't so much high literature as it is business—big business, pardner."[34]

If his foes saw him as a conceited best seller muscling in on their territory, some of the aspiring writers in the university program saw him as a genuine supporter of their ambitions. Emerging student writers such as Stephen Harrigan and Elizabeth Crook profited greatly from Michener's financial and emotional support of the creative writing program at the university. Random House even asked him to promote one of its young authors named Cormac McCarthy, whom they were touting as the next William Faulkner. Jim gladly obliged almost all requests to help beginning writers.

True to form, Michener's ten-gallon epic *Texas* covered everything of major and minor importance in Texas history: from the age of the conquistadors, the Spanish adventurers, and the early Christian missions to the battles of the Alamo, Goliad, and San Jacinto to the boom-and-bust cycles of the twentieth century. He also worked in the rise of the Ku Klux Klan, problems of illegal immigration, and the plight of the lowly armadillo as it struggles to survive in the increasingly crowded landscape. Of all the two hundred or so characters in the novel—among them Davy Crockett, Jim Bowie, and Stephen Austin—Michener felt the most kinship with the fictional Emma Larkin, a young woman who is stolen by the Comanches and horribly abused. She has her ears and nose cut off and survives through courage and determination, later achieving a gracious acceptance of her difficult life.

"That kind of person represents what I think," stated Michener in an interview with Caryn James of the *New York Times Book Review*. James pointed out that an unusual aspect of Larkin's character is that she turns away the boy born as a result of her rape by the Comanches, "a rejection that her Quaker husband cannot comprehend."[35] After James mentioned the novel's similarity to Michener's own rejection of his adopted son, Mark, in the mid-1950s, she asked Michener to comment. Michener suddenly grew silent, as if trying to sort through his confusion. He then said: "I always wanted the child, but it didn't work out. . . . The whole thing became rather muddled," he said of Mark. "I cabled from Europe that I would take it. But it never happened. It went back into the system. It was the ward of the orphanage, and it was simply easier for the orphanage to get the abandonment to go through, and they found another home for it." Obviously, Jim had forgotten, or not wished to accept the fact, that both and he and Mari had made a conscious decision not to take Mark in or to take any steps to ensure his welfare beyond returning him to Pearl Buck's Welcome House. As with most disappointments in his life, his treatment of his legally adopted son was indicative of how he dealt with guilt and pain. The unfortunate references to the child as "it" in Michener's comments further emphasize his compelling need to rid the matter from his conscience. "I think we reach a point," remarked Michener, "in which the errors of the past are just done with. And everything associated with them is wiped out. It's harsh, even cruel, but I do think that it represents a lot of life experience."[36]

Although not on par with *Centennial, The Source,* or *Chesapeake, Texas* succeeds in bringing the state's history to life. It does not, however, get to the heart of Texas. Michener again returns with a plethora of detail about Texas's sordid past: constant murders, swindles, wipeouts, massacres, scams, bonanzas, corrupt courts, and government scandals. He slyly indicts the gun craze, the wholesale slaughter of Mexicans in border wars, the slave system, anti-intellectualism, and the ludicrous hunting of game park animals. With its panorama of landscape and characters, *Texas* meanders through the various eras in an absorbing fashion.

With the publication of *Texas,* Michener had given up hope that he would achieve unanimous critical acclaim. Like Dickens, he was happy to write for the public, and to hell with the critics. He believed in the words of Mark Twain: "In the end it is the public that is the only critic that really matters."[37] If the national and international critics shunned him, Texans still adored him. Michener received more than three hundred fan letters for *Texas* and was constantly invited to banquets and library gatherings. The same year that *Texas* was published, Larry McMurtry's *Lonesome Dove,* the real Texas epic, also appeared and went on to win the Pulitzer Prize. Afterward, Michener's novel lost much of its luster. But devoted Texans still remembered the years of the 1980s when Michener traveled around the state, made contributions to the University of Texas, wore his Stetson and bolo tie, and became an honorary Texan. Although he would travel again to points around the world—the South Pacific, Europe, and Alaska—Jim was in Texas to stay.

CHAPTER 18

New Frontiers

G iven the limitations of his age, the vast distances needed to be traveled, the rigors of the climate, and the proximity to other Pacific cultures, Michener probably should have begun work on his Alaska novel sometime in his fifties or after he finished writing *Hawaii.* But in April 1984, as Jim and Mari circled above the state in an Alaska Airlines jet, age, experience, or any physical weakness suddenly did not matter. He seldom was happier—or had more stamina—than at the beginning of a new venture. Once, when someone asked him about the importance of risk in his life, he answered: "I am opposed to playing it safe in all aspects of life. People who attempt to play it safe, especially in the arts but also in love and games and work, most often lose. Ironically taking full risks is the real strategy for playing it safe."[1]

Like *Texas,* the Alaska project was suggested by an outsider—in this case, the president of Sheldon Jackson College in Sitka, Alaska, Michael Kaelke—who wrote Michener in 1983 offering the author the use of the campus for his research. Even Alaska's governor invited him to visit and write a novel of the state. A year passed. In April 1984 Michener wrote Kaelke, asking him if he and Mari could visit, which they did shortly thereafter.

The original concept for a novel on Alaska actually originated as early as 1947, when Phil Knowlton, Michener's boss at Macmillan, thrilled Jim with his tales of northern adventure. "Often in those and subsequent years I toyed with the idea of heading for the far north to tackle Alaska but always refrained because I thought at forty I was much too old to brave the horrendous low temperatures that Knowlton had spoken of." Knowlton made Michener shudder by reporting that on clear mornings, he could see steam rising from the outhouses twenty miles away. Not ready for such temperatures, Michener "decided regretfully" that he would never write his novel of Alaska.[2]

Over the years, however, Michener frequently entertained the idea, and he only needed Kaelke's prodding to finally decide to do it. The college president offered Michener the use of a log cabin on campus and the title of Distinguished Faculty Scholar. Michener would have no obligations other than to conduct his research and write. Since Jim believed in total immersion in a project, he picked a frigid time of year to take the plunge into Alaska's vastness. On December 11, 1984, he and Mari left a balmy Austin for Sitka, on Alaska's southeast coast, which had a temperate climate and was usually drenched in rain during the winter. "I loved Alaska," he confessed, "the terrifying solitude of the empty north, the lonely salmon fisheries of the farthest south, the gold fields at the Canadian border, and above all that dramatic chain of little Aleutian islands reaching out toward Russian Siberia." During that Alaskan winter, he planned numerous outdoor activities that would augment his archival research. On the eve of the winter solstice, December 22, he was in the Arctic Circle, hanging out at a remote hotel in Fort Yukon, while the temperature outside plummeted to fifty-two degrees below zero. "It wasn't bad— but the only part I disliked was the constant putting on and taking off of the five layers of clothing that such cold required, but when the temperature rose to a minus twenty-two it was so congenial I went about only in a heavy shirt."[3]

There were other journeys to Prudhoe Bay and Nome. "I think I know about the frozen arctic," he remarked. "I've been to Prudhoe Bay and I've walked down on the Arctic Sea about a mile. But until you see Nome with those great blocks of arctic ice heaving up from the Bering Sea, well, it's just ice prior to that. And after that, it's something else. It's a living thing."[4] In Nome, with the help of an able guide, he bundled himself into a heavy parka and slipped into a dog-sled, and he and the guide mushed their way several miles through the forest. When the weather warmed, he flew out to the western-most point in the United States, Attu Island, where he boarded an American tour ship, *World Discoverer*, en route to a daring transit of arctic waters from Nome to Halifax, Nova Scotia. The ship visited seven of the loneliest islands, including Little Diomede, located only two miles from Soviet Russia. "The island is almost inaccessible," reported Michener. "Ski planes land on the Bering Sea ice in winter. We landed in rubber boats called Zodiacs, and ashore we met a wonderful mix of Eskimos, school teachers from the lower Forty-eight, and workmen building a watertank so the inhabitants could at last have drinking water from a safe source."[5]

On Little Diomede, Michener found copies of his early books. He became so engrossed in signing them for people who had wonder-ful stories to tell that he forgot the passage of time. When he finally returned to the shore, he saw with sickening clarity the *World Discoverer* sailing away without him, unaware that he was not on board. Thinking quickly, one of the Eskimos prepared his walrus-hide boat, helped Michener into it, and within a few minutes was heading out to over-take the ship. "We could not have done so," remarked Michener, "had not several keen-eyed passengers noticed the unusual craft heading for Soviet Russia. At this moment, I rose, steadied myself, and started waving violently. At last someone taking photographs realized we had not come out merely to bid the *Discoverer* bon voyage." Soon, the ship's engines ceased, and an entranceway was opened in the side of the ship. That night Michener joked to a ship's passenger: "My books may not do too well in Boston or Detroit, but they're real big on Little Diomede."[6]

The literary inspirations for the writing of *Alaska* ranged from Jack London, Rex Beach, and poet Robert Service to contemporary authors Joe McGinnis and John McPhee. Michener found McGiniss's 1980 nonfiction work *Going to Extremes* and John McPee's 1977 travel narrative *Coming into the Country* exceptional introductions to Alaskan culture and the famed Alaskan wilderness. "I read them both early on and thought they were corking good books," Jim remarked.[7] Of the two, Michener preferred McPhee's careful journalistic rendering, as the author focused on the tiny arctic hamlet of Eagle, Alaska. But the microcosm of Alaska as reported by McPhee would not work for Michener, who needed the historical record of the whole Alaskan peninsula and the Pacific Rim to tell his story.

Using his theory of the proper "weight" of subject matter, Michener thought Alaska had it all: the native peoples—Athabascans, Eskimos, Aleuts, Southeast Indians—and the geography, with the strategic importance of the arctic and the bridging of the two continents. "I know many interesting areas," Michener commented, "but I don't know any that play a keystone role in as large a hunk of earth as Alaska does." The settlement of Alaska by early peoples attracted him the most. "You see," Jim observed, "you can write about the Sioux Indians in Nebraska or the Cherokee without spending a lot of time speculating on where they came from. They're there. You can't do that in Alaska. The very nature of the people calls for some statement about how they got there." Also in his intellectual plan of the novel was a significant Russian and Canadian component. "I particularly desired to acquaint Americans with the role that neighboring Canada had played and still does play in Alaskan history."[8]

Settling into his log cabin on the Sheldon Jackson campus, Michener continued his work on the first draft of *Alaska* through January and February of 1985. He stuck to his usual writing regimen: at the typewriter by 7:00 or 7:30, steady work until noon, seven days a week. He spent the afternoons sauntering around the streets of Sitka, pausing to talk to residents or in nice weather to ruminate about things on a park bench. A soft Alaskan rain—not an Austin tempest—usually drummed on the roof through the winter. While he typed out *Alaska*, he got periodic requests from Erskine for revisions on *Texas*. This mixing of projects often led to confusion in the process. Once, Michener inadvertently typed out "Austin, Alaska" in the upper right hand corner of a letter to Erskine.

His view from Sheldon Jackson became his window on Alaska. He loved listening to Stravinsky and looking out the window at the volcanic islands poking out of the silver, motionless sea, the mists coiling like serpents around their summits. When the rain clouds abated, great slivers of sunlight lay on the water, and the headlands flashed green in the bright light. Situated on the Pacific side of Baronof Island, Sitka was the perfect place to write about the two Alaskas: the rugged evergreen wilderness of the interior and the lands fronting the sea made temperate year-round by the Japanese Current.

In January 1986 Michener underwent quintuple bypass heart surgery. Five weeks later he returned to writing *Alaska*. On May 10, 1986, feeling particularly proud of himself, he wrote Erskine and Laster: "With carefully modulated elation, I inform you that as of this afternoon I have completed in quite solid form the twelve chapters which comprise my Alaska novel." Michener further commented that it totaled 1,602 pages, which in book form would run just over 800 pages. He expected more cuts when Erskine went to work on it. "I will listen attentively to any of Erskine's suggestions for cuts," Jim noted. His health had also improved. "I went to a social gathering for the first time tonight. It was also the first time I wore a suit in almost four months. It felt rather trim. My weight has dropped from 194 to 169 and the doctors are trying to fatten me up. I rather like things as they are."[9]

The previous year the Micheners had moved into a new house on Mount Laurel Lane near the University of Texas. John Kings continued to conduct Jim's business affairs from Austin. Debbie Brothers, an editor at the State House Press in Austin, became his new secretary, replacing Nadia Orapchuck, who had retired. For the most part, however, operations had shifted to Sitka while Jim worked on *Alaska*, ably assisted by Kim Bogart-Johnson, a Stanford graduate and local secretary who typed out a clean copy of the manuscript and worked with Erskine on changes.

Back in Sitka on the first of June, Michener recuperated and returned to polishing *Alaska*. Limited in his exercise, he remained inside and spent days at the typewriter, gobbling more information from books and keeping up with his correspondence. He missed his Royal elite typewriter, which he had left in Austin. In its place he used a borrowed

Olympia, with pica type. "It seems billboard size when looking down at it," Jim commented.[10]

The summer proved to be a difficult one for the Alaska project. Albert Erskine, Jim's able editor, took ill in the middle of June and had to be hospitalized for several weeks. His recovery at home in Connecticut further delayed him returning to work and reviewing Jim's manuscript. "Under no conceivable circumstances," Jim told Laster, "will I do anything to put pressure on Erskine."[11] Jim had to rely on Owen Laster for suggestions while Erskine recuperated. Laster, who by his own admission considered himself a businessman and not an editor, found this a difficult role. Jim wanted him to read certain chapters but thought that Laster should be in Sitka to understand fully the Alaskan experience before passing judgment on the novel. "You can leave New York," Jim remarked, "and be in Sitka in time for tea at five."[12] Laster flew to Alaska on August 3 and for a solid two days read Jim's manuscript. At that point the manuscript totaled twelve chapters at 1,606 pages; some parts, however, were still with readers, so Laster read 600 of the 1,158 pages available to consider. After offering his support and making some important suggestions, Laster returned to New York.

On September 21 Michener wrote Erskine, who had since returned to work: "Herewith I send you the last four chapters of the book . . . you now have the complete manuscript as it leaves my hands after considerable revision. . . . I hope you have fun with the material. It's a tight novel but I will carefully listen as in the past to any of your suggestions for cutting."[13] Within a month, however, Erskine, after conferring with several other editors, wrote Michener with the news that Random House was urging that the entire Canadian section be deleted. "The Canadian episode," wrote Erskine, "is not only too long but it plays no generic part in the story in that it deflects attention from Alaska in a non-productive way. We recommend that it be eliminated completely. Its absence will be neither noted nor missed."[14] Michener considered this decision "devastating." He had thought this Canadian section was an integral part of the novel, and its omission would harm the project. Moreover, he wanted to depict Canada's significant role in the history of Alaska, and the idea of not being able to include it in the novel troubled him greatly. Indignant that Random House would unilaterally decide to cut the Canadian material, Michener sought out a Toronto publisher for it. Published in 1988 under the title *Journey*, the novel of Canadian high adventure was one of Michener's best short works.

In late 1986 and the opening months of 1987, Michener finalized *Alaska* with Erskine and Krantz. After a brief trip to London in mid-November, he took up residence in Coral Gables, Florida, ready to complete the Alaska novel while he outlined his next one, *Caribbean*. As early as the summer of 1986 he had made plans to write about the Caribbean, and on November 29 of that year he and Mari had settled into a modest house near the University of Miami.

On January 21 he underwent surgery in Miami for a replacement hip. In his datebook for January 25 he recorded: "Went for a walk in the hall. Met Jose Ferrer. Hallucination. Long walk with cane."[15] The next few weeks he progressed with only a few setbacks.

Michener turned eighty on February 3, 1987, and while most people were thinking of absolute rest at such an age, Michener was in full swing, his body and heart well conditioned, his mind as sharp as ever. While he recuperated from surgery through May and June, he worked on revisions for *Alaska* with Erskine. After several months of back-and-forth correspondence with Erskine and Krantz, and with several cuts and revisions, *Alaska* was ready to go into galleys by early 1988. The galleys were always a pleasure and a difficulty for Michener to pore over. "I wish that every aspirant writer," he wrote,

> who dreams of kicking out a quickie that will stun the world could look at these galleys and see in his or her mind's eye the stupendous amount of hard work that needs to be done before inspiring words appear in a finished book. . . . I realize that there could be easier ways than those I follow; all one needs is blazing talent, volcanic inspiration, a faultless touch, complete mastery of the English language, and [a] hell of a lot of good luck. I have lacked those qualities, but with other attributes one can still produce books worth reading.[16]

Released in June 1988 in an appropriately gold-colored hardcover, *Alaska* had a first printing of eight hundred thousand copies, a record both for Michener and for the publishing industry. In most ways, the novel fulfilled Jim's ambition of writing an adventure novel covering the Alaska experience. Like *Centennial, Alaska* reaches into the distant past and provides abundant details of geologic and natural history. And like *Centennial,* the novel features the life of a creature—Matriarch, the woolly mammoth. In succession, the chapters discuss the arrival of the earliest peoples, who reach Alaska by land bridge from Asia. Next come the Russian traders, English sailors, and American whalers. The Russians move into southeast Alaska, establishing New Archangel, the early name for Sitka. After Alaska becomes an American possession in 1867, the stage is set for the discovery of gold in the 1890s. These are some of the best parts of Michener's novel, as the gold-crazed Klondike turns ordinary people into malevolent, subhuman wrecks. The chapter titled "Gold" (originally named "Stampede") introduces the characters of Buck and Tom Venn and Melissa "Missy" Peckham, one of Michener's notable creations in the novel. It could be said that strong-willed and independent women dominate *Alaska.* While the men are absorbed in their various distractions, the women build a civilization in this harsh and forbidding land. There are several major heroines in *Alaska*—the Aleut girl Cidag, Missy Peckham, and teacher Kendra Scott—who find that the terrain, climate, and people of Alaska transform their lives. They form a long line of Michener's courageous women stretching back to Ellie Zendt, Emma Larkin, and ultimately to Mabel Michener.

Although *Alaska* contains the familiar Michener ingredients— exploration, conquest, subjugation, exploitation, warfare, courage, endurance, and tenuous harmony among peoples—it does not necessarily result in the same old product. It has some masterful touches in the "carry" sequences of the narrative. Michener distinguished between the "carry" and "scene" parts of storytelling. Calling it the "more cerebral segment," he defined "carry" as the part of the narrative in which he conveys background information, important ideas, or what characters strive for in their lives. "Done well, it can be marvelously rewarding, and the carry segments of *War and Peace* are among the best ever written," Jim observed. Carry sequences contain little or no dialogue. Scene segments, on the other hand, show character interaction, such as "a Stendhal argument or a Jane Austen tea party."[17] Writers, Jim maintained, usually favor one over the other. In his case, he excelled in carry sequences, but in scene sequences he was often deficient, resorting to dialogue that was wooden, contrived, or simply unrealistic.

The editing of *Journey* and *Alaska* marked the end of the Erskine-Michener relationship. Suffering from health problems, Erskine decided to retire after editing *Journey* for American publication. As one of Random House's finest editors, he was close enough to Michener not only to often read his mind but also to anticipate what would happen in the narrative. Random House had groomed a young editor, Kate Medina, to take Erskine's place.

Michener arrived at the University of Miami with the academic title of Distinguished Visiting Professor of English. Although he did not need academe—he once said that all he needed was a desk, a library, and an airport—he welcomed the idea of being a part of a university or college. In his suburban home in Coral Gables, with his banged-up Oldsmobile station wagon in the driveway, Michener worked on *Caribbean*, which was published in late 1989.

Michener projected that his novel would once again be a blend of fact and fiction, beginning with tribal conflicts on the island of Dominica and the arrival of Columbus and stretching into the modern era. Important historical personages would be featured throughout the story, among them the indefatigable seadog Sir Francis Drake, the nefarious buccaneer Henry Morgan, and the young, venal Horatio Nelson. Later in the book, Michener would have one of his characters interview Fidel Castro. The novel would also present the rise of the Jamaican sugar plantations, the violent 1800 slave revolt in Haiti, and the eventual freedom from slavery throughout the Caribbean islands.

The publication of *Caribbean* in the autumn of 1989 was the culmination of a decade that was nothing less than extraordinary. In the 1980s Michener published six major novels—*The Covenant, Space, Poland, Texas, Alaska,* and *Caribbean*—and two shorter novels and *Journey*—

moved four times, served on three committees, traveled continuously, had two operations, read religiously, and still found time to take in operas and symphonies. He continued to confound critics and the publishing industry alike. In creating the Michener phenomenon—and there is no other word to describe it—Jim avoided trends, researched constantly, relied on his keen intuition and classical training, blended forms, guided the creative process in most instances with unwavering integrity, and produced blockbuster after blockbuster. In never cheapening his product, he created his own niche in the publishing industry, a niche that most other writers could only envy from afar.

CHAPTER 19

Portrait of the Artist

Throughout his career Michener developed many important professional relationships with editors and publishers. With magazines, the *Reader's Digest* association had been strong and cordial. Their relationship began in the early 1950s, when he and *Digest* founder De Witt Wallace and Senior Editor Hobart Lewis sat down and hammered out a long-standing agreement. His first article for *Reader's Digest* appeared in 1950 and his last in 1993. With newspapers, his association with the *New York Times* was especially positive over the years. His op-ed pieces, feature articles on international relations, and book reviews were particularly welcomed by the *Times*. However, just as welcome were articles about Michener by other authors. Between 1946 and 1992, 120 articles appeared in the *New York Times* featuring an aspect of Michener's life or career, this in addition to articles about Michener appearing in the *New York Times Book Review* and the *New York Times Magazine*.

In book publishing, Random House had been his mainstay since 1949, when he first walked into the offices on Madison Avenue with the manuscript of *The Fires of Spring* tucked under his arm and met the lanky, chain-smoking editor Saxe Commins. Working with Bennett Cerf, Albert Erskine, Bert Krantz, and a host of other staffers over the years had made him especially close to the Random House name. In March 1990, however, the relationship became jeopardized by a series of changes at the firm. Erskine and Krantz had retired. Random House's president, Robert Bernstein, a close Michener ally, had been forced to resign the previous December. Another ally, Andre Schriffrin, was also forced to resign as managing director of Pantheon Books, a subsidiary of Random House. Bernstein's successor was Alberto Vitale, whom Michener described as an "able number-cruncher, but not a man reared in the traditions of American publishing." Michener also criticized Vitale's record of having fired six hundred people at Doubleday. "Now," claimed Michener, "everybody is waiting for the other shoe to drop at Random House."[1]

In issuing a three-page statement about the matter, Michener threatened to pull up stakes at Random House and head for "some small house, obedient to the old traditions." Michener had already placed works with smaller houses, including *The Eagle and the Raven* with State House Press, which was codirected by Debbie Brothers, his secretary in Austin; *Six Days in Havana* with the University of Texas Press; and *Pilgrimage* with the Rodale Press in Emmaus, Pennsylvania.

Michener, confident his reputation was in top form, asked Owen Laster to attempt to shop his two manuscripts, "The Novel" and "The World Is My Home," to three other major publishers. "To my astonishment," said Michener, "considering my track record of decades of successful publishing, no house wanted the manuscripts. The first publisher did not care to publish either of the books. The second house said it 'might consider the autobiography but would not care for the other.' The third house, less magisterial than the other two, declared: 'Michener is a nice fellow, but his day is passed.'"[2] The rejections were "mortifying" to Michener. Beaten and humiliated by this turn of events and not willing to enter a wrestling match with Random House, he agreed to talk to the publisher's new executives and see if a compromise could be worked out.

Vitale and S. I. Newhouse, whose family-owned Advance Publications owned Random House, headed off a threatened mutiny by scheduling a meeting in Washington, D.C., with one of their most treasured authors. At the meeting, Michener made it clear that he did not wish to leave Random House. All it would take for him to sign a new contract was for the two men to "define their understanding of how the world's largest English language publisher should conduct its business."[3] The negotiations were cordial but businesslike. When Michener left Washington, he was satisfied that he had gotten the best deal he could. Shortly thereafter, his next two books—*The Novel* and *The World Is My Home*—went under contract with Random House.

That *The Novel*, a book about the New York publishing industry, should have been written at this crucial time in Michener's career was completely coincidental. Michener had first thought of the idea more than thirty years earlier, but the seeds of it go back to the early 1940s, when Michener worked in the editorial offices of Macmillan and got his first glimpse of the vicissitudes of the trade. In the 1960s he toyed with the idea of a first-person narrative of a writer coping with the publishing industry but made no attempt to begin writing the book. In February 1978 he took a red notebook and outlined the novel "in great detail, proposing to write it shortly thereafter." He laid it aside to begin work on *The Covenant* and further postponed it as he wrote his novels of the 1980s. In March 1989, having completed *Caribbean* and the draft of *The World Is My Home*, he once again picked up the idea and wrote *The Novel* in first-draft form. "The scenes have altered enormously in the last eleven years," he noted, "but that makes it increasingly interesting and I shall hope to capitalize on the new environments of international cartels and shifting allegiances, none of which do I approve. . . . My four characters remain unsullied and ought to provide me with much interest."[4] He considered writing it in the third person but finally settled on a first-person narrative, each section in turn related by one of his four characters: the writer, the editor, the critic, and the reader.

The Novel was begun in Miami and finished at Michener's home on Mount Laurel Lane in Austin. Periodically he picked up his work and headed to his office at the University of Texas. Michener explained the move from Florida to Texas: "Bewildered by the University of Miami to decide what to do about the proposed writing school, and receiving mixed signals from various professors, I decided following two longs talks with Mari to throw my lot heavily with Texas, move there in September, and use my time writing the novel."[5] Sitting in his khaki shorts, his socks pulled up over his white calves, he delighted in this particular project to show his fans that he was capable of other topics and to tweak critics who lay in wait for his next novel.

In late 1989 he had been invited by Eckerd College in St. Petersburg, Florida, to use the facilities of the college during the winter months and to assist in the writing program. On April 13, 1990, he announced to his many friends that he and Mari intended to apportion their year as follows: "Autumn semester at Eckerd, spring semester at Texas, and summer at our condominium near Bowdoin College in Brunswick, Maine."[6] Jim insisted that they would maintain their primary residence in Austin. However, its torrid summers had prompted him to buy a condominium in "The Pines," an upscale complex thirty miles north of Portland near the Maine coast.

Michener was well aware that publishers stayed in business by retaining big names like his, while young talented writers went begging or remained unpublished. This pained him greatly. As early as the 1950s he alluded to this despairing fact in the article "The Chances against the Beginning Writer," in which he demonstrated the mathematical odds of getting a first novel published.[7] In the 1980s, as a seasoned pro, most of the writing fellowships he sponsored stipulated that monies be earmarked for talented writers in programs in which they could focus totally on their writing. Shortly before his death in 1997, Michener defined himself as a writer "who has been able to entertain and instruct millions of readers in all languages, and in doing so help to keep a publisher solvent so that he could afford to print books of fine writers who did not find large audiences."[8]

He wrote *The Novel* to be read on several levels: as a comment on the contemporary state of American trade publishing; as a swipe at the critics who had dogged him all his career; as a sentiment of the harried and tenuous career of a trade book editor; and as an appraisal of a writer reaching the end of his career. In this sly and calculated departure from his previous work, Michener offers the reader one Lukas Yoder, a prolific writer who at age sixty-seven is about to publish his most anticipated novel. Yoder's career has seesawed over the years, but he has achieved best-sellerdom and fame with a series of novels about the Amish. At the onset of the novel, he is about to cap his illustrious career with what he claims is his final book, the last in the Amish series. The novel's setting is the Pennsylvania Dutch country north of Philadelphia, an area known intimately to Michener.

Prepublication chatter predicts that Yoder's novel, *Stone Walls*, will be a disappointment, largely because it departs from the author's customary style and approach. Yoder is subjected to criticism by his agent, his editor, and the moguls at the financially strapped publishing house. They all plead with Yoder to revise the book and appease the demands of his adoring public. Yoder's agent tells him that the book business expects great things from its talented writers and that his publisher, Kinetic, has invested heavily in Yoder's future. If his new book can be saved, Yoder should make every effort to do so. If Yoder's book fails, the publishing house will be subject to a takeover, thus ending the career of Yoder's loyal editor, Yvonne Marmelle. Marmelle relates the second part of the novel, while Karl Streibert, the critic, relates the third. Streibert, a college professor imprisoned by his own inadequacy and failure as a writer, also shares Yoder's editor, Yvonne Marmelle. His literary career, along with that of a bright student, rests on the decision of an author whom they loathe. Finally, a faithful reader of Yoder unites them and helps solve a crime that has torn the region apart.

Michener's enmeshed foursome of author, editor, critic, and reader forms the nucleus of the wacky and diabolical world of publishing: from what the writer writes, to what the agent and editor expect, to what the reviewer likes, and to what the public reads. Will Yoder bow to pressure? Who ultimately holds the power in the publishing process? With over forty years' experience at the center stage of his own drama, Michener provides some compelling and surprising answers.

Like his protagonist, Lukas Yoder, Michener always wondered if his current book would flop and thereby end his long and distinguished career. Still insisting that he never read reviews of his books, he often planned to be out of the country when a book made its debut. Valid criticism did not bother him, but unqualified critics irked him greatly. He kept numerous clippings of good and bad reviews of his work. Some were sent to him by friends and fellow writers. When an interviewer asked him if *The Novel* was his attempt to take revenge on his critics, he flashed an enigmatic smile and changed the topic.[9]

The Novel, Michener's thirty-seventh book, was published in March 1991. The *Washington Post* called it "ghastly," the *San Francisco Chronicle*, "disastrous." The general consensus among those who said positive things about the book was that it was a refreshing glimpse at the publishing business and at one writer's self-analysis. Most of the negative comments centered on Michener's oaken style, creaky dialogue, and one-dimensional characters. Michener's "last" novel went on to roaring success, becoming one of the top-selling books of 1991 and convincing him that he was still the master with the Midas touch.

In the 1990s James Michener was a wealthy man, but instead of spending or hoarding his money, he used his time searching for suitable institutions and charities to which to donate large portions of it. In June 1990 the Micheners announced that they were gifting $3 million to the University of Texas Center for Writers. In announcing the donation, Michener declared: "We are totally committed to helping young writers. Several existing writing programs have distinguished records, and it would give me enormous satisfaction to see the Texas Center for Writers become one of the nation's best. I am devoting my energies and extra income to that purpose."[10] Michener's generosity had already been felt at the university. The center annually awarded five James A. Michener Fellowships to students who had completed master's degrees and were close to getting substantial writing projects published. Each student received $8,000 plus tuition and fees.

After *Caribbean* was written, several projects were on Michener's desk. Among them were *The Novel*, an art article, and his autobiography, a project that had been in his mind for some time but whose introspective nature had scared him away. Since the 1970s friends and professional colleagues had urged him to write his autobiography. He wanted to write it. Every passing year persuaded him that he should. One thing, however, stood in his way: he would be obliged to reveal his troubled marriages, his personal relationships, his failures and weaknesses as well as his successes. In short, he would have to be vulnerable, and this shocked him almost as much as financial ruin or the sudden eclipse of his career.

Until 1988 he delayed the project. Finally, his physical condition convinced him to begin. On February 25, 1988, he jotted in his notes: "Last night at about midnight I reached the decision to write as my next book a set of recollections, the first seven chapters dealing with my private life from birth to age 81, written as if I had never written a book of any kind or even thought of doing do. . . . It will be as careful and honest an account as I can make it."[11] He finally settled on a structure for this autobiography in which he could sidestep vulnerability. Instead of chronological structure, he settled on a memoir by subject, each chapter with his famous one-word title. Among them are: "Vice," "Travel," "People," "Ideas," "Health," "Wealth," and "Meanings." Using this random and digressive structure, he could be in total control of the material—a vintage Michener trait.

If introspection was taboo, self-analysis was literary suicide. The idea that the deepest parts of his being might yield some slithering monster as well as some surprising creative ideas scared Michener more than anything. "I've seen people get sadly tangled in that psychological morass and eviscerate themselves," Michener claimed. "They brood and lose all their capacity to grapple with things. The artistic life is very tenuous. You can analyze away your own sense of commitment." This unwillingness to examine the deeper layers of self, many critics believe, led to some predictable results in his fiction. "Michener has trouble getting inside characters' heads," critic Lynn Rosellini observed, "and difficulty dealing with emotion and the nuance of human behavior. Too often the characters are cardboard and the dialogue jarringly wooden and cliché-ridden." To this charge, Michener responded: "Just as I am not interested in analyzing myself, I am not interested in analyzing my characters."[12]

While Michener was involved in examining his past, he could have solved the mystery of his parentage, the greatest, darkest mystery of his life. He never chose to do this. He could have hired a professional sleuth to track down his father's identity and could have used mitochondrial DNA testing to establish that Mabel Michener was indeed his birth mother. However, he chose to close the door on this aspect of his life in his late teens and never reopened it. "He will go out of this world not knowing who he was or where he came from," John Kings remarked.[13] For Michener, such mystery was just fine.

Working from his home in Austin, he wrote his autobiography, *The World Is My Home*, between early 1988 and early 1989. His working notes reveal that the chapters were written out of final sequence. For instance, chapter 12, titled "Health," begun on February 29, 1988, was the first to be written. Next came "Wealth" on March 6, "Meanings" on March 14. The first two chapters, "Mutiny" and "Tour," were written in May. The last chapter to be written in first draft was "Politics," which was finished in late August 1988. When the book was put into its final sequence, Michener focused on his most pleasurable memories and then moved into material requiring more philosophical reflection. The first ninety pages deal with Jim's wartime experiences in the South Pacific, as he relates his arrival on Espíritu Santo and his introduction to the characters and customs of the tropics. Here, too, was his initiation into the loneliness and tedium of naval duty, subjects that he had turned to his advantage in his first novel.

Despite all of its trials and deprivations, Michener's childhood was a magical time. As recalled in the chapter "Vice," it was a time when he discovered music and art, travel and sports, ice-cream makers, Victrolas, and the temper of his beloved uncle Arthur. In this part, Michener confesses that operatic music helped to delude him into writing about the human struggle in more dramatic terms than situations might dictate. Although it distorted his perceptions, he cited the influence of opera, which he called "passionate, absurd, and illogical," as the most powerful force behind his creative talent. "My love of the operatic aria," he maintained, "has encouraged me to allow my characters to declaim at length when a brief speech might be more effective, and my enormous respect for the great duets tempts me to have two characters speaking to each other just a bit longer than the literary scene would warrant." For critics who always sensed that Michener's style bordered on grandiosity, it was immediate confirmation of their suspicions.

In subsequent sections, Michener relates the most important people who influenced him, his attractions to politics and political theory, his literary gods, his writing philosophy, and his days spent as a textbook editor for Macmillan in New York. In each part, however, amid occasional flights of hubris, the master storyteller emerges. Michener divulged several of these anecdotes over the years during interviews. Many, though, were first told in this memoir.

The most secret stories involved Michener's service in government and on government committees. Most Americans were unaware that during Michener's reign as a preeminent writer in American life, he also served with distinction in several key groups. One, of course, was the USIA during the Nixon administration; another was his involvement with the NASA Advisory Board; and third was his association with the Board for International Broadcasting. One affiliation that gave him particular satisfaction—and frustration—was the U.S. Postage Stamp Committee, which decides what postage stamps the government will issue. He served on the committee during the mid-1970s to the late 1980s.

Michener ends his autobiography by telling the reader how he would like to be remembered. Included among his most noble accomplishments were the libraries and art museums named after him, his financial legacy to young writers, the rooms that bear his name in three hotels (the Aggie Grey in Samoa, Raffles in Singapore, and the Oriental in Bangkok), and his ultimate triumph, "that solid row of books that rest on library shelves throughout the world."[14]

The World Is My Home received great fanfare before publication. Michener's reading public had waited for years for the master to reveal his secrets about writing, his background, his personal relationships, and the things that made him tick as a person. Most readers were happy with the result, although many were disappointed by the quiet exclusion of most of Michener's emotional life. Published in the early days of 1992, *The World Is My Home* became a Book of the Month Club main selection. Writing in the club's "Book News," historian David McCullough claimed Michener's memoir read "just like a classic Michener novel. It's big and colorful, crammed with a lifetime's experiences, well stuffed with curious bits of information and liberally peppered with opinions that range from the crotchety to the profound."[15]

The book went on to receive the most complimentary reviews that Michener had experienced since the days of *The Source, Hawaii, Iberia,* and *Centennial.* Herbert Mitgang, writing in the *New York Times,* praised the autobiography and declared "no other American writer has made the world the subject of his writing with such sympathy for the universal nature of people everywhere. . . . He's a great story-teller and a keen educator."[16] While acknowledging the book as being an important glimpse into Michener's personal life, *Publishers Weekly* declared: "This is a frustrating book, then, because one wishes to know Michener better than he seems to know himself, but it will probably delight his fans, even if it misleads them."[17] *Kirkus Reviews* observed: "Altogether engaging and a decidedly selective reminis-cence from the peripatetic writer who's one of the world's most suc-cessful storytellers. . . . The idiosyncratic format permits him to comment at length on topics of his choosing and to avoid subjects he finds painful or none of the reader's business."[18]

As *The World Is My Home* went on to popular success—not at the top of the best-seller list but in "the respectable suburbs"—Michener viewed his attempt to leave Random House with some amusement. If any of the three major publishers he approached had taken *The Novel* and his memoir, he surmised, they would have automatically been in line to receive his next two novels—a gold mine in terms of revenue for any publishing house. Instead, he remained with Ran-dom House, who continued to reap the benefits from its star author.

CHAPTER 20

The Tough Old Bird

Michener always believed in serendipity, and the events of spring 1991 seemed to confirm that his career was blessed with a string of charmed coincidences. Albert Erskine, during the last years of his tenure at Random House, expressed to Jim on several occasions that resurrecting the Mexico manuscript, which Jim had aborted in 1961, might be a viable option. For all Jim knew, however, the manuscript was buried in some vault at the Library of Congress, and retrieving it might be too difficult. Moreover, at the time, he had no interest in reviving the Mexico project.

Mari was also interested in the project. She volunteered to go to Washington, D.C., and retrieve the manuscript herself. Michener turned down her request. In the late 1980s his agent, Owen Laster, discovered that there still was a contract with Random House for a manuscript titled "Festival," the original name of the novel about Mexico. "When he read the legal papers," remarked Jim, "he sprang into action, for if the manuscript could be finished he would have an unexpected ready-made novel when my books were doing well."[1] While Michener pursued other projects, Laster spearheaded a search for the lost manuscript. Laster believed that the manuscript was either at the Library of Congress, perhaps misfiled there, or, for some odd reason, still at

Michener's home in Pipersville. The Micheners had not lived in the Pipersville home since the summer of 1976, so any search would have to be done through rooms stacked with stored items. Laster went on to other business matters at William Morris.

In the spring of 1991 the Mexico project was in limbo. Random House had asked Jim for some old family photographs to accompany *The World Is My Home*. These photos, Jim knew, were part of the shipment along with the Mexico material that he had sent to the Library of Congress in 1961. After a search of Michener's papers at the Library of Congress turned up nothing of the photos or the Mexico manuscript, Jim wondered if they ever left his Pipersville home in the first place. He telephoned his cousin, Virginia Trumbull, who lived in Salisbury, Maryland, and asked her to drive up to Pipersville and try to find the photographs in the Micheners' home. Additionally, he asked her to look around for the Mexico materials, which inadvertently might have been stored rather than mailed to the Library of Congress.

Two weeks later Michener received a phone call from Trumbull confirming that she had found both the old photographs and the Mexico manuscript. Both would be in the mail to Austin shortly. Michener was flabbergasted. "When I opened the box," he reported, "I found my original typing of the first ten chapters, my secretary's clean retyping in condition ready for editors, two fat notebooks . . . and a third notebook crammed with well over a hundred photos I'd taken of the bullfight milieu in Mexico and Spain. . . . It was a treasure that contained everything I remembered, everything I needed to complete the remaining chapters. It was an invitation to start work. It was a miracle."[2]

After combing the pages and chapters, he found his three-decade-old manuscript to be remarkably vital and contemporary. "Unfinished and unpolished they were," he observed, "but they were real writing about real characters and significant historical events. They formed a solid base on which to build further. He outlined his vision for the new project on paper. "In a ruthless process of elimination and consolidation and devising new chapters," Michener came up with a workable template for the novel.[3]

With this material in hand, the novel *Mexico* begged to be finished. Other projects, however, were nearing completion. Among them was the draft of *Miracle in Seville,* which was not published until 1995. If he resumed *Mexico* directly, they would have to be laid aside. "I am engulfed with projects," he remarked, "manuscripts everywhere, things I have a keen desire to do, but none exceeds the excitement I feel when I read these wonderful Mexico chapters."[4] He decided to finish the remaining chapters of *Mexico* and ready it for publication, which Random House undertook in November 1992.

There were other pressures affecting his decision. During a recent exam, Mari discovered a lump in her breast. A biopsy proved that it was cancerous. The Micheners agonized over treatments. Some doctors and patients recommended lumpectomies and some radical cutting. Other experts recommended radiation and still others chemotherapy. After consulting numerous sources, the Micheners settled on mastectomy followed by radiation. Mari entered the hospital in late June 1991 to have her operation, followed by an intensive six-week radiation program. While she was there, Jim planned to work fifteen-hour days to complete the Mexico project. "My work would prove therapeutic for both of us," Jim reasoned. "Mari could be sure I wasn't fretting myself into despair, while I could be sure that she was doing the right thing."[5]

Working in the hot Austin summer, the drapes pulled against the glaring sunlight, Michener discovered that the sudden finding of his project evoked vivid memories of Mexico, made even more poignant by Mari's current absence from their home. "It seemed at times that Mari and I were back in Mexico City," Jim wrote, "making our expeditions into the countryside, and to Guanajuato, the scene of my imaginary city of Toledo. . . . There were the mariachis I had loved, the flamenco dancers who had charmed me, the museum, the catacombs with ranks of standing mummies all in colonial costume. . . . Mari and I were once again in the old Hotel Cortes and the decades vanished, leaving me with the burgeoning enthusiasm I had known in those days of dedication."[6]

May 1992 found the Micheners in Austin, prepared to make another sizable philanthropic contribution to the University of Texas. On May 19 it was announced that the couple was donating 172 American paintings to the university, this in addition to the 107 works that had been on loan since 1968 as part of the Mari and James A. Michener

Collection. Valued at $20 million, the collection was one of the most prestigious in America. In accepting the donation, University of Texas president William Cunningham called the gift "a monumental assemblage of American paintings." When all the works were finally hung in the Archer M. Huntington Art Gallery on campus, it was considered the finest collection of American art at any university in the United States.[7]

As he amassed his collection of Bentons, Hoffmans, and Sloans in the 1950s through the 1980s, painting was never far from Jim's heart. As late as 1991 he yearned to write another art book, one that could be placed beside his five books on Japanese prints. He entered into negotiations with Milton Esterow, editor and publisher of *Art News Magazine,* with the idea of writing a substantial book on his own involvement in the world of art. Tentatively titled "Painting and the Writer," the book would follow his tutelage in the world of art, from his initial collecting of postcard-size prints to his mature assembling of one of the country's finest private collections. He would include his education haunting the great museums of the world and discuss how he refined his own critical eye regarding great paintings. As it turned out, the project was dropped by the publisher because of inadequate funding, but Jim remained committed to getting his story out. Unfortunately, there was never another chance.

Three months following his gift of American art to the University of Texas, Michener announced that he was donating yet another $15 million to the University of Texas Center for Writers. Officials expected the program, which included monies for luring top-caliber writers and graduate students as well as awarding master of fine arts degrees in creative writing, would be up and running by the fall of 1993. Until Michener's donation the center operated on a modest budget and awarded no degrees. With Michener's assistance the program hoped to take a giant leap forward and challenge the writing programs at other universities, most notably the big-gun programs at the University of Iowa, the University of Southern California, and Columbia University.

Michener set strict guidelines for the use of the funds. He specified that none of the monies could be used for resident faculty salaries, to erect buildings, or to pay for "a Caribbean conference." Stressing that he did not want to pay for an "unrestricted cornucopia," he was not above patrolling the halls of the English department, rapping on doors, and asking the director how the funds were being spent.[8]

Additional gifts to other universities followed, including $600,000 to the University of Northern Colorado to endow the library named after him and $1 million to Eckerd College to endow scholarships. A year earlier Michener gave Swarthmore $5 million.

By the fall of 1992 it appeared that Michener was divesting his fortune, giving it away at a time when he still had a sound mind and body to make good financial decisions and also rewarding those institutions that had helped him. He was amused by how closely fundraisers followed aging donors. "There is a little man somewhere," he mused, "that sits in a room with a calendar. And on the first of January every year, he rings a bell and says, 'Hey fellas, he or she is eighty-six years old this year. You better get to work right away.'"[9]

John Bear, in his book *The No. 1 New York Times Bestsellers*, published in the spring of 1993, declared James Michener the heavyweight champion of best sellers. Ever since the New York Times Bestseller List originated in August 1942, 484 titles had reached the number-one position. While Stephen King had more number-one titles—sixteen— Michener's works, taken together, spent 207 weeks at the top of the lists, more than any other author. King was a distant second with 100 weeks.

Over the fifty-year span, Michener sustained a mastery of the New York Times Bestseller List that was truly impressive. Four of his novels— *The Source* (1965), *Centennial* (1974), *Chesapeake* (1978), and *The Covenant* (1980)—finished in the number-one position for the year. *Hawaii* (1960), *Space* (1982), *Poland* (1983), and *Texas* (1985) ended the year in second place. Additionally, *Caravans* (1962) was fourth; *Alaska* (1988) and *Caribbean* (1989) were fifth; and *Return to Paradise* (1952), *The Drifters* (1972), and *Mexico* (1992) finished in eighth place. The remainder of his books, including *Tales of the South Pacific*, *The Fires of Spring*, *The Bridges at Toko-Ri*, *Sayonara*, and *Iberia*, also generated outstanding sales figures.

One of the contradictions of Jim's character that perplexed people the most was his handling of finances. On one hand, he found it difficult to pay for dinner at a restaurant or buy a pair of socks; on the other, he seemed to have no trouble giving away enormous sums of money to universities and charities. Raised in poverty, when he wondered where his next meal was coming from, Jim had a deprivation mentality throughout his life. He seriously questioned the most minor of purchases. At the same time, his gifts to universities were usually accompanied by strategically orchestrated press conferences. In other words, Jim liked to spend huge amounts of money if people knew he was doing it. Power and ego were a large part of Jim's philanthropy. The silent gift of $5,000 to support a program was not as significant to him as the announcement in front of a crowd of people, journalists, television crews, and university administrators that he was donating $5 million or $10 million to a worthy cause. Such orchestrations soothed his ego, turned the focus on him, and made him feel noteworthy.

He could, however, be quietly generous. Throughout 1993 he continued to give in such a fashion. The beneficiaries of his charity included the Doylestown Art Museum, James A. Michener Art Muscum, Mercer Museum (Doylestown), Bucks County Library, Authors League Fund for Older Writers in Need, George School, and Hill School. By the time of his death in 1997, he had given away over $117 million.

In the autumn of 1993 the Micheners, along with their friends the Silvermans, had planned to drive to Nova Scotia for a brief vacation. In September, however, Mari learned that Holland America Lines had offered Jim and her a complimentary cruise around the world. All Jim had to do was give a brief series of lectures at various points and mix with the other passengers.

In October they were on board the SS *Rotterdam* leaving Los Angeles for points in Russia and Asia. On the voyage, Jim developed severe shortness of breath, which limited his activity, although he could carry on cordial conversations with passengers while seated. His legs and ankles were swelling up, causing his doctors on board to put him on a salt-free diet. After stops in Vladivostok, Russia; Muroran, Japan; and Pusan, Korea, the ship's doctors urged him to seek medical attention in America. Consequently, the Micheners reluctantly gave up their cruise in Hong Kong and flew home to Austin on October 21, where Jim was taken by wheelchair from the plane.

At the hospital in Austin, his doctors regulated his heartbeat with a pacemaker and treated him for kidney failure with dialysis. Slowly and painfully, Jim recovered for the next few months. "My legs were like oak trees," Jim remarked, "enormous things and hard as wood. I also found that accumulations of liquid had invaded my stomach and thoracic activity. . . . After four weeks of highly-skilled dialysis, my legs looked like legs again, my weight dropped to 147 pounds, and I was a new man."[10] Jim learned, however, that his dialysis treatment would have to continue, three hours a day, three days a week, for the foreseeable future. Limited by this "onerous" schedule for what could be the rest his life, he predicted that he could write one more good book. He also planned to return to his schedule of going to Maine in the summer and then on to Florida in the fall.

When he left the hospital and returned home to Mount Laurel Lane, two nurses arrived three days a week and performed dialysis. "The machine is quite miraculous," explained Michener about his treatment. "You have a catheter in your body somewhere, your arm or chest. They hook up two plastic tubes, one red and one green. The red takes the blood out of your body and green pumps it back in. The machine performs the function of the urinary tract."[11] By summer it was clear to Jim that the machine would be part of his life forever. It was ironic that the man who tried to maintain control of every situation was also given the opportunity to choose his own death if need be.

Mari Michener was seventy-four in the summer of 1994. In August, after complaining of pain, she was diagnosed as having a form of heart disease, aortic stenosis, or the narrowing of a heart valve. A short time later in the hospital, an X-ray disclosed even more distressing news. At 11:00 in the evening, Mari's doctor telephoned Jim at home and requested to come over. The ashen-faced doctor stood in the Michener living room and said, "Jim, you and Mari have always wanted the truth up front. Are you of the same mind?"

When Jim nodded, the doctor said, "We've found that Mari's entire internal system below her navel has been invaded by a monstrous cancer. All the vital organs have been attacked: spleen, liver, kidneys, digestive tract. Half a dozen of us agreed that it was inoperable. It would be totally impossible."

"Inoperable?" asked Michener. "Is that the same as terminal?"

"Yes."

"How long?"

"Months, not years. And maybe weeks, not months."[12]

The Micheners had recently signed living wills that directed their doctors not to keep them alive by "heroic measures" if their days were clearly numbered. The doctors had suggested that radical chemotherapy, Mari's only hope, might put the cancer in remission. Jim took her to the cancer center in Houston, where she underwent the procedure. In mid-September, however, after little or no improvement, Mari returned to Austin to spend her last days in her own home, surrounded, as Jim put it, by "scores of personal friends who made her sick room a kind of social salon." On Sunday, September 25, after visiting with several friends, Mari told Jim and a few close relatives: "I have loved you so much." At 7:00 in the evening, after "a placid day," recalled Michener, "she left."[13]

Even though he considered himself a "tough hombre," Michener was knocked to his knees by Mari's death. "I was devastated to watch that really tough-spirited little girl, sixty inches tall, maintaining her courage to the end." He did not sleep a second or eat a meal for two long nights. Finally, on the third morning, he asked a friend to take him to the morgue. Although the custodians protested, Michener gained access and viewed Mari's body. "She was beautiful," he said, "and as I kissed her for the last time I whispered: 'So long, Cookie. We had a great tour together.' And she was gone."[14]

Early in the 1970s Jim and Mari had made a pact that when they died, they would like to be buried near that spot, no matter where in the world it was. For Mari, it was a little cemetery in Austin. After cremation, she was laid to rest under a tree, her grave marked with these words in Kentucky limestone:

Mari Sabusawa Michener
1920–1994
Philanthropist
Art Lover
Wife

After Mari's passing, Jim endured a month of paralyzing grief, seldom leaving the house. By December, however, he admitted to friends
that he was once again interested in attending social gatherings and
heading out for an evening of country music. His new housekeeper
was Amelia Valdez, who had moved into the home to take care of
him. His assistants, John Kings, Debbie Brothers, and Susan Dillon,
were also on hand to chauffer him around Austin or to pick up a pre-
scription at the pharmacy.

Friends dropped in to wish him well, among them Larry Grobel,
a freelance writer who had conducted the interview with Jim for
Playboy magazine in the early 1980s. Grobel had also written several
books that Michener enjoyed: *Conversations with Capote* and *Conversations with Brando;* Grobel planned to write a similar book with Michener
(*Talking with Michener*), which, after an extensive question-and-answer
session lasting many months, would yield a candid, unguarded side
of the author.

When Grobel arrived in late 1994, he found Michener sitting at
his desk clipping out stories about Mari for his scrapbook. Instead
of finding a lonely, grief-stricken old man, he found one surprisingly
energetic and hopeful. "I had a fantastic evening the other night,"
said Michener. "Willie Nelson was in town to give a concert. Five piece
band with a lead guitar. Electronics like you never heard before. After
the show we went into his traveling bus and sat around for forty minutes
recalling old times, new problems." As the time approached for his
dialysis treatment, Michener growled: "You'll see me wince like hell
when they put the bloody needles in, but three minutes later everything's working."[15]

Grobel's interviews with Michener extended into 1997. In the book,
Michener is perhaps the most relaxed and freewheeling as in any
interview he ever gave. "I held nothing back," he told Grobel. "I'm

not saving anything for a sequel."[16] But despite the often bitter and confessional asides about conservatives, Nobel Prize winners, and fanaticism in general, he did hold material back. Very little again is mentioned of Jim's personal life—his marriages, his adoptions, his friendships—the usual items that Michener kept locked away in a strongbox at the bottom of the ocean. Michener could be quite forthcoming and direct about issues that touched him: the Middle East, the writing process, publishing, sports, travel, bullfighting, education, and censorship. To that end, Grobel's book is a revealing and beguiling journey through Michener's career.

Michener spent the remaining years and months of his life in predictable routine: writing, dialysis treatments, eating regularly, a trip to the university to view his American art collection, perhaps an afternoon matinee, and in bed and asleep by 7:30 in the evening. While he felt tied down, his heart longed again for the open road. He told Buzz Potter of the *Hobo Times* that he was still "a bum at heart. I long to hit the road again to go anywhere on any project, but alas, I've been hit by a troublesome health problem which keeps me tied to one spot, but in memory I travel everywhere."[17] *Miracle in Seville* appeared on October 1, 1995, and directly behind it in line was *This Noble Land*, which Jim originally gave the gloomy title "Lament for the Noble Land." Dedicated to his editor, Kate Medina, the book was his last for Random House and also marked the last of Jim's books designed by Carole Lowenstein, who had given each Michener title since 1978 her personal signature. Lowenstein's assistance in making Michener a perennial best seller was often overlooked by readers and critics, but her distinctive book designs were significant and noteworthy.

This Noble Land: My Vision for America, published in August 1996, was met with guarded praise. Most critics recognized it as Michener's farewell volume and were not eager to dismiss it lightly. Still, people who had followed Michener's populist writings in magazine and newspapers throughout his career would find few surprises in the book. Here were the vintage Michener topics: education, race relations, American wealth, health care, machismo in society, the importance of art, and the family in crisis. After defining a noble country as one capable of stability, courage, and vision, Michener delineates the major weaknesses of American culture and how Americans can strengthen them. Although these are well-trodden areas in Michener's writing, his passion and concern for his country are evident. Describing himself as "a near-term optimist," he predicts greatness for America until the year 2050—"then the beginning of twilight." "Our kinetic power, already in action, will carry us forward for half a century. I doubt we could make enough errors in that time to hinder our forward motion."[18]

Criticism was generally favorable toward the book. *Publishers Weekly* commented: "Michener's style is straightforward and congenial, informed by myriad personal examples and energized by the passion of his hopes and fears for his beloved country."[19] The *Library Journal* was less enthusiastic: "A tepid mélange of meliorism and wishful thinking that only reinforces the melancholy induced by Michener's eloquent delineation of the nation's woes."[20]

Like many people, Michener loved the rhythms and music of poetry before he understood what the poems meant. As a schoolboy, he was made to memorize a vast range of poetry, from Longfellow and Lowell to Hardy and Keats. He calculated that he had to memorize four poems a year for twelve years. On his own, however, he committed to memory "perhaps six times that number."[21] It was not until he reached college that the poems began to make sense. At Swarthmore, Shakespeare, Byron, Shelley, and Wordsworth entered the picture, shaping and enriching his maturing language ability. Ultimately, Shakespeare's sonnets became his favorite and endured down the decades. He kept a volume of them in his drawer, frequently referring to them as the occasion arose.

Throughout his career, Michener wrote his own poems, mostly amateurish in nature, some in the form of haiku and others in the form of his beloved English sonnet. In 1996 he and State House Press publisher Debbie Brothers decided to polish the sonnets and publish them the following year to mark his ninetieth birthday. Housebound in Austin, Michener chose 112 of his best sonnets for the volume, sonnets that reveal, in many people's minds, more about the man than his autobiography disclosed. His first poem was written in 1927, when he was an undergraduate at Swarthmore, and the last shortly before his death. In between, he wrote of war, love, sexuality, writing, religion, and travel. At least five of his finished sonnets were written on the aborted 1993 ocean voyage to Alaska, Russia, and Asia.

A Century of Sonnets is, perhaps fittingly, Michener's last book, his love song to the world that nurtured him, wounded him, stimulated him, and ultimately provided him a feast of storytelling material. Here is his despair, his awakening mind, his vagrant youth, his love of music and learning, and his knowledge and appreciation of the world's cultures.

Ever since Thomas Wyatt introduced the Italian sonnet form into English and Shakespeare modified it into the distinctive English form, the sonnet has enjoyed wide popularity among poets such as Wordsworth, Keats, Meredith, Barrett Browning, and Frost. Michener was challenged by the grammatical, intellectual, and musical demands of the sonnet, often spending numerous hours working out the complicated structure like a jigsaw puzzle. "The sonnet is an elegant invention," he wrote in his second sonnet,

> For disciplining thought and fey confession
> Its structure expedites its main intention
> Which is: "Move thought in orderly progression."[22]

For a man who loved form, convention, and a good brainteaser, the sonnet was perfectly suited to him.

Michener lived in physical pain throughout his adult life. He wrote in pain, walked in pain, communicated in pain. His hip aggravated him constantly. By Jim's ninetieth birthday in February 1997, his dialysis treatments had weakened him considerably, but he bore up under them, seldom if ever complaining to Amelia, his housekeeper, whom he had taken to calling "Dear." She called him "Sweetie."

On that special day, John Kings wheeled him into the spacious art gallery at the University of Texas, where 357 people applauded and cheered him. Jim was presented with a bronze bust of himself and a special copy of his sonnets, which had just come off the press. Many filed by, shook his hand, and wished him well. Among the guests were

Lady Bird Johnson, three university presidents, two former governors, the students from the writing program he helped to fund, and a crowd of people who just showed up to celebrate his birthday.

Michener's will was signed and filed on November 7, 1996, designating the Library of Congress and the University of Texas as the official repositories of his writings. Swarthmore was named the main beneficiary of the estate, receiving the rights and royalties to all of Michener's books. But in July 1997 Michener signed an important codicil to his will, eliminating the University of Texas and naming the University of Northern Colorado as the official repository of his writings. Swarthmore remained the primary beneficiary. For the University of Texas, it was a significant loss.

Months earlier, the university had offended Jim by taking money from an important trust in Austin and, instead of naming the art museum after Michener, opted for naming the building after the trust's president. Jim was livid. "Go ahead and grab the money," Jim told the university. "I already have my name on a museum—it's in Doylestown."[23] While he appeared indifferent about the matter, he felt rejected by the university. Since forgiveness was not a Michener quality, he took sudden and drastic action by removing the university from his will.

The summer of 1997 was a difficult one for Michener. Each physical movement seemed a labor. His weight had dropped to below ninety pounds. Moreover, his once indestructible will to live was diminishing. Throughout his career, he had greeted each morning with wonder and joy, eager for work. In early October it all seemed futile. On October 4 he decided to terminate his dialysis treatment, opening the way for his imminent death. The master of control, the man with a methodical style, had made perhaps his most profound move.

On October 9, resigned to death, he wrote his friends: "I approach this sad news with regret, but not with any panic. I am surrounded by friends who support me in these final moments with the same high spirit they have displayed in the past. . . . What a full life [these memories] made. And what a joy they bring me now; what a joy your recollection of them gives me now. It is in this mood that my final days are being passed. And I thank you all for your thoughtfulness." He signed the letter, "fondly, James. A. Michener."[24]

Throughout his later years, Michener had drawn inspiration from the life and words of the great Japanese woodblock artist Katsushika Hokusai, who believed that he had accomplished more in his golden years than he had in his youth and middle age. At the age of seventy-five, Hokusai wrote: "From the age of six I had a mania for drawing the forms of things. By the time I was fifty I had published an infinity of designs; but all I produced before the age of seventy is not worth taking into account. At seventy-three I learned a little about the real structure of nature—of animals, plants, trees, birds, fishes, and insects. Thus, when I am ninety I shall penetrate the mystery of things. And when I am a hundred and ten everything I do, be it a dot or a line, will be alive."[25] For all his accumulated learning and for all his travel and literary accomplishments, Jim, like Hokusai, wanted to believe he was only beginning to penetrate the mystery of life.

Having said his farewell, Jim spent his final days at home in peaceful, gradual decline. Around him in his study were the reminders and souvenirs of a lifetime in writing. His Royal typewriter, one of a fleet of machines he had around the country, stood on his desk. He was most proud of his row of books, some of which he believed would endure for a long time. *Iberia, Centennial, The Source, The Covenant,* and *Hawaii* were among them. He was one of the best-selling authors of the twentieth century. But then, the generations had a way of forgetting such luminaries. How would he ultimately be judged? Fellow writers like John Barth had their opinions: "Nobody did his homework more thoroughly than Michener as his muse shuttled him from the South Pacific to Hawaii, Korea, Spain, Poland, Chesapeake, Texas and even Outer Space—but one may respectfully question the long-term staying power of those knowledgeable and enormously popular place-novels of his."[26] Other critics, such as Pearl K. Bell, saw him as a unique author who was hard to categorize and therefore found it difficult to identify his place in American letters:

His shortcomings of style and characterization, the stilted dialogue, the sentimental indulgence in what-might-have-been if at some point in those 15,000 years someone had been farsighted enough to act in a way that would, as he likes to put it, "have altered the course of history"—why hit Michener over the head with all this when he modestly refuses to inflate his talents? Though one might wish his devices less simplistic, it is surely not dishonorable that along with all the self-improving information he offers his readers, he tries to improve their hearts as well by exposing, as he has done in many of his books, the torment and destruction caused by racial intolerance and religious bigotry.[27]

To many readers during the long span of his career, Michener was known as "America's storyteller"; to other readers, he became the voice of their generation; to still others, who disliked textbook histories, he was their guide through the epochs. He never played it safe in his writing. Who but Michener would dare to preface a novel with entire chapters on the planet's geologic beginnings or give a seventy-year-old diplodocus the status of a main character?

William Faulkner once remarked that his ambition was "to put everything into one sentence—not only the present but the whole past on which it depends and which keeps overtaking the present."[28] It could be said that Michener's goal was to include everything in one book, by gathering up all things important, like Noah assembling his animals in the ark, and setting sail on an epic voyage to someplace and somewhere in time. To readers who went with him, no one did it better.

On a personal level, Michener was pleased that success had not destroyed him the way it seemed to doom other writers. Ross Lockridge, Tom Heggen, and Ernest Hemingway had committed suicide. Here was Jim Michener, age ninety, poking along with Quaker forbearance, turning out best seller after best seller, quietly building his legacy word by word, phrase by phrase. Jim Michener: foundling, hobo, scholar, art collector, politician, philanthropist, traveler, husband, writer—survivor. By anyone's standards, it was a noble journey.

On October 16, seven days after sending out his farewell letter, Jim died of kidney failure at home in Austin.

Notes

The correspondence of James A. Michener is collected and archived at two principal locations: the Library of Congress in Washington, D.C., and the University of Northern Colorado (UNC), in Greeley. There are also letters in private collections. The UNC collection, however, has microfiche copies of the Michener letters at the Library of Congress. Unless otherwise indicated in the notes, all correspondence is archived at UNC. It was Michener's wish to have his papers centralized at UNC, and that is gradually happening. Michener kept copies of his outgoing mail, so the collection has correspondence both sent and received. The manuscripts and related materials for *Tales of the South Pacific* (1947) through *The Drifters* (1972) are located at the Library of Congress. The original manuscripts beginning with *Centennial* in 1974 and ending with *This Noble Land* in 1996, except those in private collections, are at UNC. Eventually, all of Michener's papers will be located at UNC.

Chapter 1. The Boy

1. Hayes, *James A. Michener*, 12
2. Day, *James A. Michener*, 15.
3. Hayes, *James A. Michener*, 15.
4. Michener, *The World Is My Home*, 495.
5. Michener, *A Century of Sonnets*, 18.
6. Michener, *The World Is My Home*, 477
7. Dybwad and Bliss, *James A. Michener*, 58
8. Michener, *The World Is My Home,*, 93.

9. Ibid., 95.
10. Ibid., 103.
11. Ibid., 108.
12. Ibid., 111.
13. Hayes, *James A. Michener*, 13–14.
14. Michener, *The Fires of Spring*, 8.
15. Ibid., 11.
16. Hayes, *James A. Michener*, 14–15.
17. Michener, *The Fires of Spring*, 20.
18. Ibid., 14.
19. Hayes, *James A. Michener*, 16.
20. Michener, *The World Is My Home*, 440.
21. Ibid.
22. Ibid., 442.
23. Hayes, *James A. Michener*, 18.

Chapter 2. The Young Drifter

1. Michener, *The World Is My Home*, 116.
2. Ibid., 484.
3. Ibid., 117.
4. Ibid., 118–19.
5. Ibid., 120.
6. Ibid., 122.
7. Hayes, *James A. Michener*, 22.
8. Michener, *The World Is My Home*, 444.
9. Dybwad and Bliss, *James A. Michener*, 19.
10. Ibid., 20.
11. Hayes, *James A. Michener*, 30.
12. Dybwad and Bliss, *James A. Michener*, 30.
13. Michener, *The World Is My Home*, 96–97.

Chapter 3. The Mind's Journey

1. Newman, *The Idea of a University*, 30.
2. Hayes, *James A. Michener*, 34–35.
3. Ibid., 35.
4. Schlesinger, *The Almanac of American History*, 454.
5. Michener, *The World Is My Home*, 299.
6. Dybwad and Bliss, *James A. Michener*, 26.
7. Ibid., 10.

8. Hayes, *James A. Michener*, 39.

9. Ibid., 40.

10. Michener, *Collectors, Foragers.*

11. Ibid., 39–40.

12. *New York Times*, Apr. 4, 1951.

13. Michener, *The Fires of Spring*, 278.

14. Hayes, *James A. Michener*, 46.

15. Dybwad and Bliss, *James A. Michener*, 48.

16. Ibid., 51.

17. Grobel, *Talking with Michener*, 18.

18. Hayes, *James A. Michener*, 47.

19. Michener, *The World Is My Home*, 150.

20. Ibid., 150–55.

21. Ibid., 155.

22. Dybwad and Bliss, *James A. Michener*, 74–75.

23. Hayes, *James A. Michener*, 52.

24. JAM to G. Walton, n.d.

25. JAM to G. Walton, July 25, 1935.

26. Michener, *The Fires of Spring*, 188.

Chapter 4. Sojourn in the Rockies

1. G. Walton to S. P. Koon, July 6, 1935.

2. JAM to G. Walton, Mar. 30, 1936.

3. G. Walton to W. Wrinkle, July 15, 1936.

4. Hayes, *James A. Michener*, 52.

5. Ibid.

6. Ibid., 55.

7. Michener, *Literary Reflections*, 98.

8. Hayes, *James A. Michener*, 58.

9. Michener, *About Centennial*, 55–57.

10. Michener, *The World Is My Home*, 176.

11. Ibid.

12. Ibid., 178.

13. Ibid., 179.

14. Ibid.

15. Kings, *In Search of Centennial*, 24.

16. Michener, *My Lost Mexico*, 5.

17. Ibid., 3.

18. Ibid.

19. JAM to H. Wilson, May 21, 1941.

20. Ibid.

21. Hayes, *James A. Michener*, 37.

Chapter 5. The Amateur Hero

1. Michener, *The World Is My Home*, 277.

2. Ibid., 278.

3. Ibid., 268.

4. Ibid., 272–73.

5. *Progressive Education*, Nov. 1941.

6. G. Walton to JAM, Nov. 3, 1941.

7. JAM to G. Walton, Nov. 3, 1941.

8. JAM to W. Murra, Sept. 14, 1942.

9. Michener, *The World Is My Home*, 16.

10. Ibid., 17.

11. Ibid. 21.

12. Ibid., 20.

13. Hayes, *James A. Michener*, 61.

14. JAM to P. Koon Michener, June 3, 1944.

15. Michener, *Tales of the South Pacific*, 2.

16. Ibid., 139.

17. Michener, *The World Is My Home*, 149.

18. Ibid., 33.

19. Ibid., 42.

20. Ibid., 37.

21. Hayes, *James A. Michener*, 62.

22. Ibid., 63.

23. Ibid.

24. Michener, *The World Is My Home*, 90.

25. Ibid., 265.

26. Ibid., 266.

27. Hayes, *James A. Michener*, 66.

28. Michener, *The World Is My Home*, 267.

29. Michener, *Tales of the South Pacific*, 1.

30. JAM to G. Brett, Mar. 18, 1945.

31. Michener, *The World Is My Home*, 278–79.

32. Ibid., 27.

33. JAM to G. Brett, May 4, 1945.

34. G. Brett to JAM, June 7, 1945.

35. Michener, *The World Is My Home*, 455.

36. JAM Correspondence Navy File, 1946, LOC; copy UNC.

37. Day, *James A. Michener*, 22.

38. G. Brett to JAM, June 7, 1945.
39. H. Latham to JAM, July 8, 1945.
40. JAM to H. Latham, Nov. 23, 1945.
41. G. Brett to JAM, Oct. 8, 1945.

Chapter 6. Nobody Shouted "Author!"

1. JAM to R. Vavra, June 2, 1972.
2. Osmond Molarsky, qtd. in Hayes, *James A. Michener*, 73.
3. Michener, *The World Is My Home*, 279.
4. *New York Times*, Feb. 3, 1947.
5. *Yale Review* (Apr. 13, 1947).
6. *New York Times*, Feb. 3, 1947.
7. *Quarterly Book List*, June 1947.
8. Michener, *The World Is My Home*, 282–83.
9. Michener, "Conscience of the Novel," in Hull, *The Writer's Book*, 112.
10. Ibid., 122–23.
11. Hayes, *James A. Michener*, 77.
12. Michener, *The World Is My Home*, 290.
13. Ibid., 456.
14. Ibid.
15. S. Commins to JAM, Mar. 9, 1948.
16. JAM to G. Brett, Mar. 12, 1948.
17. G. Brett to JAM, Mar. 18, 1948.
18. JAM to C. Scott, Mar. 31, 1948.
19. Michener, *The World Is My Home*, 284.
20. Ibid., 286.
21. Ibid., 287.

Chapter 7. The Page and the Stage

1. *World Herald*, May 10, 1948.
2. R. Bendiner, "Truth about the Pulitzer Prizes."
3. Strauss, *A Talent for Luck*, 99.
4. Silverman, *Michener and Me*, 32.
5. Ibid., 33.
6. Michener, *The World Is My Home*, 360.
7. Michener, *The Fires of Spring*, 574.
8. Michener, *The World Is My Home*, 364.
9. *Current Biography*, 1948, 450.
10. *Yale Review*, Feb. 6, 1949.
11. *Atlantic*, Apr. 1949.

12. *New York Times*, Feb. 15, 1949.

13. *Saturday Review of Literature*, Apr. 28, 1949.

14. *Christian Science Monitor,* April 28, 1949.

15. *Library Journal*, May 1949.

16. JAM to F. Merrill, Oct. 8, 1941.

17. Secrest, *Somewhere in Time*, 288.

18. Silverman, *Michener and Me*, 43.

19. Secrest, *Somewhere in Time*, 292.

20. Michener, *The World Is My Home*, 165.

21. Secrest, *Somewhere in Time*, 290–91.

22. Michener, *The World Is My Home*, 165.

23. Michener, *Tales of the South Pacific*, 48.

24. Silverman, *Michener and Me*, 44.

25. JAM to H. Silverman, spring 1949.

26. Strauss, *A Talent for Luck*, 102.

Chapter 8. The Occasional Husband

1. Kings, *In Search of Centennial*, 24.

2. Michener, *About Centennial*, 18.

3. H. Lewis to J. Hayes, July 10, 1980.

4. Hayes, *James A. Michener*, 98.

5. Ibid.

6. Michener, *A Michener Miscellany*, 14.

7. H. Lewis to JAM, June 24, 1952.

8. Michener, *Literary Reflections*, 124.

9. Ibid.

10. Ibid.

11. Ibid., 125.

12. Strauss, *A Talent for Luck*, 106.

13. H. Lewis to JAM, June 24, 1952.

14. D. Wallace to JAM, Nov. 3, 1952.

15. H. Strauss to D. Wallace, Nov. 30, 1952.

16. JAM to R. Vavra, May 3, 1972.

17. Minutes of the Asia Foundation, Nov. 5, 1954.

18. Ibid., Dec. 16, 1954.

19. Michener, *The World Is My Home*, 367.

20. Ibid., 366.

21. Ibid.

22. Day, *James A. Michener*, 75.

23. Hayes, *James A. Michener*, 107.

24. *New York Times*, July 2, 1953.

25. *Saturday Review,* July 11, 1953.

26. *New Republic,* July, 1953.

27. *New Yorker,* Aug. 1, 1953.

28. Strauss, *A Talent for Luck,* 105.

29. Kronenberger, *Brief Lives,* 360

30. Prescott, *In My Opinion,* 66.

31. Ibid.

32. Ibid., 153.

33. Ibid.

34. Michener, *Literary Reflections,* 129.

35. Ibid., 131.

36. JAM to V. Michener, Jan. 20, 1956.

37. Ibid.

38. Ibid.

39. Ibid.

40. JAM to V. Michener, May 10, 1955.

41. Michener, *A Michener Miscellany,* 104.

42. JAM to D. Selznick, Dec. 13, 1952.

43. Strauss, *A Talent for Luck,* 109.

Chapter 9. The Writer at Large

1. JAM to G. Day, Nov. 15, 1954.

2. JAM to H. Silverman, June 5, 1955.

3. Michener, *A Michener Miscellany,* 166.

4. Michener, "Afghanistan: Domain of the Fierce and the Free."

5. Michener, *A Michener Miscellany,* 174–75.

6. Ibid., 230.

7. Michener, notes to Random House, Sept. 8, 1988.

8. JAM to H. Silverman, July 20, 1955.

9. Ibid.

10. JAM to H. Silverman, n.d.

11. *Honolulu Star-Reporter,* Apr. 26, 1956.

12. Silverman, *Michener and Me,* 50.

13. Hayes, *James A. Michener,* 129–30.

14. E. Shoemaker to JAM, Nov. 22, 1956.

15. M. Michener to P. Buck, Nov. 22, 1956.

16. Day, *James A. Michener,* 97.

17. M. Michener to P. Buck, Nov. 22, 1956.

18. Qtd. in *New York Times,* Nov. 1, 1956.

19. JAM to E. Deakman, Dec. 29, 1976. See also Michener, *The World Is My Home,* 390.

20. *New York Times Book Review,* JAM interview with Robert Clurman, Mar. 3, 1957.

21. *Greeley (Colo.) Tribune*, Feb. 16, 1957.

22. Michener, *A Michener Miscellany*, 377.

23. JAM to E. Deakman, Dec. 29, 1976.

24. Ibid.

25. Ibid.

26. B. Cerf to G. Day, Dec. 23, 1956.

Chapter 10. Islands in the Sun

1. JAM to H. Lewis, Jan. 20, 1957.

2. H. Lewis to JAM, n.d.

3. Prescott, *In My Opinion*, 154.

4. Michener, *The World Is My Home*, 377.

5. *Honolulu Star-Bulletin*, Apr. 26, 1956.

6. Michener, *The World Is My Home*, 322.

7. Michener, notes on *Hawaii*.

8. Silverman, *Michener and Me*, 78.

9. JAM to Grove Day, Mar. 22, 1957.

10. *Honolulu Star-Bulletin*, June 6, 1959.

11. Ibid.

12. Taylor, "Michener and Names."

13. Ibid.

14. Ibid.

15. Ibid.

16. Michener, *Hawaii*, 513.

17. Birmingham, *The Late John Marquand*, 124.

18. Strauss, *A Talent for Luck*, 114.

19. Michener, *Report of the County Chairman*, 5.

20. Ibid., 6.

21. *Honolulu Star-Bulletin*, Nov. 1, 15, 1959.

22. Ibid., June 6, 1959.

23. Michener, *Report of the County Chairman*, 9–10.

24. Ibid., 10.

25. JAM to W. Vitarelli, Feb. 20, 1960.

26. B. Cerf to JAM, Dec. 26, 1959.

27. *New York Herald Tribune*, Nov. 16, 1959.

28. *New York Times Book Review*, Nov. 22, 1959.

29. *Chicago Sunday Tribune*, Nov. 15, 1959.

30. *Saturday Review*, Nov. 21, 1959.

31. *Catholic World*, Jan. 20, 1960.

32. *Spectator*, Dec. 13, 1939.

33. *Kirkus Reviews*, Nov. 26, 1959.

34. *Honolulu Star-Bulletin*, Oct. 24, 1959.

35. *Honolulu Advertiser*, Oct. 25, 1959.

36. Qtd. in Leonard Lyons, "The Lyon's Den," *New York Times*, Feb. 18, 1960.

37. Sutton, "The Strange Case of James Michener."

38. Hayes, *James A. Michener*, 150.

39. Michener, *Report of the County Chairman*, 13, 17.

Chapter 11. A Different Drummer

1. Michener, *Report of the County Chairman*, 21.

2. Michener, *My Lost Mexico*, 5

3. JAM to R. Vavra, May 2, 1972.

4. Michener, *My Lost Mexico*, 16.

5. Ibid.

6. Ibid., 20.

7. Ibid., 61.

8. Ibid., 65.

9. Ibid., 66.

10. Hayes, *James A. Michener*, 179.

11. Ibid., 177–78.

12. Michener, notes to "The Sharif of Koristan."

13. *Publishers Weekly*, Apr. 10, 1972.

14. Michener, *Caravans*, 23.

15. Strauss, *A Talent for Luck*, 253.

16. *Time*, Aug. 9, 1963.

17. *America*, Aug. 31, 1963.

18. G. Bell to her father, Mar. 30, 1902.

19. Michener, *A Michener Miscellany*, 232–33.

20. Ibid.

Chapter 12. "Noiseless, Patient Spider"

1. *Writer's Digest*, August 1968.

2. Michener, *About Centennial*, 46.

3. Michener, *The Source*, 766.

4. *Philadelphia Bulletin Magazine*, Dec. 22, 1963.

5. Grobel, *Talking with Michener*, 196.

6. Michener, *A Michener Miscellany*, 277.

7. JAM to R. Vavra, June 2, 1972.

8. A. Erskine to JAM, July 21, 1964.

9. JAM to E. Mizrachi, Feb. 2, 1964.

10. *Chicago Jewish Forum*, 284.

11. *Congress Bi-Weekly*, June 14, 1965.

12. Fiedler, *Collected Essays*, 85.

13. Michener, *The World Is My Home*, 414.

14. Ibid., 418.

15. JAM notebook, Dec. 1965.

Chapter 13. A Traveler in Spain

1. Grobel, *Talking with Michener*, 206–207.

2. JAM notebook, July 1966.

3. Michener, *Iberia*, 346.

4. Ibid., 36–37.

5. Michener, datebook, July 20, 1966.

6. Michener, *Iberia*, 590.

7. Ibid., 585.

8. JAM to R. Vavra, June 2, 1972.

9. Michener, "Running with the Bulls."

10. JAM to R. Vavra, June 2, 1972.

11. Michener, *Iberia*, 375.

12. Ibid., 680.

13. Ibid., 469.

14. *Christian Science Monitor*, May 9, 1968.

15. JAM to R. Vavra, Sept. 1, 1969.

16. Michener, *Iberia*, 708.

17. Ibid., 937–38.

18. Ibid., 848.

19. Ibid., 850.

20. Ibid.

21. Ibid., 938–39.

22. JAM to A. Erskine, Jan. 24, 1967.

23. Michener, notes on *Iberia*.

24. *Time*, May 17, 1968.

25. *Washington Post Book World*, May 5, 1968.

26. JAM to R. Vavra, Sept. 1, 1969.

27. *Saturday Review*, May 4, 1968.

28. *Philadelphia Inquirer*, May 10, 1968.

29. *Wall Street Journal*, May 6, 1968.

30. JAM to R. Vavra, Sept. 1, 1968.

Chapter 14. Shine, Perishing Republic

1. Nixon, *The Memoirs of Richard Nixon*, 317.
2. Michener, "The Collector."
3. Silverman, *Michener and Me*, 150.
4. JAM to R. Vavra, May 2, 1972.
5. Michener, "Running with the Bulls."
6. Ibid.
7. JAM to R. Vavra, July 6, 1970.
8. R. Vavra to JAM, June 12, 1973.
9. H. Lewis to JAM, Nov. 18, 1969.
10. *New York Post*, Apr. 30, 1971.
11. Michener, *The World Is My Home*, 168.
12. Haldeman, *The Haldeman Diaries*, 211.
13. F. Shakespeare to JAM, July 10, 1972,. UNC.
14. Michener, *The World Is My Home*, 199.
15. Ibid., 198.
16. Ibid., 200–201.
17. Michener, "What the F.B.I. Has On Me."
18. *Anchorage (Alaska) Daily News*, May 27, 1973.
19. *New York Times*, July 1, 1973.
20. Ibid.
21. *Anchorage (Alaska) Daily News*, May 27, 1973.
22. JAM private notes—Honolulu to Guam, en route, UNC.
23. *Reader's Digest*, July 1972.
24. JAM private notes, Peking. China Trip, UNC.
25. *Reader's Digest*, July 1972, 280.
26. JAM to F. Shakespeare, June 30, 1972.

Chapter 15. One Man's America

1. Kings, *In Search of Centennial*, 63.
2. Ibid., 24.
3. Michener, *About Centennial*, 27.
4. Ibid., 36.
5. JAM to H. Lewis, n.d.
6. Kings, *In Search of Centennial*, 14.
7. Michener, *About Centennial*, 35.
8. Ibid., 30.
9. Kings, *In Search of Centennial*, 76.
10. Ibid.
11. Michener, *About Centennial*, 41.

12. Ibid., 44.

13. Ibid., 47–48.

14. Ibid., 49.

15. JAM to J. Kings, Feb. 2, 1974.

16. Michener, notes on *Centennial.*

17. JAM to J. Kings, Feb. 2, 1974.

18. *New York Times,* July 1, 1973.

19. Ibid., Nov. 11, 1973.

20. JAM to J. Kings, Feb. 2, 1974.

21. *Palm Springs Life,* Oct. 28, 1974.

22. *Washington Post,* Sept. 29, 1974.

23. *New York Magazine,* Oct. 10, 1974.

24. Grobel, *Talking with Michener,* 213.

25. *Philadelphia,* June 1981.

26. *Family Weekly,* Oct. 10, 1982.

27. Michener, *Sports in America,* 315.

28. J. Avenick, e-mail to author, Oct. 11, 2003.

29. Michener, *The World Is My Home,* 395.

30. J. Avenick, interview by author, Aug. 5. 2003.

31. JAM to J. Avenick, Feb. 27, 1976.

32. Avenick, interview.

33. JAM notebook, July 2, 1976.

34. *Baltimore Sun,* July 24, 1977.

35. *Baltimore News American,* July 3, 1977.

36. JAM to R. Vavra, June 2, 1972.

37. *Baltimore Sun,* July 24, 1977.

38. Ibid.

39. J. Avenick, e-mail to author, Aug. 29, 2003.

40. *Baltimore Sun,* July 24, 1977.

41. Piszek, *Some Good in the World,* 168.

42. *San Francisco Chronicle,* Mar. 21, 1978.

43. *Hollywood Star-Reporter,* June 21, 1977.

44. *Baltimore Sun,* July 7, 1977.

45. *Washington Post,* July 9, 1978.

46. *New Hope (Pa.) Gazette,* July 27, 1978.

Chapter 16. The Covenant

1. Random House press release, Oct. 1980.

2. Ibid.

3. Michener, notes on *The Covenant.*

4. JAM to T. Oursler, Apr. 1978.

5. E. Uys, e-mail to author, Aug. 26, 2003.

6. Ibid.

7. Ibid.

8. JAM to T. Oursler, June 15, 1978.

9. Athena.english.vt.edu.

10. Ibid.

11. Philip Bateman, notes on *The Covenant.*

12. Ibid.

13. E. Uys to JAM, July 1978.

14. JAM to E. Uys, n.d.

15. JAM to M. Michener, Aug. 1978.

16. JAM to N. Orapchuck, Sept. 13, 1978.

17. www.errol.uys.com.

18. E. Uys to JAM, Sept., 28, 1978.

19. E. Uys to JAM, Dec., 18, 1979.

20. E. Uys to JAM, Mar. 9, 1979.

21. Michener, notes on *The Covenant.*

22. *Ibid.*

23. Ibid.

24. Tobias to JAM, Jan. 31, 1979.

25. E. Uys to JAM, no date.

26. E. Uys, e-mail to author, Aug. 26, 2003.

27. Grobel, "Playboy Interview."

28. JAM to E. Uys, Feb. 2, 1980.

29. *Natal Daily News* (South Africa), Aug. 20, 1980.

30. Ibid.

31. F. Uys, e-mail to author, Oct. 1, 2003.

32. *Washington Star,* Feb. 11, 1980.

33. *Washington Post,* Nov. 2, 1980.

34. E. Uys, e-mail to author, Oct. 1, 2003.

35. *New York Times,* Nov. 14, 1980.

36. *Rand Daily Mail* (South Africa), Sept. 6, 1980.

37. *Baltimore Sun,* Dec. 14, 1981.

38. *New York Times,* Dec. 7, 1980.

39. *Time,* Feb. 9, 1981.

40. *Columbus (Ohio) Dispatch,* Nov. 23, 1980.

41. Michener, notes on *The Covenant.*

42. *Rand Daily Mail,* Sept. 6, 1980.

43. Grobel, *Talking with Michener,* 171–72.

Chapter 17. The Great Ennobler

1. The first airplane crash was in the harbor of Manus Island, New Guinea, in 1944; the second occurred shortly thereafter in New Caledonia. The third crash, mentioned here, occurred in 1957.

2. *Washington Times*, Oct. 12, 1982.

3. *Washington Post*, Sept. 19, 1982.

4. *New York Times*, Sept. 19, 1982.

5. *Los Angeles Times*, Oct. 3, 1982.

6. *The Bulletin*, May 17, 1981.

7. Piszek, *Some Good in the World*, 187.

8. Ibid., 213.

9. Ibid., 213–14.

10. E. Piszek to JAM, July 19, 1981.

11. Michener, notes on *Poland.*

12. Ibid.

13. *Los Angeles Times*, Sept. 4, 1983.

14. Hayes, *James A. Michener*, 5.

15. Michener, *The World Is My Home*, 205.

16. Ibid., 206.

17. U.S. Government Accounting Office, NSIAD, 85–93, June 24, 1985.

18. Michener, *New York Times*, July 5, 1987.

19. *Chicago Tribune*, June 27, 1985.

20. JAM to L. Kaufman et al., May 6, 1983.

21. *Writer's Digest*, Feb. 1985.

22. John Kings, notes on *Texas.*

23. Ibid.

24. Ibid.

25. Michener, *A Michener Miscellany*, 5.

26. Michener, *Texas*, 3.

27. Ibid., 3–4.

28. JAM to O. Laster, Oct. 1, 1983.

29. Kings, notes on *Texas.*

30. Michener, *The World Is My Home*, 385.

31. *The Reporter* (Royersford, Pa.), Sept. 27, 1984.

32. University of Texas press release, Oct. 12, 1984.

33. *Chicago Tribune*, Oct. 13, 1985.

34. *Los Angeles Times*, Dec. 21, 1985.

35. *New York Times Magazine*, Sept. 8, 1985

36. Ibid., 58.

37. Qtd. in De Voto, *Mark Twain's America*, 138.

Chapter 18. New Frontiers

1. JAM to R. Vavra, June 2, 1972.

2. Michener, *The World Is My Home*, 429.

3. Ibid., 430.

4. *We Alaskans*, Aug. 4, 1985.

5. Michener, notes on *Alaska.*

6. *New York Times Magazine*, Mar. 16, 1985.

7. *We Alaskans*, Aug. 4, 1985.

8. Ibid.

9. JAM to A. Erskine, May 10, 1986.

10. JAM to J. Kings, Nov. 16, 1984.

11. JAM to O. Laster, June 24, 1986.

12. JAM to O. Laster, July 7, 1986.

13. JAM to A. Erskine, Sept. 21, 1986.

14. A. Erskine to JAM, Oct. 20, 1986.

15. JAM datebook, 1987.

16. Michener, notes on *Alaska.*

17. Michener, *The World Is My Home*, 319.

Chapter 19. Portrait of the Artist

1. *New York Times*, Mar. 20, 1990.

2. Michener, *My Lost Mexico*, 163.

3. *New York Times*, Mar. 20, 1990.

4. Michener, notes on *The Novel.*

5. Ibid.

6. JAM to A. Buchwald, Apr. 13, 1990.

7. Michener, "The Chances against the Beginning Writer," in Hull, *The Writer's Book*, 102–113.

8. Grobel, *Talking with Michener.*

9. *U.S. News and World Report*, June 17, 1991.

10. *Austin (Tex.) American-Statesman*, June 24, 1990.

11. Michener, notes on *The World Is My Home.*

12. *U.S. News and World Report*, June 17, 1991.

13. Ibid.

14. Michener, *The World Is My Home*, 511.

15. Ibid., 10.

16. *New York Times*, Jan. 12, 1992.

17. *Publishers Weekly*, Feb. 20, 1992.

18. *Kirkus Reviews*, Mar. 13, 1992.

Chapter 20. The Tough Old Bird

1. Michener, *My Lost Mexico*, 69.
2. Ibid., 75.
3. Michener, *My Lost Mexico*, 69–70.
4. Michener, notes on *Mexico*.
5. Michener, *My Lost Mexico*, 77.
6. Ibid., 70.
7. *Austin American-Statesman*, May 20, 1992.
8. Ibid., Oct. 5, 1992.
9. *Chronicle of Higher Education*, Jan. 13, 1992.
10. JAM to H. Silverman, Feb. 15, 1994.
11. *Austin American-Statesman*, Aug. 25, 1995.
12. JAM open letter to friends, Dec. 15, 1994.
13. Ibid.
14. Ibid.
15. Grobel, *Talking with Michener*, vxi.
16. Ibid., xx.
17. JAM to B. Potter, Oct. 27, 1995.
18. Michener, *This Noble Land*, 238.
19. *Publishers Weekly*, Oct. 15, 1996.
20. *Library Journal*, Nov. 1996.
21. Grobel, *Talking with Michener*, xvii.
22. Michener, *A Century of Sonnets*, 2.
23. Silverman, *Michener and Me*, 215.
24. JAM open letter to friends, Oct. 9, 1997.
25. Michener, *A Michener Miscellany*, 274.
26. J. Barth to author, Mar. 3, 2003.
27. *Commentary*, Apr. 1981.
28. Kazin, *Bright Book of Life*, 31.

Works by James A. Michener

Books

Tales of the South Pacific (Pulitzer Prize). New York: Macmillan, 1947.
The Fires of Spring. New York: Random House, 1949.
Return to Paradise. New York: Random House, 1951.
The Voice of Asia. New York: Random House, 1951.
The Bridges at Toko-Ri. New York: Random House, 1953.
Sayonara. New York: Random House, 1954.
The Floating World. New York: Random House, 1954.
The Bridge at Andau. New York: Random House, 1957.
(with A. Grove Day) *Rascals in Paradise.* New York: Random House, 1957.
The Hokusai Sketchbooks. Rutland, Vt.: C. E. Tuttle, 1958.
Hawaii. New York: Random House, 1959.
Japanese Prints: From the Masters to the Modern. Rutland, Vt.: C. E. Tuttle, 1959.
Report of the County Chairman. New York: Random House, 1961.
The Modern Japanese Print: An Appreciation. Rutland, Vt.: C. E. Tuttle, 1962.
Caravans. New York: Random House, 1963.
The Source. New York: Random House, 1965.
Iberia: Spanish Travels and Reflections. New York: Random House, 1968.
Presidential Lottery. New York: Random House, 1969.
America vs. America: The Revolution in Middle-Class Values. New York: New American
    Library, 1969.
Facing East. New York: Random House, 1970.
The Quality of Life. Philadelphia: Girard Bank, 1970.

Kent State: What Happened and Why. New York: Random House, 1971.

The Drifters. New York: Random House, 1971.

A Michener Miscellany: 1950–1970. New York: Random House, 1973.

Centennial. New York: Random House, 1974.

About Centennial: Some Notes on the Novel. New York: Random House, 1974.

Sports in America. New York: Random House, 1976.

Chesapeake. New York: Random House, 1978.

The Watermen. New York: Random House, 1979.

The Covenant. New York: Random House, 1980.

Space. New York: Random House, 1982.

Collectors, Forgers—and a Writer: A Memoir. New York City: Targ Editions, 1983.

Poland. New York: Random House, 1983.

Testimony. Honolulu: White Knight Press, 1983.

Texas. New York: Random House, 1985.

Legacy. New York: Random House, 1987.

Alaska. New York: Random House, 1988.

Journey. New York: Random House, 1989.

Caribbean. New York: Random House, 1989.

(with John Kings) *Six Days in Havana.* Austin: University of Texas Press, 1989.

The Eagle and the Raven. Austin: State House Press, 1990.

Pilgrimage: A Memoir of Poland and Rome. Emmaus, Pa.: Rodale Press, 1990.

James A. Michener on the Social Studies. Silver Spring, Md.: National Council for the Social Studies, 1991.

The Novel. New York: Random House, 1991.

The World Is My Home: A Memoir. New York: Random House, 1992.

James. A. Michener's Writer's Handbook. New York: Random House, 1992.

South Pacific: As Told by James A. Michener. San Diego: Harcourt Brace, 1992.

Mexico. New York: Random House, 1992.

My Lost Mexico. Austin: State House Press, 1992.

Creatures of the Kingdom. New York: Random House, 1993.

Literary Reflections. Austin: State House Press, 1993.

Recessional. New York: Random House, 1994.

William Penn. Morrisville, Pa.: Pennsbury Society, 1994.

Miracle in Seville. New York: Random House, 1995.

Ventures in Editing. Aliso Viejo, Calif.: James Cahill Publishing, 1995.

This Noble Land: My Vision for America. New York: Random House, 1996.

A Century of Sonnets. Austin: State House Press, 1997.

Selected Articles and Stories

"Afghanistan: Domain of the Fierce and Free." *Reader's Digest,* November 1955.

"After the War: Victories at Home." *Newsweek,* January 11, 1993.

"All for One: A Story from Korea." *Reader's Digest*, July 1952.

"Aloha for the Fiftieth State." *New York Times Magazine*, April 19, 1959.

"American in Tahiti." *Paradise of the Pacific*, January 1953.

"Australia." *Holiday*, November 1950.

"Bach and Sugar Beets." *Music Education Journal*, September 1938.

"Birth of Hawaii." *Life*, October 26, 1959.

"A Bizarre, Extraordinary Convention." *U.S. News and World Report*, July 30, 1984.

"Books That Gave Me Pleasure." *New York Times Book Review*, December 5, 1982.

"The Book That I'm Writing." *New York Times Book Review*, June 12, 1983.

"The Bridge at Andau." *Reader's Digest*, March 1957.

"The Bridges at Toko-Ri." *Life*, July 6, 1953.

"A Buoyant, Optimistic Convention." *U.S. News and World Report*, September 3, 1984.

"China Diary." *Reader's Digest*, May 1972.

"Circles in the Sea." *Holiday*, May 1950.

"The Collector." *Texas Quarterly*, spring 1970.

"Confessions of a Political Candidate." *Reader's Digest*, November 1962.

"Death and Daring on the Moon." *People Weekly*, September 27, 1982.

"Denver to New Delhi: A Writer's Moves." *New York Times*, March 17, 1982.

"Don't Knock the Rock." *Reader's Digest*, February 1966.

"The Education of James Michener." *American Educator*, summer 1983.

"The Empty Room." *Ladies' Home Journal*, September 1947.

"Fiji." *Holiday*, June 1950.

"Five Warring Tribes of South Africa." *New York Times Magazine*, January 23, 1972.

"Forgotten Heroes of Korea." *Saturday Evening Post*, May 10, 1952.

"Four Miracles and a Masterpiece." *Reader's Digest*, November 1966.

"Giving It Away." *Arts and Antiques*, March 1989.

"God Is Not a Homophobe." *New York Times*, March 30, 1993.

"Guadalcanal." *Holiday*, August 1950.

"Hardest Working Woman in the World." *Reader's Digest*, March 1959.

"Hawaii." *Holiday*, May 1953.

"Hawaii the Fiftieth State." *New York Times Magazine*, April 19, 1961.

"Hermitage: Russia's Fabulous Art Palace." *Reader's Digest*, March 1965.

"Historic Meeting in Indonesia." *Reader's Digest*, August 1955.

"How to Lose an Election." *Honolulu Star-Bulletin*, November 15, 1958.

"In and Out of Books." *New York Times Book Review*, January 22, 1961.

"Inside Kennedy's Election." *Look*, May 9, 1961.

"Introducing Hemingway." *Publishers Weekly*, January 11, 1985.

"Is America Burning?" *New York Times Magazine*, July 1, 1973.

"Japan." *Holiday*, August 1952.

"Keep the Radios Broadcasting to the East." *New York Times*, July 5, 1987.

"Kent State: Campus under Fire." *Reader's Digest*, March 1971.

"Lament for Pakistan." *New York Times Magazine*, January 9, 1972.

"Looking toward Space." *Omni,* May 1980.

"Madrid's Fabulous Prado." *Reader's Digest,* June 1969.

"Main Line." *Holiday,* April 1950.

"Memoirs of a Pacific Traveler." *Saturday Review,* June 1980.

"Mexico's Mild-Mannered Matador." *Reader's Digest,* July 1961.

"Music in the Social Studies." *Music Education Journal,* September 1938.

"My Other Books." *Harper's,* January 1961.

"New Guinea." *Holiday,* October 1950.

"New Zealand." *Holiday,* January 1951.

"The 1980's: The Ugly Decade." *New York Times,* January 1, 1987.

"The Old Man and the Southern Sea." *Los Angeles Times,* May 17, 1992.

"One and Half Cheers for Progress." *New York Times Magazine,* September 5, 1971.

"People of the Pacific." *Saturday Review,* November 12, 1960.

"Polynesia." *Holiday,* March 1951.

"Publishing on a Sub-Tropical Island." *Publishers Weekly,* July 1, 1968.

"Reading before Writing." *Saturday Review of Literature,* April 30, 1949.

"The Red Kimono." *New York Times Magazine,* November 26, 1972.

"Reflections of a Nesomaniac." *Reader's Digest,* June 1978.

"Revolution in Middle-Class Values." *New York Times Magazine,* August 18, 1968.

"Running with the Bulls." *Esquire,* December 1970.

"Sex Education: A Success in Our Social Studies Classes." *Clearing House,* summer 1938.

"Should Artists Boycott New York?" *Saturday Review,* May 5, 1961.

"Six against the Heavens." *People Weekly,* September 20, 1982.

"The South Pacific." *Saturday Review,* October 17, 1959.

"Soviet Jewry." *New York Times,* September 16, 1972.

"Spain's Secret Wilderness." *Holiday,* April 1968.

"This I Believe." *Reader's Digest,* July 1954.

"To Moscow: A Mission for Peace." *Reader's Digest,* September 1972.

"The Way It Is in Korea." *Reader's Digest,* January 1953.

"What America Means to Me." *Reader's Digest,* February 1976.

"What Are We Fighting For?" *Progressive Education,* November 1941.

"What Every Candidate Should Know." *New York Times,* September 23, 1962.

"What If Biblical Edicts Were Enforced?" *Oklahoma Observer,* June 25, 1993.

"What the F.B.I. Has on Me." *Esquire,* December 1971.

"When the Mandate of Heaven Has Been Lost." *New York Times,* November 11, 1973.

"While Others Sleep." *Reader's Digest,* October 1957.

"Who Is Virgil T. Fry?" *Clearing House,* October 1941.

"Why I Am Running for Congress." *Saturday Evening Post,* May 5, 1962.

"Why I Collect Art." *Reader's Digest,* May 1970.

"Why Man Explores." *Omni,* November 1981.

"The Writer's Public Image." *Esquire,* December 1965.

"Writer's War." *Saturday Review,* January 22, 1955.

Partial and Unpublished Manuscripts (UNC Collection)

"Jefferson." 1937–1950.
"The Sharif of Koristan." 1955–1958.
"Russia." 1964–1966.
"The Fortune Teller." 1980–1981.
"The Writer and the Critic." Circa 1985.
"Morning in America." 1990–1992.

Selected Bibliography

Armory, Cleveland. "Trade Winds." *Saturday Review*, May 15, 1971.

Baker, Carlos. *Ernest Hemingway: A Life Story*. New York: Scribner's 1968.

Baker, Joan Stanley. *Japanese Art*. New York: Thames and Hudson, 1991.

Beans, Bruce E. "The Source." *Philadelphia*, June 1981.

Becker, George J. *James A. Michener*. New York: Ungar, 1983.

Bell, Pearl K. "James Michener's Docudramas." *Commentary*, April 1981.

Bendiner, Robert. "Truth about the Pulitzer Prizes." *McCall's*, May 1966.

Birmingham, Stephen. *The Late John Marquand*. Philadelphia: Lippincott, 1972.

Briet, Harvey. "Talk with Mr. Michener on the Role of Literature." *New York Times Book Review*, May 22, 1949.

Davies, Peter. *The Truth about Kent State*. New York: Farrar, Strauss, 1973.

Day, A. Grove. *James Michener*. Boston: Twayne, 1977.

De Voto, Bernard. *Mark Twain's America*. Boston: Houghton Mifflin, 1936.

Dybwad, G. L., and Joy Bliss. *James A. Michener: The Beginning Teacher and His Textbooks*. Albuquerque: The Book Stops Here, 1994.

Eron, Carol. "James A. Michener: Life and Literature." *Washington Post Book World*, September 19, 1976.

Esterhaus, Joe, and Michael Roberts. "James Michener's Kent State: A Study in Distortion." *Progressive*, September 1971.

Fiedler, Leslie. *Collected Essays*. New York: Stein and Day, 1971.

Frieland, Eric. "Michener and His Source." *Chicago Jewish Forum*, summer 1996.

Galvez-Hjornevik, Cleta. "James Michener: Educator." Ph.D. diss., University of Texas, Austin, 1984.

Gilbert, Martin. *Israel*. New York: William Morrow, 1998.

Grobel, Lawrence. "Playboy Interview." *Playboy*, September 1981.

———. *Talking with Michener*. Jackson: University Press of Mississippi, 1999.

Groseclose, David. *James A. Michener: A Bibliography*. Austin: State House Press, 1996.

Guttenplan, D. D. "Michener's Harsh Reading." *Newsweek*, January 16, 1984.

Haldeman, H. R. *The Haldeman Diaries: Inside the Nixon White House*. New York: G. P. Putnam, 1994.

Hayes, John. "James Michener." *Writer's Digest*, April 1972.

———. *James A. Michener: A Biography*. Indianapolis: Bobbs-Merrill, 1984.

Hull Helen, ed. *The Writer's Book*. New York: New Direction, 1953.

James, Caryn. "The Michener Phenomenon." *New York Times Magazine*, September 8, 1985.

Kings, John. *In Search of Centennial*. New York: Random House, 1978.

Kazin, Alfred. *Bright Book of Life*. Boston: Little, Brown, 1973.

Kronenberger, Louis, ed. *Brief Lives: A Biographical Companion to the Arts*. Boston: Little, Brown, 1971.

Latham, Harold. *My Life in Publishing*. New York: Dutton, 1965.

Levine, Beth. "Our Man in Havana." *Publishers Weekly*, July 14, 1989.

Logan, Joshua. *Josh: My Up and Down Life*. New York: Delacorte Press, 1976.

Morton, H. V. *In Search of England*. London: Methuen, 1930.

McCormick, Bernard. "Portrait of the Artist as an Elder Statesman." *Philadelphia*, April 1, 1968.

Mitgang, Herbert. "Why Michener Never Misses." *Saturday Review*, November 1980.

Newman, John Henry. *The Idea of a University*. New York: P. F. Collier and Son, 1969.

Newquist, Roy. "An Interview with James Michener." *Writer's Digest*, August 1968.

Nixon, Richard. *The Memoirs of Richard Nixon*. New York: G. P. Putnam, 1979.

Piszek, Edward J. *Some Good in the World*. Boulder: University Press of Colorado, 2001.

Prescott, Orville. *In My Opinion*. Indianapolis: Bobbs-Merrill, 1952.

"Pulitzer Boy." *New York Times Book Review*, May 16, 1948.

Reynolds, Michael. *Hemingway in the 1930's*. New York: W. W. Norton, 1997.

Roberts, F. X., and C. D. Rhine. *James A. Michener: A Checklist of His Works*. Westport, Conn.: Greenwood Press, 1995.

Rossellini, Lynn. "The Man Who Loves Facts." *U.S. News and World Report*, June 17, 1991.

Schlesinger, Arthur M., Jr., ed. *The Almanac of American History*. New York: Barnes and Noble, 1993.

Secrest, Meryle. *Somewhere in Time*. New York: Knopf, 2002.

Severson, Marilyn, *James A. Michener: A Critical Companion*. Westport. Conn.: Greenwood Press, 1995.

Shahin, Jim. "The Continuing Saga of James A. Michener." *Saturday Evening Post*, March 1990.

Silverman, Herman. *Michener and Me*. Philadelphia: Running Press, 1999.

Sorensen, Ted. *Kennedy*. New York: Harper and Row, 1965.

Strauss, Helen. *A Talent for Luck.* New York: Random House, 1979.

Stuckey, W. J. *The Pulitzer Prize Novels.* Norman: University of Oklahoma Press, 1981.

Sutton, Horace. "The Strange Case of James Michener." *Paradise of the Pacific,* September 1963.

———. "Michener: Man of the Pacific." *Saturday Review,* June 1980.

Taylor, Clarice B. "Michener and Names." *Paradise of the Pacific,* October 1959.

Ubbelhohde, Carl. *A Colorado History.* Boulder, Colo.: Pruett, 2001.

Warga, Wayne. "James A. Michener's Imagination." *Washington Post Book World,* September 8, 1974.

Index